Please return/renew this item by the last date shown
on this label, or on your self-service receipt.

To renew this item, visit **www.librarieswest.org.uk**
or contact your library

Your borrower number and PIN are required.

Libraries**West**

D1345160

4 5 0011988 8

ICY
GRAVES

The remembrance of these experiences makes one almost fear to encourage good and brave men to penetrate these forbidding regions. But it is not all gloom and depression beyond the Polar circles. Sunshine and lively hope soon return.

Dr John Murray
Naturalist on the *Challenger* Expedition (1872–76)
'The Renewal of Antarctic Exploration'
Geographical Journal, January 1894

Thus, as knowledge grows, the power of the explorer increases, and the old-time hardships that we read of seem curious fantasies or epics of heroic men battling blindly with ignorance.

Dr Robert Rudmose-Brown
Naturalist on the *Scotia* Expedition (1902–04)
'Some Problems of Polar Geography'
Scottish Geographical Magazine, 1927

The great mystery of the South ever challenges to one fight more, and here death, dressed in storm, darkness, and cold, bandages no man's eyes.

Admiral Richard E. Byrd
'Our Navy Explores Antarctica'
National Geographic, October 1947

ICY GRAVES

EXPLORATION AND DEATH
IN THE ANTARCTIC

STEPHEN HADDELSEY

For the brothers Haddelsey,
Richard and Martin

First published 2018

The History Press
The Mill, Brimscombe Port
Stroud, Gloucestershire, GL5 2QG
www.thehistorypress.co.uk

British Library Cataloguing in Publication Data.
A catalogue record for this book is available from the British Library.

ISBN 978 0 7509 8255 9

Typesetting and origination by The History Press
Printed and bound in Great Britain by TJ International Ltd

CONTENTS

ACKNOWLEDGEMENTS

In examining the circumstances of so many fatalities it has, of course, been impossible not to form judgements regarding certain decisions made in the field. In doing so, I have been acutely aware of the potential criticisms that might ensue. After all, I was not there – and I do not claim first-hand familiarity with the challenges of operating in Antarctic conditions. For this reason, as well as basing my accounts very closely upon contemporary diaries, letters, reports, inquests and interview transcripts, I have repeatedly sought the opinion of those who *were* there, and who have experienced the conditions for themselves. I am, therefore, particularly grateful to the following Antarctic veterans for sharing their recollections and views, and, in some cases, for reading portions of the manuscript: Ray Berry (FIDS), Ken Blaiklock OBE (FIDS & Commonwealth Trans-Antarctic Expedition), Dr John Dudeney OBE (BAS), Peter Gibbs (FIDS), Professor Rainer Goldsmith (Commonwealth Trans-Antarctic Expedition), John Hall MBE (BAS), Dr Graham Hurst (BAS), Dr Des Lugg (Australian Antarctic Division), Dr David Pratt CBE, FIMechE (Commonwealth Trans-Antarctic Expedition), Roderick Rhys Jones (BAS & British Antarctic Monument Trust), Pete Salino (BAS), the late Professor William Sladen MBE (FIDS), and Dr Yoshio Yoshida (Fourth Japanese Antarctic Research Expedition). Any opinions expressed, and mistakes committed, remain the sole responsibility of the author.

In addition, I have benefited enormously from the assistance of Billy-Ace Baker (American Polar Society), James Brooks (Head of Court and Tribunals Service, the Falkland Islands Government), Brian Dorsett-Bailey (brother of Jeremy Bailey), Mrs Irene Gillies (sister of Alistair 'Jock' Forbes), Dr Henry Guly (BAS Medical Unit), Derek Gunn (son of Bernie Gunn), Professor

Matthew Hall (Professor of Law & Criminal Justice, University of Lincoln), David Harrowfield, Dr David Keatley (School of Psychology, University of Lincoln), the Coroner's Office of the Falkland Islands Government, Dr Peter Marquis (BAS), Mayumi Miyashita (National Institute of Polar Research, Japan), Richard McElrea (New Zealand Coroner), Gary Pierson (South-pole.com), Mrs Jocelyn Sladen (wife of Professor William Sladen), Robert B. Stephenson of the Antarctic Circle website (www.antarctic-circle.org) and Ivar Stokkeland (Norwegian Polar Institute).

In particular, I should like to express my gratitude to Ieaun Hopkins, Jo Rae and Beverley Ager of the British Antarctic Survey's Archives Department, whose expertise and generosity with their time have made researching this book infinitely easier than it might otherwise have been.

Finally, I should like to thank my wife, Caroline, and my son, George, for all their love and support – and for heroically resisting the temptation to roll their eyes when I began to regale them with yet more anecdotes relating to the exploration of Antarctica.

Stephen Haddelsey
Halam, Nottinghamshire
September 2017

AUTHOR'S NOTE

In writing this book my intention has not been to provide a comprehensive list of every fatality suffered during the exploration of Antarctica, for such a list I refer the reader to John Stewart's excellent *Antarctica: An Encyclopedia* (Jefferson: McFarland & Company, 1990). Instead, I have sought to identify a range of accidents which, arranged thematically, should serve to highlight some of the more common hazards faced by those who, over the course of the last century or so, have been actively engaged in pushing back the boundaries of our geographic and scientific knowledge of the continent.

For a number of reasons, which include language, accessibility and the comprehensiveness of the British Antarctic Survey (BAS) Archives, many of the examples cited are from the United Kingdom; however, so far as has been practicable, I have included representative stories from as many nations as possible, including Argentina, Australia, Brazil, France, Japan, New Zealand, Norway, South Africa, the Soviet Union, Sweden, the United Kingdom and the United States.

Finally, I have chosen, quite deliberately, to restrict myself to deaths that have occurred during expeditions dedicated to the exploration and scientific investigation of the continental landmass, the vast majority of these being government sponsored. Excluded, therefore (with only two exceptions), are casualties sustained at sea, during tourism, and in privately organised small-scale ventures where tests of human endurance are the aim rather than a consequence of the exercise.

INTRODUCTION

On the morning of 22 January 1913, a party of eight men struggled to the summit of Observation Hill on the south-west tip of Ross Island, Antarctica. Between them they carried a 3.5m-long cross of Australian mahogany gum tree, or *Eucalyptus marginata*, a densely grained hardwood known to the Aborigines as *jarrah*. 'It was a heavy job,' wrote the amateur zoologist Apsley Cherry-Garrard that evening, 'and the ice was looking very bad all around, and I for one was glad when we had got it up by 5 o'clock or so.'[1]

Once slotted into a hole dug the previous day, the white-painted cross stood 2.5m tall, commanding McMurdo Sound on one side and the barren white wasteland of the Ross Ice Shelf, or the 'Great Barrier' as it was then known, on the other. 'It is really magnificent,' Cherry-Garrard enthused, 'and will be a permanent memorial which could be seen from the ship nine miles [14.5km] off with a naked eye … I do not believe it will ever move.'[2]

The cross commemorates the sacrifice of Captain Robert Falcon Scott, Dr Edward Wilson, Lieutenant Henry Bowers, Petty Officer Edgar Evans and Captain Lawrence Oates, and the men who raised it intended that it should endure; what they could not have foreseen was that this landmark would become the single most recognisable icon, certainly of British, and arguably of all, 'Heroic Age' Antarctic exploration. Nearly half a century later, recalling his own very recent initiation into polar exploration, Sir Edmund Hillary would write:

My ideas of the Antarctic were hazy in the extreme and, if I thought about it at all, I imagined a sombre land of bitter cold and heroic suffering, of

serious men dedicated to impossible ideals, and of lonely crosses out in the snowy wastes.[3]

In January 1957 Hillary had established his own winter quarters almost in the shadow of Observation Hill, so there can be no doubt that he was thinking of Scott's memorial.

In the sixty years since Hillary wrote his account of his essential, but highly contentious, part in the Commonwealth Trans-Antarctic Expedition (CTAE) of 1956–58, our perceptions of the expeditions launched by the Edwardian polar explorers have changed remarkably little. Just like Hillary, we anticipate stories of frostbitten heroes slogging across barren landscapes, hauling unbearably heavy sledges towards impossible goals. And, in our imaginings, they usually die in the process, lying in sodden reindeer skin sleeping bags, exhausted, emaciated and with their hands and faces blackened with frostbite. No matter whether their labours are seen as heroic and noble (as they were by Scott's hagiographic early biographers) or futile and ill-judged (as many revisionist historians argue), suffering and death sit at the core of our perception of the first Antarctic explorers.

The identification of death as a defining characteristic of their expeditions began with the very earliest commentators. The British polar historian James Gordon Hayes, who coined the term the 'Heroic Age' in his 1932 book *The Conquest of the South Pole*, described the period as beginning when Scott embarked on the *Discovery* in 1901 and ending with Shackleton's *Endurance* Expedition in 1917.

Although the phrase is now commonly applied to a slightly wider period, beginning with the Sixth International Geographical Congress of 1895 and terminating with Shackleton's death at the outset of his *Quest* Expedition in 1922,[4] its main features, as summarised by Hayes, remain unchanged. Its work was accomplished 'for the most part under difficult conditions'; its successes were achieved with imperfect means, 'the man was greater than the machine'; its stories form a record of how 'for the last time in human history, large parts of an unknown continent have been unveiled'; and, finally, its prosecution was acutely dangerous, particularly for the British explorers whose footsteps 'were continually dogged by disaster'. For Hayes, these attributes, or shortcomings, appeared to render the exploits of the explorers of the first quarter of the twentieth century more perilous, more romantic and therefore intrinsically more appealing than the expeditions that followed.

And yet a comparison of the earlier and later expeditions reveals that they had much more in common than we might suppose – and this is nowhere more evident than in their casualty statistics.

Of the 664 men estimated to have taken part in the expeditions launched between 1895 and 1922,[5] nineteen died – approximately 2.9 per cent of the total.[6] Of these, seven died of starvation, hypothermia or vitamin deficiencies while on long-distance sledging expeditions; three drowned or were killed in shipboard accidents; five succumbed to disease; three died on local sledging expeditions; and one died in a crevasse fall, during a long-distance sledging expedition but on the outbound journey, while in good health and with ample supplies of food and fuel. Expressed another way, this means that each man who took part in an Antarctic expedition between 1895 and 1922 faced a one in thirty-five chance of death. Although the risks varied significantly depending upon the exact duties of the individuals involved, with a base cook less likely to die than a long-distance sledger, these odds do not appear to be too unfavourable, given the harshness of the environment, the pioneering nature of the work, the limitations of the equipment and knowledge then available and the distance of the expeditions from external aid.

As Hayes acknowledged, a higher proportion of British explorers 'purchased their discoveries with their lives',[7] and of the 155 men involved in the shore-based operations of the British expeditions launched between 1901 and 1921, ten died – 6.5 per cent of the total, equivalent to a one in sixteen chance of death. As might be expected, the year that generated the highest number of casualties was 1912, simultaneously the *annus mirabilis* and *annus horribilis* of Heroic Age exploration, when five expeditions were in the field. In total, eight men died between 17 February and 14 December, of whom all but one was British.[8]

It's difficult to calculate accurately the total number of fatalities for all nations during what we might, for convenience, describe as the 'Post-Heroic' period, but we do have detailed figures for British and US operations. Between 1922, the year of Shackleton's death, and 1961, the year in which the International Antarctic Treaty was ratified, the United States lost thirty-one men and the British lost eleven,[9] with all these casualties sustained between 1946 and 1961.

At first glance, the loss of forty-two lives in just fifteen years seems excessive, especially when compared with the nineteen lost during the twenty-seven years of the Heroic Age, but this perception does not take into account the huge increase in activity in the same period. For instance, during the austral summer of 1946–47, the United States sent 4,700 men south as part of its colossal Cold War exercise, Operation Highjump. Of these, just four died (a casualty rate of 0.09 per cent). Although numbers reduced after the operation, with just 179 men divided between twenty stations operated by eleven different nations during 1955, they increased exponentially during the International Geophysical Year (IGY) of 1957–58, with a winter population of 912 men, rising in the summer months to approximately 5,000.[10] In that period, Britain sustained three casualties (2.4 per cent of the total British personnel of 127, or a one in forty-two chance of death) and the United States sustained nine (2.7 per cent of 339 personnel, or one in thirty-eight).

Given our perception of the heightened dangerousness of the early period of Antarctic exploration, it's surprising to see that the difference in the chance of death during the Heroic and Post-Heroic eras is not as great as we might expect – particularly when those deaths are considered as percentages of the personnel as a whole. Writing of the casualties sustained during the IGY, Walter Sullivan, who reported on the enterprise for *The New York Times*, opined:

> Such mishaps were due, essentially, to the novelty of the environment in which men and equipment had been called upon to operate. Had the nature of the hazards been fully understood, they would not have been much greater than those confronting the man who tries to dash across Fifth Avenue against the lights. The difference was that the jaywalker, however foolhardy, has usually lived with city traffic all his life.[11]

Of course, the hazards referred to by Sullivan are essentially the same for all Antarctic expeditions and in order to understand the enduring appeal of polar exploration we must first recognise the uniqueness and the challenges of the environment in which that exploration was, and is, prosecuted.

A continent of more than 8 million square kilometres, Antarctica is the coldest, driest, highest and windiest land mass on the face of the globe, with 98 per cent of its surface area permanently covered in ice and snow to depths that can exceed 3km. Mean temperatures range between −40°C and −70°C during the long, dark winter months, while winds that gust at well over 322kph not only reduce visibility by hurling clouds of drift snow into the air but also, through the phenomenon known as the 'wind chill factor',[12] remove heat from a body so that it quickly cools to the current air temperature. In these conditions, exposed flesh freezes almost immediately, resulting in damage that, in the worst cases, can mean the loss of extremities such as fingers, toes, nose and ears. Eyelashes freeze together, gluing eyes shut, and exhaled breath and nasal mucous congeal to form heavy 'ice masks' that must be thawed or cut away. Even teeth will split with the cold, as happened to Edward Wilson's Cape Crozier party during the *Terra Nova* Expedition.

On clear days, the power of the sun, the lack of water vapour in the air and the reflective glare of the ice, will combine to severely burn unprotected skin. If goggles are not worn, the eyes, too, will burn, causing photokeratitis, or snow-blindness, a temporary but acutely painful loss of vision that makes the sufferer feel as though their eyes are full of sand. On cloudy days, even during the summer months, perception can be massively distorted as a result of the loss of the visual clues usually provided by colour and contrast: objects lying only a foot away can appear to be far distant, and vice versa. Frank Bickerton, mechanical engineer on Mawson's Australasian Antarctic Expedition (AAE) of 1911–14, memorably compared this phenomenon of 'white-out' to 'living in a spherical tent made of sheets, except for the wind. Such days were an outrage to our senses.'[13] If forced to endure such disorientation for long, he thought, 'you would soon go mad'.[14]

In these conditions travel, whether by foot or vehicle, becomes impossible or, at best, extremely perilous – particularly where crevasses are present. These fissures are formed as the ice sheets flowing down from the Polar Plateau buckle and split as they collide with underlying surface inequalities, with mountains, and with each other. Over time, the mouths of the crevasses are plugged by drift snow that renders them largely invisible and therefore doubly dangerous. The strength of the snow bridges formed in this fashion is dependent upon a number of factors including depth, width and air temperature and, in the event of a collapse, the larger crevasses are quite capable of swallowing a man, a dog team or even a motor vehicle. During the IGY, a series of fatalities sustained during routine vehicle movements close to base demonstrated just how vulnerable tractor drivers could be, with the result that long-distance motorised parties often travelled no faster than the man-hauled sledges of the Heroic Age – a fact that caused the US scientist Palle Mogensen to remark dolefully, 'With all this horsepower and modern equipment, we can't do better than they did – twenty miles a day!'[15]

A combination of white-out, high winds, tidal changes and fluctuations in temperature also significantly increases the risk of travelling on sea or bay ice, as two members of Shackleton's *Endurance* Expedition discovered to their cost when, on 8 May 1916, the young sea ice on which they were travelling from Hut Point to Cape Evans broke up during a blizzard. They were the first Antarctic explorers to die in such a fashion, but many more followed, and in the twenty-four years between 1958 and 1982, the break-up of sea ice claimed no fewer than seven lives from Britain alone.

The changes wrought in the landscape by such conditions can also prove fatally disorienting, as happened on 23 February 1951, when three members of the Norwegian–British–Swedish Antarctic Expedition drove their Studebaker Weasel over a newly formed and invisible ice edge, straight into the killingly cold waters of the Weddell Sea.

As well as causing the destruction of sea ice, the action of the strong katabatic winds sculpts the surface ice into sastrugi, wave-like crests that can be up to 1.5m tall and as hard as iron. It is these sastrugi that have caused so many explorers to compare the Antarctic landscape to a frozen sea and they constitute a major obstacle, not only to those travelling over the surface but also to anyone trying to land an aircraft, as Hillary and his RNZAF pilot, John Claydon, found on 25 January 1957 when they only narrowly avoided ripping the skis from their de Havilland Beaver.

Where the scouring action of the wind is absent, soft snow collects in layers so deep that a man on foot will sink to his groin, making every step a struggle. If this accumulation occurs on floating ice, its weight can be sufficient to push the underlying ice beneath the surface of the water, so that anyone attempting to cross it is likely to suffer from wet as well as cold feet. During Operation Tabarin, a top-secret wartime expedition designed to re-establish British sovereignty in the face of Argentine incursions, a sledging party encountered this phenomenon while traversing Erebus and Terror Gulf on the eastern side of the Antarctic Peninsula. In temperatures of −34°C, their feet became encased in solid casts of ice as soon as they lifted them from the deep snow, significantly increasing the risk of frostbite.

To further exacerbate the difficulties of those navigating without the benefit of the Global Positioning System, the close proximity of the Magnetic South Pole renders magnetic compasses erratic and unreliable while, on overcast days, the alternative sun compass becomes equally useless. In these conditions, even an experienced polar traveller can stray unwittingly from his chosen course and enter a crevasse field, with potentially devastating results.

Finally, and of particular relevance to those seeking to reach the South Pole – the primary objective of many, though not all, early expeditions – the lifeless interior of the continent rises to around 4,267m above sea level. At this altitude, the atmosphere becomes so rarefied that the performance of men, dogs and motor vehicles is seriously inhibited, and for many years aircraft trying to take off from the Amundsen–Scott South Pole Station could do so only with the aid of Jet Assisted Take-Off (JATO) solid-fuel rockets.

★ ★ ★

These, then, are the natural conditions common to all Antarctic expeditions; it is in their knowledge, equipment and tactics that they differ. In fact, though we often think of the early explorers as ordinary men, striving against extraordinary obstacles with only the most primitive aids to support them, innovative technology formed a part of every Heroic Age British foray into Antarctica: Scott's National Antarctic (*Discovery*) Expedition of 1901–04 carried a hot air balloon; Shackleton's 1907 British Antarctic (*Nimrod*) Expedition included a four-cylinder, 15hp Arrol-Johnston motor car in its equipment; and Mawson purchased both a Vickers REP monoplane and the latest wireless sets for his 1911 expedition. Scott and Shackleton would both take motorised sledges on their later expeditions and a de Havilland Gipsy Moth biplane became central to Mawson's plans for his British, Australian and New Zealand Antarctic Research Expedition (BANZARE) of 1929–31.

In choosing to adopt the very latest technology available to them, the Heroic Age explorers were quite deliberately following the example of some of the earliest expeditions into Antarctic waters, most notably James Cook's second voyage of discovery (1772–75), during which the canny Yorkshireman made full use of a copy of John Harrison's revolutionary fourth chronometer to establish his longitude.[16] Just like Cook, Scott, Shackleton and their peers all believed that technology could ease their labours and make their objectives more attainable. So far as motor vehicles were concerned, Scott was 'convinced of their value',[17] while Shackleton put up a fierce defence when the utility of his motor-sledges was challenged by a sceptical committee of the Royal Geographical Society in March 1914. These men were not temperamentally or philosophically wedded to a bygone age, but all too often the latest products of the industrial age failed to live up to their expectations and forced them to revert to more primitive but tried and tested methods.

Temperamental though it might be, it is also true that no casualty on the early expeditions was directly attributable to the experimental technology: balloons ascended and descended without an explorer plummeting to his death, and while the motorised sledges broke down with tiresome regularity, they did so without exploding or carrying an unwary driver through the sea ice or into the depths of an unseen crevasse. Indeed, the closest a Heroic Age explorer ever came to being killed by new technology was when, on 5 October 1911, the AAE's Vickers monoplane fell to earth, injuring both Frank Wild, the veteran English explorer, and the pilot, Hugh Watkins. Ironically, however, this accident occurred not in Antarctica but at the Cheltenham Racecourse in Adelaide, weeks before Mawson's expedition sailed south. In reality, it was only with the advent of more reliable motor vehicles and aircraft that the first deaths began to occur, though most resulted from human error rather than from mechanical failure.

With the gradual refinement and improvement of technology over the coming decades, entirely new challenges and fresh variations to old dangers were encountered, many of which could not have been foreseen. The CTAE, for example, would almost certainly have failed without the Tucker Sno-Cats that became the mainstay of Vivian Fuchs's transcontinental journey. Powered by a 200hp Chrysler V8 petrol engine and with a top speed of 24kph, the Sno-Cat's greatest advantage was its unique traction system, which provided almost 100 per cent traction even when turning in soft snow. But its design also contained a number of flaws. In particular, a complicated lubrication system meant that the convoy had to stop every few days so that a grease gun could be applied to each vehicle's 320 individual grease nipples – a tedious job even in a heated garage, and triply so on the Polar Plateau, with a temperature of −29°C and a wind blowing at 40kph. 'And imagine what a grease gun does in a stiff breeze,' one expeditionary recalled with a shudder, 'you get oil everywhere, all over your anoraks – filthy!'[18] Worse still, fabric impregnated with grease cannot breathe properly and body moisture becomes trapped. This means that clothes lose their insulation value and their wearers become more prone to frostbite and hypothermia, despite having taken all the usual precautions.

Problems such as these meant that many of the non-engineering staff of both Heroic and Post-Heroic expeditions came to regard their vehicles with uncertainty and even antipathy. After watching the trials of Shackleton's propeller sledge in Norway in May 1914, expedition artist George Marston remarked pessimistically, 'Perhaps it will go for twenty min[utes]',[19] while, for his part, when asked about the potential for the development of emotional ties with the machines used a little over forty years later, CTAE surveyor Ken Blaiklock recalled, 'Most people just regarded them as a lump of metal to get from A to B ... No, I don't think there was any attachment in that way.'[20] Dog-drivers like Blaiklock were also keen to point out that dogs on a fan trace will almost always stop safely in the event of one of their number falling into an unseen crevasse; the same could hardly be said of a 3–tonne Sno-Cat.

Similarly, while it might seem perfectly reasonable to suppose that the introduction of wireless telegraphy would constitute an unequivocal boon to polar explorers, the evidence reveals that, from the outset, its psychological effects were mixed. When preparing for his *Terra Nova* Expedition, Scott considered including a transmitter and a generator in his equipment, but eventually he was dissuaded by their size and combined weight. Instead, Mawson made the pioneering experiment, taking two complete sets of Telefunken apparatus on his AAE.[21] He knew that if the expedition succeeded in sending and receiving messages via a relay station on Macquarie Island some of the doubt and uncertainty inherent in Antarctic exploration would be effectively removed and for the first time an expedition would be able to announce to the outside world both its achievements and, perhaps more importantly, its exact location.

During the AAE's first year success was extremely limited, with the operator on Macquarie Island able to pick up only disjointed words and phrases from the messages dispatched from Cape Denison on the Antarctic mainland. But, after the erection of a new aerial mast, communication improved during the second year and an important precedent was set. And yet, surprisingly, the wireless seemed to make so little difference to the explorers' lives that Archie McLean, the medical officer, observed, 'We ... scarcely think about the fact that it is the first time any Polar expedition wintering has been in wireless communication with the outside world.'[22] Mawson's insistence that his men should pay for sending personal messages – a decision forced on him by the parlous condition of the AAE's finances – further discouraged use and, finally, the senior operator's descent into madness turned the wireless into a liability when he began to send garbled and paranoid transmissions to the outside world and to hide or deliberately mistranslate incoming messages. As a result, the introduction of wireless to the Antarctic has become inextricably linked with one of the most florid of all examples of mental illness in the polar regions.

The double-edged nature of wireless communication continued to be apparent in the Post-Heroic period. In a curious and probably unique inversion, when sitting comparatively snug and secure in their hut on the northern tip of the Antarctic Peninsula, the personnel of Operation Tabarin found themselves listening, courtesy of the BBC's live broadcasts from London, to the profoundly disturbing sounds of German bombs falling on their homes in England – an experience hardly likely to reconcile them to their separation from family and friends. Even in less extreme circumstances, many explorers discovered that wireless increased rather than reduced their feelings of isolation, with some finding that their day-to-day lives had become so different to the routine experiences of those at home that they had little or nothing to say to one another. After one exchange, Rainer Goldsmith, the physiologist with the CTAE's Advance Party, observed dejectedly, 'They have very little understanding of the sort of things that we might be interested in.'[23] Blaiklock, the Advance Party's leader, also acknowledged that, in their isolation, explorers become:

> … very parochial … five minutes after the outbreak of the Vietnam War, for example, you're discussing have we got enough dog meat? You're very self-centred shall we say? You're concerned with your own problems, the whole base's problems, not the world's.[24]

All too often, the fact that wireless changed explorers' expectations regarding the frequency and content of communications was entirely lost upon officials at home and in a paper entitled 'Cold Weather Hazards', Eric Back, the medical officer to Operation Tabarin, stated:

> In order to keep up the morale of isolated parties they should be kept informed of the work in hand … The sense of frustration experienced by men completely isolated in the cold and given no information about future plans can be extremely galling and is often not appreciated by those at home.[25]

But, as Fuchs learned during the CTAE, the reverse could also be true. Having embarked upon one of the most hazardous portions of his journey, he found himself so distracted by the clamour of the BBC and his expedition committee for daily updates and press releases that he feigned wireless blackouts in order to bend his mind to rather more pressing matters.[26]

The impacts of wireless, then, have been much more complex than might have been expected and some studies have even shown that parties working in the most remote, isolated and demanding environments actually perform better, both physically and mentally, than those more subject to outside influences. Though it would be wrong to suggest that its role was in any way decisive, there is even evidence that wireless, and the responsibilities its maintenance entailed, played some part in the suicide of Arthur Farrant at Deception Island in November 1953.

Without doubt, the technological innovation that truly transformed Antarctic exploration was the advent of powered flight. Hubert Wilkins, Richard E. Byrd, Hjalmar Riiser-Larsen, Douglas Mawson, John Rymill and Lincoln Ellsworth all successfully used aeroplanes in the Antarctic during the 1920s and 1930s, but their operations were on a tiny scale when compared with the post-war era. The frequency and duration of flights during the IGY dwarfed anything that had gone before – as can be gauged from the fact that, in the three months between 20 November 1956 and 21 February 1957, the United States Navy airlifted 772 tonnes of cargo to the South Pole in sixty-five separate sorties.

For all its benefits, such a colossal expansion of air activity in polar conditions must itself increase the likelihood of accidents, and throughout the 1950s and 1960s the death toll from aircraft accidents rose exponentially. Add to the unavoidable environmental factors, including white-outs, high winds and poor surface conditions, the fact that much of the flying was completed in large aircraft, such as the Douglas C-124 Globemaster and the Lockheed P2V Neptune, and the probability of multiple casualties being sustained in just one accident also increased. This reality was tragically proved on 18 October 1956 when a Neptune crashed at McMurdo, killing four, and again on 16 October 1958 when six men died in a Globemaster crash in the Admiralty Mountains. However, the potential for air accidents to skew the figures was most potently demonstrated on 28 November 1979 when, in the worst of all disasters in the Antarctic, an Air New Zealand McDonnell Douglas DC-10 ploughed into the slopes of Mount Erebus, killing all 257 passengers and crew.

★ ★ ★

Even if we discount such 'freak' catastrophes as the loss of Air New Zealand Flight 901, air crashes account for more deaths in the Antarctic than any other single cause. But, of course, it is also true that the vast majority of the casualties sustained during routine flights in support of Antarctic operations have been suffered by the United States, the scale of whose air activity is vastly greater than that of any other nation.

For countries with a smaller presence in the Antarctic, environmental conditions continue to pose the greatest threat. For example, of the twenty-seven casualties sustained by the Falkland Islands Dependencies Survey (FIDS) and its successor, the British Antarctic Survey (BAS), between 1948 and the present day, a total of twenty-two are directly attributable to drowning, the break-up of sea ice, crevasse falls (including five in, or on, vehicles), exposure or climbing accidents. Of the remaining five, two men died in a fire, one suffered a heart attack, one committed suicide and one was struck by a low-flying aircraft. Neither FIDS nor BAS have suffered any deaths among the passengers or crew of their aircraft, though there have been innumerable narrow escapes, usually as a result of forced landings.

Inevitably, the environmental conditions that have caused so many fatalities can also generate psychological and physiological responses that can seriously affect the mental well-being of those engaged in exploration and research. Causes and effects are generally much better understood today than they were a century ago, but prevention is still problematic, and debate continues about the effectiveness of the psychological profiling of candidates for Antarctic field work. The phenomenon known colloquially as 'cabin fever', for instance, is a well-documented condition directly attributable to long periods spent in isolation and winter darkness. Its onset is marked by restlessness, irritability, irrational frustration, disturbed sleep patterns and paranoia, and it is now known to result from a lack of sunlight, which in turn accelerates the pineal gland's secretion of melatonin. Its seriousness varies according to the individual but on a small base its effects, if not managed carefully, can be highly disruptive and even catastrophic – particularly when they are combined with other factors, such as a poor or insufficient diet, lack of privacy, limited recreation, absence of sex, poor communications, personal incompatibility, and pre-existing mental conditions such as depression.

In the event of trauma or death, post-traumatic stress can be added to this catalogue – and the impact of a fatality on a small, close-knit and mutually dependent community should not be underestimated, however much the mechanisms and support for dealing with the emotional aftermath might change over time. It is a telling fact that, where fatalities have been sustained, survivors generally have chosen not to erect memorial crosses until the point of their own departure – perhaps because they were keen to avoid living in the shadow of such depressing reminders. A parallel might be found in the habit of wartime squadrons not to allow empty chairs at the mess table or to discuss the fallen. How much worse, then, is the position when bodies are recovered and where the facilities available to modern expeditions enable the *eventual* repatriation of corpses. In these situations, those in mourning must continue their work, knowing that the bodies of their companions are held in storage just a few metres from where they continue to eat, sleep and work.

Given this occasionally toxic cocktail of environmental and psychological factors it is surprising that suicide remains a highly unusual phenomenon on polar bases. Murder is absolutely unknown, though the death, on 12 May 2000, of Dr Rodney Marks, a 32-year-old Australian astrophysicist, gave rise to much speculation. Marks died from imbibing methanol but, according to the New Zealand Coroner's inquest, 'there was no suggestion of suicide',[27] and no satisfactory explanation of how and why he drank the methanol has ever been forthcoming. The coroner, Richard McElrea, found that the death was 'unintended', but the mysterious disappearance from Marks' room of 'a weird bottle, with the prawn on the side',[28] and the fact that his poisoning highlighted 'an unsatisfactory hiatus as to the proper investigation of a death occurring in Antarctica under these circumstances'[29] inevitably resulted in many newspapers reporting the death as potentially 'the first South Pole murder'.[30]

★ ★ ★

In spite of the overwhelming evidence that the early Antarctic expeditions were only marginally riskier than those that followed, in popular perception the Heroic Age remains a distinct period, defined by tragedy and sacrifice. The Post-Heroic period, on the other hand, is seen as comparatively 'safe' and its activities not only routine but also facilitated by the unequivocally beneficial impacts of modern technology. James Gordon Hayes was quite definite on the subject, asserting that it was because of the early explorers' sacrifices that he 'suggested that this period should be known as the Heroic Age'.[31] He also argued that the expeditions that followed the death of Shackleton were quite different – and while Hayes' work is now largely forgotten, the taxonomy of polar exploration that he defined lives on.

In recent years, cultural historians like Stephanie Barczewski and Max Jones have done much to chart the process by which Scott and his companions achieved virtual canonisation in the years immediately after their deaths, embodying as they did all the qualities of heroism and self-sacrifice so beloved of the empire.[32] And while public perception of imperial heroes has undergone substantial revision over the course of the last century – a process begun by Lytton Strachey, but nowhere more noticeable than in the movement from the hagiographic early biographies of Scott by writers like Harold Avery and Stephen Gwynn to Roland Huntford's vitriolic debunking in *Scott and Amundsen* – these changes have done nothing to stifle interest in the Heroic Age.

An unfortunate consequence of Hayes' categorisation and of our obsession with the Heroic Age – an obsession fuelled, in part at least, by our mistaken conviction that its risks exceeded those of later periods – is that the achievements, personalities and sacrifices of the Post-Heroic phase of Antarctic exploration have been largely obscured. While the parallel careers of Scott and Shackleton have spawned a quite extraordinary number of biographies, narrative histories, management studies and deconstructions, books on the most important British expeditions of the later period have been limited to the official accounts published in the immediate aftermath of those ventures.[33] There is, for instance, no popular narrative history of Rymill's British Graham Land Expedition (BGLE) of 1934–37, despite its being widely acknowledged as one of the most important and successful British expeditions of the first half of the twentieth century. Similarly, only in very recent years have Operation Tabarin and Fuchs's CTAE received any attention from popular historians.[34]

And yet it is an irrefutable fact that the vast majority of the Antarctic continent was explored not by the men of the Heroic Age, but by their successors. During the CTAE alone, Fuchs's Advance and Crossing parties discovered two new mountain ranges and traversed for the first time the seemingly endless wilderness that lies between Vahsel Bay and the South Pole. On the other side of the continent, George Marsh and Bob Miller of Hillary's Ross Sea Party discovered another two new mountain ranges, proved that the Queen Alexandra Range was made up of five distinct chains, and located four new glacier systems. Meanwhile, Richard Brooke and his Northern Party sledged well over 1,000 miles and climbed an astonishing thirty-one mountains, most of which had never previously been scaled.

The explorers of the Post-Heroic phase also achieved a number of important 'firsts': the first flight to the South Pole (Byrd, 1929); the first transcontinental flight (Ellsworth and Hollick-Kenyon, 1935); the first motorised journey to the Pole (Hillary, 1957–58); and the first surface crossing of the continent (Fuchs, 1957–58). Nor could these achievements be described as the 'dregs' left by the explorers of the Heroic Age. Completion of a surface crossing, in particular, was an ambition of Bruce, Scott, Shackleton and Filchner, and held by many to be at least equally desirable as reaching the South Pole. Indeed, while it had long been accepted that a traverse of the continent would have undeniable scientific and geographical benefits, not least the ability to determine whether Antarctica was a continent or a huge archipelago, a sizeable contingent of 'scientific explorers' saw little intrinsic value in the conquest of the pole.

In all probability, men like Scott, Shackleton, Byrd, Rymill and Fuchs would have considered themselves fellow travellers in a historical and exploratory continuum. Each was keen to use the best equipment and techniques available to him – but each knew that the environment in which he operated could render that equipment and those techniques futile, redundant and even dangerous. Certainly, we can be confident that the phrase 'Heroic Age', a retrospectively applied collective term, would have meant nothing to the men who took part in the expeditions of the period. Indeed, the term 'hero' tends to sit far more comfortably with the dead than with the living and it is very doubtful that Scott and his companions would have accepted it willingly.

Similarly, the later explorers did not recognise the existence of an unbridgeable gulf between themselves and their predecessors; instead, they saw themselves as inheritors of the 'heroic tradition'. George Lowe, official photographer on Fuchs' expedition, was quite typical when, in the immediate aftermath of the CTAE, he looked back to the expeditions of Scott and Amundsen as the benchmark by which to measure Fuchs' achievement. 'Although we used vehicles we still clung to camping and eating rules of the past ...' he wrote in *The Mountain World*:

> Then, Amundsen with his dogs or Scott on foot walked the 1,800 desperate miles. Amundsen averaged 17 miles a day with his dog teams and returned according to plan; Scott averaged a dozen miles a day and died tragically within a hundred miles of his base ... in the future there will be no place for the lightly equipped hardy dash which was the spirit in which our expedition was conceived.[35]

For his part, Rainer Goldsmith described the CTAE as, quite simply, 'the last of the heroic expeditions – full stop!'[36]

To this day, curious and intrepid men and women continue to explore, research and document the Antarctic continent, and while an improved understanding of the risks involved, a tightening of safety procedures and swifter evacuation all mean that death is no longer ever-present, it is still a regular visitor. To evidence this fact, one need only look at the tally of casualties among the various international Antarctic programmes during the twenty-first century: one British (in 2003); one Russian (2008); two South African (2006 and 2009); two Brazilian (2012); and one Australian (2016).

Recognising the high and continuing cost in human lives of Antarctic exploration, on 10 May 2011 the British Antarctic Monument Trust unveiled a new memorial of Welsh slate and Carrara marble in the crypt of St Paul's Cathedral, dedicating it to all 'those who lost their lives in Antarctica'. Fittingly, the memorial makes no distinctions regarding roles, ranks, gender, causes of death or the period in which those deaths occurred: all are commemorated equally.

In the following pages, we will meet many of those intrepid explorers and scientists, of all nations, and examine how and why they died 'in pursuit of science to benefit us all'.

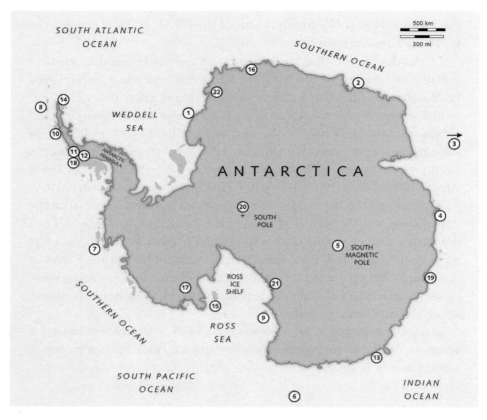

Approximate locations of fatalities mentioned in the text:

1 **HALLEY BAY**
Neville Mann – 15 August 1963
Dai Wild ⎫
John Wilson ⎬ 12 October 1965
Jeremy Bailey ⎭

2 **EAST ONGUL ISLAND**
Shin Fukushima – 10 October 1960

3 **HEARD ISLAND**
Richard Hoseason ⎫
Alistair Forbes ⎬ 26/27 May 1952

4 **MIRNY**
Ivan Kharma – January 1956
Oskar Krichak ⎫
Igor Popov ⎬ 3 August 1960
+ 6 others ⎭

5 **VOSTOK**
Aleksei Karpenko – 12 April 1982

6 **BALLENY ISLANDS**
Leif Lier ⎫
Ingvald Schreiner ⎬ 26 December 1929

7 **THURSTON ISLAND**
Max Lopez ⎫
Fred Williams ⎬ 30 December 1946
Wendell Hendersin ⎭

8 **DECEPTION ISLAND**
Arthur Farrant – 17 November 1953

9 **ROSS ISLAND**
Aeneas Mackintosh ⎫
Victor Hayward ⎬ 8 May 1916
Richard T. Williams – 6 January 1956

10 **PETERMANN ISLAND**
John Coll ⎫
Kevin Ockleton ⎬ 14 August 1982
Ambrose Morgan ⎭

11 **HORSESHOE ISLAND**
David Statham ⎫
Stanley Black ⎬ 27 May 1958
Geoffrey Stride ⎭

12 **STONINGTON ISLAND**
John Noel ⎫
Tom Allan ⎬ c. 26 May 1966

13 **PETREL ISLAND**
André Prud'homme – 7 January 1959

14 **HOPE BAY**
Oliver Burd ⎫
Michael Green ⎬ 9 November 1948

15 **LITTLE AMERICA**
Vance Woodall – 21 January 1947

16 **MAUDHEIM**
Bertil Ekström ⎫
John Jelbart ⎬ 24 February 1951
Leslie Quar ⎭

17 **MARIE BYRD LAND**
Max Kiel – 5 March 1956

18 **ROTHERA**
John Anderson ⎫
Robert Atkinson ⎬ 16 May 1981
Kirsty Brown – 22 July 2003

19 **WILKES**
Hartley Robinson – 7 July 1959

20 **SOUTH POLE**
Rodney Marks – 12 May 2000

21 **CAPE SELBORNE**
Tom Couzens – 19 November 1959

22 **VESLESKARVET NUNATAK**
Donald Voight – 22 December 2006

1

'The Worst Thing Possible'

Fire in Antarctica

Ever since manned space flight became a viable proposition, it has been widely accepted that Antarctic research stations provide perhaps the best opportunities to study many of the environmental, social and psychological conditions that astronauts might experience on long-duration missions to planets such as Mars, and during extended tours at the International Space Station.[1] In particular, psychologists have been keen to determine, first, how protracted periods of confinement in small social groups and in extreme environments can affect group and team dynamics and performance; and, second, whether there are certain personality types that prove more resilient to the stresses inseparable from life in such conditions. Some of the analogous environmental factors cited by researchers include isolation, restricted society and remoteness from external aid. However, there are also shared physical dangers that are less commonly referenced and chief among these is fire.

Robert Friedman of NASA's Lewis Research Center has written that, in space, 'Fire events, even though they have a very low probability of occurrence, are considered serious threats and [are] greatly feared', and he cites the lack of room available in spacecraft cockpits for the storage of firefighting equipment and 'the limited understanding of the unusual characteristics of incipient fires in the low-gravity, weightless environment of orbiting spacecraft' as two of the most important contributing factors.[2]

Neither of these particular problems has been encountered in Antarctic expedition huts, but they, too, have suffered from their own unique and environment-specific fire risks: manufactured almost entirely of wood, the

early expedition huts were heated by solid-fuel burners and lit by liquid fuel lanterns; most expedition personnel smoked tobacco; and, in the winter months, accumulations of drift snow could quickly block windows and doors.

In the near-total absence of any naturally occurring combustible materials,[3] the risk of fire in Antarctica is a man-made phenomenon – but the prevailing environmental conditions, including high winds, the desiccating effects of low humidity and the absence of liquid water for dowsing flames, all increase the threat substantially. For much of the twentieth century, building materials and operating practices meant that the consequences of a base fire could be catastrophic, destroying in a few devastating minutes accommodation, fuel, food, clothing, scientific, survey and construction equipment, wireless sets, scientific collections and written records – to say nothing of the lives of the men themselves. Even today, the United States' Antarctic Fire Department acknowledges that, at McMurdo, 'the loss of a single structure could effectively shut down a significant portion of station operations, if not the entire station altogether', while at the Amundsen–Scott South Pole Station, 'every square inch is vital to station operations. Damage from fire could have catastrophic consequences for station operations.'[4] And yet, despite the introduction of non-flammable and fire-resistant materials, better firefighting equipment and training, and improvements to base design, including the wide separation of buildings, all too often the best way to react to a well-established fire is still to stand back and let it burn.

★ ★ ★

The first accidental fire recorded in Antarctica occurred during the *Southern Cross* Expedition of 1898–1900, the second of the expeditions launched after the Sixth International Geographical Congress of 1895, and the first nominally British expedition of the Heroic Age.[5]

Under its Norwegian-British leader, Carsten Borchgrevink, the expedition landed at Cape Adare, on the north-western tip of Ross Island, on 17 February 1899. The prefabricated living and storage huts, and a magnetic observation hut built from spare materials were complete by the beginning of March and, after some specimen collecting and localised sledging on the sea ice of Robertson Bay, the shore party of ten men settled down for the winter. According to Louis Bernacchi, the expedition's Australian physicist, the cramped conditions within the hut and the darkness and cold without meant that very little work was done during the winter months; instead, the men 'waxed fat and apathetic out of pure inertion and sloth; it was', he opined, 'a life of merely bovine repose'.[6]

This repose was shattered in the early hours of 24 July. 'I awoke through a suffocating smoke,' wrote Borchgrevink, 'and found that one of the members had his bunk on fire.'[7] Given that some reviewers later criticised the sensationalism of his expedition narrative – a product, probably, of the influence of his sponsor, George Newnes, the newspaper magnate – Borchgrevink's account of this potentially devastating incident is both brief and surprisingly matter-of-fact. 'It gave us rather a start,' he observed, 'and I took extra precautions against fire.'[8] For his part, Bernacchi recognised that, if it had been discovered any later, the fire would have become 'a serious catastrophe' and, potentially, 'the most terrible thing that could have happened to us there':

> Being built of pine [the huts] would have been consumed in a few minutes, and we would have had little time to save anything. [Exposure] to that pitiless climate in the depth of winter would have been awful. One of the members, whose night it was to read off the meteorological instruments, carelessly left a lighted candle in his bunk close to the wall. The wall caught fire, and in a few seconds the whole bunk was wrapped in flame and dense smoke filled the room.[9]

Fortunately, the smoke woke the men before it asphyxiated them, and they succeeded in extinguishing the flames, 'but not before a fair amount of damage had been done'.[10]

Following this accident, the extra fire precautions adopted by Borchgrevink included the preparation of ten knapsacks of provisions to be picked up by the men if they evacuated the hut in another emergency. When added to a cache of food, clothing, fuel and equipment left at the foot of Cape Adare, these would enable the men to survive until the return of the *Southern Cross* from Australia in the spring. There could be little doubt that a winter under canvas, or in makeshift shelters, would be profoundly challenging and unpleasant, but later expeditions – particularly the Hope Bay contingent of Otto Nordenskjöld's Swedish Antarctic Expedition of 1901–04, the Northern Party of Scott's *Terra Nova* Expedition of 1910–13, and the Advance Party of Fuchs' Commonwealth Trans-Antarctic Expedition of 1956–58 – would prove that it was at least possible.

The introduction of these and similar measures by later expeditions, including, whenever possible, the construction of a provisioned refuge hut and the rostering of night watches, resulted in much more effective management of fire risk in the Antarctic. Of course, many of the early explorers were sailors who understood the dangers of fire at sea, particularly in wooden-hulled vessels, and the adoption of the necessary safety precautions seems to have met with very little resistance. Night duties also provided time for reading and for the sort of quiet, solitary reflection that otherwise proved so difficult in a hut filled with active young men, and many expedition diaries refer to the oasis-like tranquillity of these hours, when a man might sit 'with a leg thrust into each oven, while the amateur washing dripped on to the red hot stove'.[11]

Certainly, the tactics proved effective, because the first fatal fire in Antarctica did not occur until 1948 – nearly half a century after Borchgrevink's narrowly averted disaster. The site of that fire was Eagle House, the first permanent British shore station to be established on the Antarctic Peninsula, built by the personnel of Operation Tabarin at Hope Bay in February 1945.

★ ★ ★

Roughly 3km wide and 5km deep, Hope Bay cuts into the very tip of the peninsula's northern coastline and it had long been considered Operation Tabarin's primary destination. Jimmy Marr, who landed during a preliminary reconnaissance in early 1944, thought it a 'most delightful place',[12] and its attractions and benefits are immediately apparent to any visitor.

When viewed from the sea, its foreground is defined by a patch of stony ground, about 1.5 square kilometres in extent and stained pink with the ordure of 60,000 penguins. Behind this rocky beach lies a wall of dramatic, jagged black mountains, its hollows and crevices packed with snow. Two of these mountains, in particular, dominate the scene: on the left, or south-east, lies a wide snow-filled basin with a rocky rim, named Mount Flora by Gunnar Andersson of Nordenskjöld's expedition. Its counterpart, to the south-west, is a great round-shouldered hill named Mount Taylor, its looming brow more often than not topped with cloud, or with the streaming plumes of drift snow that indicate the onset of a blizzard. Between the two, Depot Glacier sweeps down towards a narrow inlet at the head of the bay, while, further to the right, Blade Ridge gives way to low ice cliffs, broken by a series of nunataks that resemble, in the words of one later resident, 'black rock teeth with cavities stopped with glacial silver'.[13]

Most important of all, the site offers relatively easy access to the sea ice of Crown Prince Gustav Channel, which separates James Ross Island and Vega Island from the east coast of Graham Land. Dazzled by the benign aspect of this landscape, David James, Assistant Surveyor with Operation Tabarin, wrote that it 'was all so utterly unlike any conceptions we had of the Antarctic even at its best that we all thought Hope Bay to be a land flowing with milk and honey. Yet it must be savage enough in winter.'[14]

A shore party under expedition leader Andrew Taylor chose as the site for Eagle House a spot to the south of a rocky promontory known as Seal Point. Lying at the toe of the massive sheet of inland ice, some 8m above sea level and 1km inland, it consisted of two level areas of moraine, each about 30m square and divided during the summer months by a swift-flowing glacial stream. The advantages were obvious: located some distance from the noisome penguin colonies, the site gave ready access to the glacier for sledgers; during the summer months the glacial stream provided a source of fresh water; and, at the shore, a 2m-high ice foot served as a natural jetty for offloading supplies and equipment from the ship.[15]

The expedition's main building, which Taylor and his team completed in April, was roomy, if not luxurious. At its centre stood two prefabricated wooden huts, each 5m by 11.5m, which the expedition's highly skilled carpenter, Lewis 'Chippy' Ashton, joined together to create a mess room, bedrooms and a workroom. To these, he then added a number of sizeable extensions which housed the galley, storerooms, an engine room for the radio generator, toilets, a laboratory and a carpenter's workshop.

In order to keep the interior warm, two stoves were located in the galley, with additional heaters in the mess, laboratory, survey room and bathhouse. Unfortunately, as Taylor recognised, while this large number of heaters enabled the maintenance of a comfortable ambient temperature, they also increased the risk of fire. Moreover, while the expedition had been provided with four fire extinguishers, they were not particularly well suited to Antarctic conditions. 'They were of the large cylindrical foaming water-filled type,' Taylor remarked wryly:

… on which was printed in bold letters 'Protect from Freezing'. We did the best we could in this respect, but there must have been numerous occasions in the night, after the fires were allowed to die and the temperature dropped, when their service would have been most questionable.[16]

In order to mitigate the risks, Taylor appointed Bill Flett, his second in command, as 'fire chief', responsible for inspecting the stoves every night before lights-out, and for 'giving us occasional talks on certain precautions he wanted us to take'.[17] In addition, they stored a selection of bedding, clothing, rations and radio equipment in a Nissen hut built a short distance away, along with copies of the expedition's precious scientific and survey reports. In the event of a fire, these precautions, they hoped, would give them 'a reasonable chance of replacing a part of our loss, and existing until the spring for a relief ship to arrive'.[18]

The preventative measures introduced by Taylor and Flett worked well, and the only accidental fire that the personnel of Operation Tabarin experienced during their two years in the Antarctic occurred not at Hope Bay, but at Base B, on Deception Island, when one of its two generators caught fire, probably as a result of a stray spark from a loose electrical connection igniting petrol vapour in the engine room. The flames destroyed the generator, but there were no casualties and the wireless officer, Tommy Donnachie, quickly restored communications.[19]

In Taylor's opinion, the expedition as a whole had been lucky, for he had little doubt that, if a fire had started, Eagle House would have become a death trap. In 1947, a year after his return from the Antarctic, he wrote:

> Had a fire ever caught the building in which we were living, there would have been little or no chance of extinguishing it in the high winds which so generally prevailed, and its entire contents would have been destroyed completely.[20]

His remarks would prove tragically prescient.

★ ★ ★

Between August and December 1945, Taylor's party had completed sledging journeys totalling some 1,300km along the eastern shore of Graham Land and in the vicinity of James Ross Island, but much remained to be done – in

particular, the forging of routes up onto the mountainous peninsula itself. This was the work inherited by Operation Tabarin's civilian successor, the Falkland Islands Dependencies Survey (FIDS).

On one FIDS expedition, in November 1948, Base Leader Frank Elliott and three companions set out from Hope Bay to explore the coastline between Cape Kater and Cape Roquemaurel. They made good progress, and by 18 November they had reached a point 457m above sea level inland from Cape Kjellman, the eastern entrance to Charcot Bay, which divides the Trinity Peninsula from the Davis Coast.

But Elliott was becoming increasingly concerned at his inability to establish contact with the three-man party left at Eagle House. Throughout most of the journey he had spoken with the base daily, passing weather reports and receiving messages from the Governor of the Falkland Islands, but then, 'quite suddenly, they went off the air'.[21] Elliott later admitted that, initially, he hadn't been particularly troubled by the break in communications, thinking that 'either the radio equipment had gone wrong temporarily or a generator had gone out of action. We knew they had duplicates, so it would come in again.'[22] But the silence remained unbroken.

On the evening of the 18th, he consulted 'Bunny' Fuchs, the recently appointed FIDS field commander then undertaking a journey through George VI Sound on the western edge of the peninsula, and over the radio they agreed that Elliott's party should immediately return to base. Of course, defective equipment and atmospheric interference often interrupted radio signals, but, as Fuchs himself admitted, a few days previously he had been deeply shocked to learn that Eric Platt, the 22-year-old base leader at Admiralty Bay, had died of a heart attack, and this event might well have increased his desire to understand the cause of the prolonged silence at Hope Bay.

Elliott's party set off the next day and travelled fast, covering, on average, 27km per day over five days, and 63km on their last – a record for the time of year. On 24 November, as they descended the glacier that links Duse Bay with Hope Bay, they passed a newly built cairn, but were too tired after their long journey to examine it. Shortly afterwards, the base came into view – and what they saw appalled them. When they had left a few weeks earlier, Eagle House had been completely buried by drift snow, with only its chimneys, aerials and anemometer poking through, and with shovelled channels marking the location of doors and windows. Now, in place of the expected snow-mound, all they could see was a great, ugly dark smear on the pristine snow, with nothing of the hut remaining but a few scorched timbers. '[There] was just a black hole in the snow,' recalled Elliott, 'and there was nobody there at all.'[23]

★　★　★

Three weeks earlier, on the morning of Wednesday 4 November, Eagle House had been a scene of intense, happy activity. Keen to make an early start, Elliott, John O'Hare, Brian Jefford and Stephen McNeile finished lashing their loads and then pushed the heavy sledges to the spans, where the excited dogs leapt and clawed at the snow in anticipation of their departure. 'Dick' Burd and Michael Green helped with the final preparations and Bill Sladen filmed the teams as they climbed towards the crest of the glacier.

The excitement over, the base personnel returned to the hut 'to tidy up the scene of the usual hasty departure'[24] and discuss the field party's prospects. 'The hut always seems strangely bare and empty after the sledgers have gone,' 'Doc' Sladen noted in his diary, 'but the kitchen that we move into on these occasions is friendly and cosy.'[25]

Over the next few days, the weather at Hope Bay deteriorated, with a heavy drift confining the trio to a hut which now seemed absurdly large with just three men inhabiting it. Green concentrated on completing his report on the geology of the southern portion of James Ross Island, and on labelling his rock samples. Burd, a Canadian ex-submarine officer, compiled a stores list and wrote up his meteorological observations, and Sladen developed his films and preserved his biological specimens, a process that included the dry freezing of a sample of crabeater seal milk – an exercise which, he noted with some satisfaction, had 'never been done before'.[26]

On the night of 8 November, snow still whirled past the four windows that remained unblocked by the accumulating drift, but Sladen and Burd decided that they would venture outdoors nonetheless, Sladen to continue his ornithological observations at the nearby rookery and to collect some penguin carcasses to feed the dogs, and Burd to hunt for fresh eggs for their own consumption.

According to Sladen's account, the pair left the hut at around 11 p.m., heading in different directions. By the time the doctor completed his work at 1.45 a.m., the temperature had dropped, and the wind had increased to gale force, knocking him over twice as he slogged back towards the hut, and constantly blowing his loaded sledge towards the sea. He returned to a scene of total devastation:

> The first thing I saw was a dense cloud of smoke, most of which was coming from the north end of the hut. The snow was dark with soot on the leeward as far as Hut Point. I found the door with difficulty and tried to push my way in. As soon as I opened it, billows of smoke rushed out. The door was half drifted up but I was able to reach the handle from outside. I just managed to scramble out again. I then ran round to the W/T and Laboratory windows which I knew were fairly free. They were blackened on the inside. I tried to force my way through the W/T window but was compelled to come out as the fumes were so hot and suffocating. There was no answer to frantic shouts made between breaths inside the window.[27]

At this point, Sladen noticed a red glow at the junction of the engine shed, back porch and main building, and he tried to shovel snow onto the area with his hands, in the hope of extinguishing that portion of the fire before it spread – but with Hope Bay's relentless south-westerly wind fanning the flames, it proved a hopeless endeavour.

It was now 2 a.m. and, with smoke pouring from the chimneys and from the engine room and latrine extension at the north end of the main building, Sladen ran to the Nissen hut in the hope of finding some tools with which to effect the rescue of his friends. To his dismay, he found the outward-opening door of the secondary hut blocked by drift snow, which he had neither the time nor equipment to clear.[28] Instead, he forced his way into another much smaller, corrugated iron structure, nicknamed 'Uncle Tom's Cabin' or the 'Tin Galley', which had been constructed by Chippy Ashton in 1945 as a temporary shelter for those engaged in the building of Base D. In the half-light, he managed to locate an axe, and then returned to the burning building:

> I made for the entrance again, but had difficulty in finding it as smoke was billowing out of the sides of the door and from under the roof ... I smashed into Mike's room, keeping as low as possible, but had to withdraw without finding anything.[29]

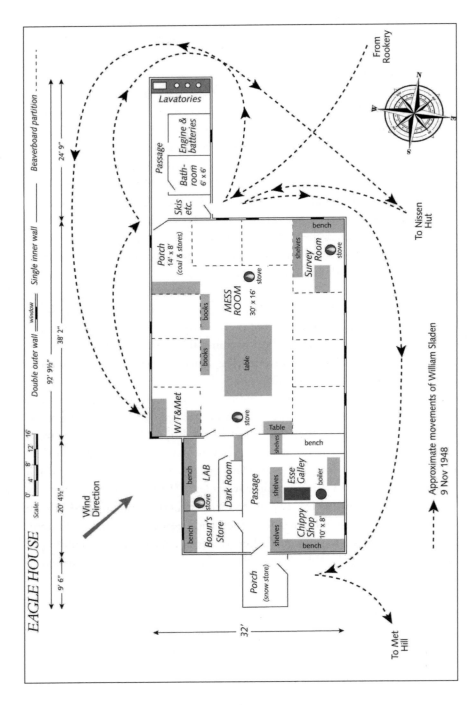

By this time the roof at the south end of the hut was also ablaze and, after a second unsuccessful attempt to break his way into the main part of the building, Sladen realised that he must abandon any hope of finding Burd and Green. 'The sinister silence,' he wrote a few days later:

> … the dark smoke torrenting down to the sea, pressed low by the gale and drift; the feeling of complete and utter helplessness; worse still, the thought of Dick and Mike with no one to save them was the most terrifying thing I have ever experienced.[30]

At 3 a.m. the main roof collapsed with a tremendous crash, sending a shower of sparks and fragments of burning wood into the air. These were then caught by the wind and blown towards the other buildings to leeward. Fearing that they, too, would be destroyed, but realising that he could do nothing but 'watch in readiness',[31] Sladen concentrated on moving the dogs, which were already blackened by the smoke. Half an hour later, the inevitable happened: a piece of burning debris landed among a pile of timber and other materials intended for a new hut. Almost immediately it was alight. Sladen approached in the hope of putting out this smaller fire before it took hold, but quickly retreated when the flames reached a stash of small arms ammunition, sending out a random fusillade. As the roof of the hut's northern extension caved in, he returned upwind to the vantage point of Met Hill where, with his arm around a dog named Whitey – a favourite of Burd's – he watched the fire complete its work, wistfully observing, 'As I gazed at the hut a Snowy Petrel, tinted pink by the glow, circled and fluttered but vanished as suddenly as it had appeared.'[32]

By 6 a.m., more than four hours after he had first discovered it, the fire had begun to die down; the roof and walls of the hut had disintegrated and only their debris and the floorboards continued to burn, the crackle of the flames frequently punctuated by the explosion of the cans of condensed milk that had been stored near the medical equipment and by the irregular crack of small arms fire at the dump. Anxious to get out of the bitterly cold wind that continued to blow at between 50–60kph, Sladen sought refuge in the Tin Galley – but still he dared not sleep, or stay for long, for fear of the fumes. Instead, after a brief respite, he paced up and down the base site, trying both to keep warm and to ensure that stray sparks did not cause any further damage to the remaining stores and structures.

At last, he felt sufficiently confident to retreat to a tent that had been pitched close to the penguin rookery in order to provide him with a modicum of comfort during his studies. A sleeping bag, a sheepskin and the Primus stove helped him to restore some warmth to his frozen limbs and then he rested for a few short hours, before returning to inspect the ruins, and the gruesome contents, of Eagle House.

Sladen began the appalling task of sifting through the still smouldering wreckage at 4 p.m. that afternoon. Though he knew they must be dead, it was, he admitted, 'nevertheless a bitter blow to find Dick Burd and Mike Green's remains. I thought it wiser to leave everything as it was until the sledge party's return, so covered them.'[33] A brief examination also confirmed that the ruins contained nothing that was salvageable of the expedition's meticulously maintained biological, geological, meteorological and survey records. Every scrap of paper had been reduced to windblown ashes, every film melted, every specimen burned to nothing or turned to unrecognisable, carbonised trash.

Besides his own escape and that of the dogs, the only positive aspect of the disaster was the survival of the Nissen hut, the loss of which, Sladen knew, 'would have been serious, for most emergency food, clothing, W/T and medical stores were there'.[34] But even this had been the merest fluke, as the Nissen hut's position to leeward of the main building had placed it in the direct path of the shower of sparks and burning debris vomited forth by the blazing hut. It remained unscathed only because it had been shielded by a thick covering of snow. 'This point,' he noted in his report on the tragedy, 'should be remembered when building Nissen huts for other bases.'[35]

Anxious to inform the sledge party of the events at Hope Bay, and to expedite their return, on the 10th Sladen tried to make contact using the emergency wireless set stored in the Nissen hut. Unfortunately, with so little experience of the equipment, he found it impossible to install the battery, so instead he climbed the glacier to Nobby Nunatak, the most obvious landmark on the final stage of the sledgers' homeward route, where he left a note inside a small cairn topped with a flag. This, he hoped, would prepare the sledgers for the spectacle that would greet them when they approached the base. 'Dear Frank,' he wrote:

I am afraid what I must write here will come as a very great shock to you. You probably hoped that our wireless sets had broken down, but I fear that the worst thing possible has happened to our home. Monday night it caught fire in a gale and I am the only one left. I cannot write more about it just now. Will you please find me before you do anything else. I am here mostly, but living in the rookery in my tent ... I am taking this note to Nobby with a flag. Bill.[36]

This, then, was the well-intentioned message that Elliott's party missed during their descent of the glacier a fortnight later.

Having done everything possible to mitigate the shock for the sledgers, Sladen trudged back down the glacier. Stretched out before him lay Antarctic Sound, a great jumble of broken sea ice clogging its waters as far as the eye could see, the whole tumbled mass moving inexorably northwards. Dark storm clouds blotted out the mountains of Joinville Island, and suddenly the doctor felt a rush of anxiety for the sledge party who might, even then, be traversing the sea ice south of Bald Head in the Crown Prince Gustav Channel. What would happen if they, too, met with an accident? Perhaps, up to this point, the need for action had prevented him from dwelling on the full horror of the catastrophe that had overwhelmed his small party. Now, he could no longer avoid 'the heavy depression that seemed to well all around me':

A feeling of great loneliness and deepest sorrow; the grim sight of utter desolation that greeted me every time I passed the still smouldering hut; the work we had struggled to do to the best of our ability under very trying conditions. Seven of us instead of nine; arriving so late and leaving so early and leaving for good; the reports so carefully prepared and containing so much of interest and experience. All this seemed as nothing when my mind turned back to the two companions we would never see again. Their quiet and unruffled outlook on life had never ceased to impress me. I felt much in need of those qualities now.[37]

Shortly afterwards, in a poignant gesture of mourning and remembrance, he picked up a few lichen-covered rocks and placed them next to the shrouded bodies of his friends. 'There seemed to be a great need for colour among those ghastly smouldering ruins and these bright vermillion clusters, which are our only form of plant life, seemed to neutralise the grimness of the surroundings.'[38]

And so began Sladen's long, lonely vigil, with only the dogs and the penguins for company. With remarkable stoicism, he decided to recommence all the scientific observations from scratch; indeed, he visited the Stevenson Screen to take the routine meteorological readings within twenty-four hours of the disaster. As well as making up for at least some of the losses, this decision would, he knew, help both to prevent him from dwelling for too long on recent events and to pass the time until Elliott's return. 'All my notes had been destroyed,' he observed in the newly begun official Base Diary, 'so I started catching my ringed birds, noting their numbers, weighing and repainting them.'[39] He also cared for the dogs and for a litter of newborn puppies, took regular ice observations and, having first improvised a temporary battery connection for the emergency wireless set, resumed the regular daily schedules, though he remained uncertain whether or not his transmissions were being heard. This extraordinary single-mindedness and dedication would result in Sladen being awarded the MBE, in recognition of his 'courage and fortitude in hazardous circumstances'.[40]

★ ★ ★

Having recovered from the immediate shock of seeing the wreckage of Eagle House, Elliott ordered the rest of his party to pitch a tent and make tea while he walked over to the penguin rookery. At this point, they had no idea of the extent of the tragedy and all expected to find Sladen, Green and Burd safe and well, if a little uncomfortable after their involuntary weeks under canvas.

When Elliott reached the tent, Sladen was inside, preparing a meal and writing up his diary and ornithological notes:

> I heard the crunching of seal skin boots on the snow outside, and the familiar words … 'Hello there'. It was Frank Elliott. My joy at knowing that the sledgers had returned safely and seeing the chaps again was turned into confusion by not knowing how to answer Frank's first enquiry … 'Are you all safe?' Apparently he had not seen the note I had left at Nobby.[41]

Elliott found the doctor 'pretty distraught and upset',[42] and little wonder. 'It was a frightful shock for us all,' wrote O'Hare after hearing the news. 'Heaven alone knows what Sladen must have suffered during the three weeks [*sic*] between the fire and our return.'[43]

They agreed not to discuss the subject any further that evening and, displaying extraordinary empathy, Sladen actually volunteered to spend another night alone in his tent at the rookery in order to allow the sledge team, close-knit now after their weeks in the field, to digest in private the shocking new reality. His presence, he knew, could only act as a constraint on their natural wish to express their feelings. 'I'll never forget how the doctor stood up to everything,' O'Hare later told a reporter from the *Daily Mail*. 'He went through hell, but he made no fuss.'[44]

One of the first duties of the reunited party must be to recover and inter Burd and Green's bodies – but high winds and thick drift made the task impossible until the end of the month. A brief respite on 29 November allowed them to complete the first stage of the operation which, in O'Hare's words:

> ... was to dig out the remains ... from the house site which is almost full of snow ... Elliott and Sladen dug, McNeile and Jefford got rocks and cleared Met Hill for the graves and I made two crosses from sledge brakes. They are very plain as there was only a hacksaw, salvaged from the fire, with which I could work.[45]

Fortunately, Sladen's equipment included a small tin of black paint that he used to mark the penguins, and this enabled O'Hare to write two simple inscriptions, recording names, roles, dates of death, and the fact that Burd and Green had died 'on duty'. But at this point the wind rose again and in no time at all the freshly dug graves had filled with drift snow, and they were forced to postpone the funeral service. For much of the following day poor weather confined the four men to their tents, but this delay at least provided them with an opportunity to cut each other's hair and to smarten their soiled and ragged clothes.

At last, on the afternoon of 1 December, the blizzard relented and the shrouded bodies of Mike Green and Dick Burd could at last be placed in their shallow graves and covered with stones. 'Elliott said a few words and a prayer,' recorded O'Hare. 'Sladen then prayed. The service was concluded with another short prayer and the Lord's Prayer.'[46]

The obsequies completed, Elliott and his companions returned to the work of sorting the surviving stores and equipment ready for what they assumed would be the imminent arrival of the *John Biscoe*. In fact, unusually poor sea ice conditions would prevent the ship from reaching them for over two months. For a field party usually bent upon the pursuit of knowledge, on this rare occasion ignorance would prove to be bliss.

★ ★ ★

What caused the fire that destroyed Eagle House? The day after they recovered the bodies, O'Hare and Sladen dug down through 3m of snow to the remains of the engine shed, and the evidence they found among the wreckage appears conclusive. 'The fuelling funnel was in the engine petrol tank,' O'Hare noted. 'I tried to find the ignition switch but found no trace of it although I located the coil and a lead which had been attached to the switch.'[47] Worsening weather curtailed their investigations, but the discovery of the funnel in this position indicates that the fire began when fuel, or its vapour, ignited during the process of topping up the tank. Elliott certainly felt convinced that the fire started in this fashion and in a later report he strongly 'recommended that all petrol generators be replaced with diesel'.[48]

Unfortunately, neither Sladen, O'Hare nor Elliott left any formal record of precisely where the bodies were located, but in a later conversation with Ken Blaiklock, who was stationed at Base E on Stonington Island at the time of the fire, Sladen mentioned that he found both bodies in the engine shed. He also stated his belief that one man had probably died while attempting to save the other.[49] At other times, he suggested that the fatal spark might have come from the pipe that Green habitually smoked.[50] Since the replenishing of a fuel tank with a 5-gallon jerrycan would usually require only one man,[51] it would appear that, in Sladen's opinion, Green started the fire while refuelling the generators, and that he might have set his clothes alight in the process. Hearing his cries, Burd ran to the northern extension where he tried to extinguish the flames – but died in the attempt.

Certainly, the fact that the two men died at all seems to support the idea that the blaze began with a catastrophic accident that involved one or both while they were in the engine room. Alternatively, perhaps the fire started in a less immediately devastating fashion, but the two men simply failed to appreciate just how quickly it would spread in the tinder-dry hut. It is also possible that they wasted precious seconds attempting to fight the blaze with the extinguishers that Andrew Taylor thought so totally unsuited to Antarctic conditions.

One last question needs to be answered: if, as seems almost certain, the fire began in the engine room, why did the roofs of the main block and southern extension collapse prior to that of the northern extension, where the engines were located? Since there is no evidence to suggest any variance in the materials used in constructing and insulating the different sections of the roof, this might suggest that the centre and southern sections of the structure were subjected to the heat and flames for a longer period. Indeed, were it not for the telltale fuel funnel, these facts might lead one to believe that that the fire had begun in the vicinity of one of the five separate stoves located in the laboratory, mess, galley and survey rooms, or at the junction of one of their hot metal chimneys with the roofing material – a known flashpoint.

To resolve this conundrum, we must return to the design of Eagle House. In his account of the hut's construction in early 1945, Andrew Taylor observed:

> The centre of the mess room was unfortunately broken by the supporting studs formed by the adjoining central partition of the two huts, which had originally been erected in juxtaposition. We could not afford to remove these supports entirely, for they carried much of the weight of the rather extensive roof, so Ashton fitted the mess room table into the studding, and we removed one or two towards each end of the room to allow for the passage of traffic from one part to the other.[52]

The early collapse of the main roof can almost certainly be traced to Chippy Ashton's decision to remove some of the central timber supports. In normal conditions, this alteration would not have been problematic; it became so only when fire was added to the equation, with the result that the structural integrity of the building was undermined much more quickly than might otherwise have been the case. However, there is no reason to suppose that the roof's early collapse caused any part of the tragedy: by 3 a.m. 9 November, the time at which the central roof caved in, Burd and Green were long since dead.

Whatever caused the fire, and wherever it started, there is certainly no doubt that the climate and topography of Hope Bay played important roles in its rapid and uncontrollable spread, the flames being fanned by the strong south-westerly wind, so that, within a very short time, practically no hope remained of saving the building. 'We had winds gusting up to 120mph

[193kph] quite often at Hope Bay,' Elliott recalled. 'There was a funnel down the glacier and it just built up the wind speed.'[53]

★　★　★

In 1952, Bernard Stonehouse, a pilot and biologist with FIDS, and one of the very few men to spend three consecutive winters in Antarctica, wrote:

> Of all the difficulties which can overtake a polar expedition, the loss of its base is perhaps the most disastrous. Nevertheless, the frequency with which such losses seem to occur suggests that there are fundamental errors in the design of the huts, as well as a tendency to underestimate the danger of fire.[54]

Naturally, he cited the 1948 disaster at Hope Bay, but he also alluded to highly destructive, though non-fatal, fires at Deception Island in 1946 and during Michel Barré's French Antarctic Expedition to Adélie Land in January 1952.

In Stonehouse's well-informed opinion, poor design and unsuitable building materials were often to blame, if not for the fires themselves, then certainly for their rapid spread. Operation Tabarin's wartime bases at Port Lockroy and Hope Bay, for instance, had not only been constructed almost entirely of wood, they had also been extended and modified, more or less according to the whim of the base leaders and carpenters, so that each eventually became 'a straggling group of interconnected rooms and passages'.[55] Later peacetime bases, such as Base E at Stonington Island, replicated many of the obvious, if also largely unavoidable, faults, including the use of timber and tarred roofing felt for construction and tarred paper for insulation, the incorporation of numerous stoves and generators, the passage of stovepipes through the outer fabric, and the storage, under the same roof, of various types of fuel. 'It is hardly surprising,' Stonehouse observed, 'that the risk of fire is so great.'[56]

Perhaps nowhere were the inadequacies of Antarctic hut design more apparent than at Mirny, a large Soviet IGY station established on the coast of Queen Mary Land in 1956. John Béchervaise, an experienced Australian base leader, visited the facility in January 1959 while en route to take command of the Australian National Antarctic Research Expedition's (ANARE) Mawson Station, and he left a detailed description of a strangely quaint establishment, oozing 'proletariat gentility':

Station headquarters is still buried to roof-level, but ramps have been 'dozed down through the snow and some of the little windows are blinking at the light. We squeeze along a narrow passage and through a dark little vestibule; then into a small room, from which two others retreat; one a bedroom, the other, a kind of office. But all space is so occupied and noisy that first impressions are embroidered many times before they crystallise … Every room is papered with mid-Victorian designs; ornately decorated chairs, lampstands, picture-frames, door-knobs, sofas with flowered chintzes, and all sorts of knickknacks … The scientific equipment was excellent and entirely modern by our standards; but almost every observatory was decoratively papered, and few suitable walls lacked their sofas … In many high windows were pot-plants …[57]

Buried in snowdrifts and with its high, inaccessible windows and small, overcrowded rooms that seemed more closely akin to a Victorian boudoir than a modern scientific station, it would be difficult to imagine an environment less likely to enable a swift exit in the event of a fire, especially when the disorienting effects of darkness and smoke were added to the mix.

In the early morning of 3 August 1960 fire did break out at Mirny and, in the worst catastrophe to engulf any polar base, eight scientists died, including six Russians, a Czech and an East German. According to Gilbert Dewart, an American observer at the base, at 5.45 a.m. the duty engineer at Mirny's central power station noticed that there had been a failure in the electrical distribution system, which he traced to Building Number Eight, the combined office and sleeping quarters of the eight-man meteorological section. The engineer called the meteorological duty officer but, receiving no reply, he then rang the section chief, Oskar Krichak, whose cabin was also in the meteorological building. Woken by the telephone at his bedside, Krichak confirmed that the electricity had failed and, far more worryingly, that he could smell smoke. He then said that he would investigate and report back.

Rather than wait for Krichak's call, the engineer alerted his supervisor who then, with the geological section chief, set out to investigate. In Dewart's words:

Yagodkin and Solovyev fought their way over mountainous snowdrifts through 120mph [193kph] gusts of wind to the meteorology building, which was on the outskirts of the base. Its roof was covered by a layer of snow six feet thick, but flames were coming out of the personnel hatch and through ominous cracks in the snow. Dense clouds of smoke were billowing from the balloon release tower, which was connected to the main building by a 120-foot [37m] tunnel. None of the residents could be seen. Unable to enter the under-snow complex, the two men stumbled back and turned [on] the general fire alarm at the nearest building.[58]

On hearing the alarm, the rest of the base personnel responded efficiently, quickly dressing and equipping themselves with extinguishers, shovels and even tractors, which they used to push snow onto the flames and away from the building's exits. But the fire had struck during the worst storm of the year at Mirny, with winds so powerful that they frequently knocked the amateur firefighters off their feet 'and kept the inferno under forced draft ... [it] remained out of control for hours'.[59]

None of the meteorologists escaped the blaze and it took several days to sift through the ruins to locate and recover the bodies. 'The men never had a chance,' wrote a traumatised Dewart, who volunteered to take part in the search:

We found Oskar lying on his back in front of what had once been a heavy wooden door separating his private room from the main hall of the house. Apparently he had been overcome by a blast of flame as soon as he had opened the door to investigate ... Olldrich Kostka and several of the others had enough time to crawl under their bunks, but they had suffocated there. The last man to be found was the tall, powerfully built Igor Popov, who had dashed through the flames to reach the tunnel that led to the balloon release tower. His terribly burned body was found seventy-five feet [23m] down the tunnel.[60]

Although the cause of the fire would remain, according to the tight-lipped Soviet authorities, 'undetermined',[61] as so often in the Antarctic, the powerful wind had undoubtedly played its part – but so too did the antiquated and quirky design of the base itself. As well as noting the crowded rooms and complicated floorplan, Béchervaise had observed that, while the Russians were eager to import the very latest equipment and ideas to support their scientific work, their 'customary ways of coping with climate – shelter and clothing – are much less susceptible to change'.[62] In other words, the traditional techniques used in the manufacture of buildings and clothing capable of withstanding an Arctic winter had been passed down from generation to generation, and the effectiveness of these methods left the Russians with very little appetite for newfangled approaches: if they functioned effectively in the far north, surely they would work equally well in the far south? Of course, the answer to this question is to be found in the death toll at Mirny: eight men either smothered or burned to death in a single incident, almost certainly because they could not escape from the nostalgic, but highly combustible labyrinth of their own creation.

★ ★ ★

In the years following the destruction of Base D at Hope Bay, a number of FIDS and BAS stations have been damaged by fire, including, most recently, the Bonner Marine Laboratory at Rothera, which was razed to the ground in September 2001. But no British personnel have been killed or seriously injured by fire since the deaths of Burd and Green. The Russians have not been so fortunate. Twenty-two years after the destruction of the meteorological observatory at Mirny, another blaze wrought such major damage at Vostok that it is little short of a miracle that the loss of life was so limited.

Established in 1957 at the Geomagnetic South Pole – 3,488m above sea level and at the centre of the East Antarctic Ice Sheet – Vostok is second only to the Amundsen–Scott South Pole Station in terms of its remoteness. Moreover, with the lowest naturally occurring temperature ever reliably recorded on the surface of the planet (−89.2°C) it also experiences arguably the harshest climatic conditions of any manned base anywhere on Earth.

During their first winter at Vostok, the Soviet scientists found the environment so punishing that they could not work safely outdoors for periods exceeding ten to fifteen minutes, despite having been issued with 40-watt pocket-sized batteries and electric heaters to warm their hands, feet and chests. Antifreeze did not prevent the ink in the self-recording instruments from freezing, diesel turned to jelly, rubber became brittle, radiosonde balloons crumbled at the slightest touch, the paint on the

motor-tractors blistered, and, most peculiar of all, water dropped onto the supercooled ice outside hissed and danced, just as it would if dropped onto a hot stove. According to one early resident, 'It was savagely cold, the frozen air searing like a flame. It was, indeed, a cosmic cold.'[63] The high altitude complicated matters still further, so that the slightest exertion would leave those who hadn't yet acclimatised, gasping. 'We ... tried to breathe as deeply as possible, but still we couldn't get enough air; it was something like trying to drink out of an empty glass.'[64]

It was here, at this almost unimaginably inhospitable outpost, that at 4 a.m. on 12 April 1982 a Soviet mechanic named Sergei Kuznetsov woke to a strong smell of burning.[65] Glancing through the window of his cabin, he saw a large plume of black smoke rising from the station's powerhouse, and he quickly roused the rest of the twenty-one-man crew. Led by the station chief, Pyotr Astakhov, the scientists and support staff donned their outdoor clothing, grabbed the available fire extinguishers, and ran outside, intent on dousing the flames before they could spread. Unfortunately, as V.S. Ignatov had remarked during his own period in command at Vostok in 1960, 'It's easier to prevent a fire than to put it out'.[66]

Fully realising that, at this time of year, they were far beyond the reach of external aid, the party fought hard, but in vain. With no oxygen masks, a strong wind fanning the flames, and with extinguishers that quite simply refused to function in temperatures hovering around −59°C, they had no chance of containing the fire before it had destroyed the entire contents of the powerhouse, including not only the station's three main diesel units but also its standby generators, which, with an extraordinary lack of foresight, had been placed in the same building. For a while, the flames threatened the station's fuel dump but, by a happy fluke, the wind direction changed just as it seemed that a huge explosion had become inevitable.

The only man to die in the fire was Aleksei Karpenko, the base's chief mechanic, who had entered the burning building in a courageous, or foolhardy, attempt to save at least one of the station's vital generators. But if the fire had claimed just one life, it now seemed that there was every likelihood of the Antarctic climate completing the work that the conflagration had left unfinished. With the generators reduced to blackened junk, the base had no power – and that meant no heat, no electric light and no means of melting snow for drinking water and cooking. The radios, too, relied upon the ruined power units – but, even if he did manage to establish contact with any of the other Russian or international bases, Astakhov knew that, with the onset of the Antarctic winter, it would be impossible for either an aircraft or a land party to relieve them until November. To survive the long months ahead, he and his men must rely upon their own initiative, resources and stamina.

Over the coming days and weeks, the twenty survivors learned something of what it had been like to take part in the very earliest polar expeditions. In order to conserve heat and light, they shared bunks in three small rooms in one of the undamaged buildings, made habitable by a kerosene-fuelled heater and small tins of diesel into which they dipped twisted wicks of asbestos fibre, much as the explorers of the Heroic Age had used homemade blubber lamps. Unfortunately, the resemblance did not stop there. Just as the unpurified seal blubber had smoked abominably, so too did the diesel lamps – a result of the lack of oxygen in the rarefied atmosphere of Vostok – and by the time their trials came to an end, the faces of Astakhov and his companions had been dyed black.

In the vicinity of the primitive heaters, the temperature hovered around 21–26°C, but outside their immediate ambit it dropped to well below freezing. The juxtaposition of naked flames and liquid fuel also increased the risk of fire and a twenty-four-hour watch must be maintained. The recovery from the station's scrapyard of a broken-down diesel generator enabled the early re-establishment of radio communication with the Soviet Molodyozhnaya Station, but this only served to confirm Astakhov's conviction that relief would not be possible until the end of the austral winter. The restoration of another superannuated generator made the preparation of food somewhat easier, but power remained at a premium and great care had to be taken to avoid an overload.

In November 1948, Bill Sladen had decided that the best way to pass the time and to prevent himself dwelling on the recent catastrophe was to continue his observations at the neighbouring penguin rookery. Thirty-four years later, Astakhov, too, decided that work would provide much-needed distraction and so, despite all the obstacles ranged against them, the scientists of Vostok resumed their studies. In addition to their routine and longstanding work on magnetism and meteorology, in recent years, and as their contribution to the International Antarctic Glaciological

Project, the Russians had been conducting a deep ice-drilling experiment. Their objective was the analysis of ice cores to retrieve information regarding temperatures and other atmospheric phenomena from centuries past. Having begun the project in 1979, the Vostok team, which included specialists seconded from the Leningrad Mining Institute, had reached a depth of around 2,130m by the time of the fire; after it, and despite the makeshift and unreliable power supply, they still managed to advance a further 82m.

The ordeal of Astakhov and the other smoke-blackened survivors finally came to an end with the arrival of the annual overland tractor-sledge convoy from Mirny on 23 November, seven and a half months after the destruction of the powerhouse. In the eulogistic words of *Pravda*, against all the odds, 'the heroic winter scientists … [had] managed to conquer the frost',[67] and now they could embark on their long journey back to Mother Russia – a journey they eventually completed nearly four months later when their ship, the *Bashkiriya*, reached the Black Sea port of Odessa.

As for the new personnel at Vostok, as well as the much-needed provisions and fuel, their giant Kharkovchanka tractors had dragged a replacement power plant from Mirny and now their primary concern was its installation. Only when this job had been completed could the full scientific programme be resumed. This time, however, they decided to locate the standby units at a safe distance from the main powerhouse. Another bitter lesson had been learned.[68]

★　★　★

Engines, generators and their fuel have been responsible for many of the fires that have damaged or completely gutted Antarctic bases, and in this respect the blaze that killed Aleksei Karpenko was no exception. A New Zealander, Robert Thomson, visited Vostok in 1962 and again seven years later, and he described the poor design and build quality of the Russian generators. They were, he wrote in 1969, 'of 1930 vintage; and the three twin-cylinder units, each of about 7 KVA, were in a very bad state … they were so badly made … they lasted only a short time, then they had to be chucked out'.[69] He also commented on the fact that the powerhouse in which these generators were located, and which later caught fire, was 'oil-saturated'.[70]

The fatal fire at Vostok did not occur until thirteen years after Thomson's last visit, but in the dying days of the Soviet Union and with the costs of the Soviet–Afghan War rapidly spiralling out of control, it seems improbable that the Vostok power plant had benefited from any significant investment in the intervening period. The fire that wrought such damage appears to have started as a result of damage to wiring insulation caused by the effects of the extreme dryness of the atmosphere.[71] It was, then, a uniquely Antarctic phenomenon, but the associated risks were clearly exacerbated by poor design and manufacturing standards.

Of course, engines and their fuel have not been the only culprits, just as engine sheds have not been the only structural losses. Discarded cigarette butts, clothing left too close to heaters, a misguided (and drunken) attempt to convert a base refrigerator into a sauna, and even arson have all claimed their victims – though, fortunately, the price has usually been paid in material terms rather than in lives lost. Usually, but not always – and in the last decade a further three fatalities have been sustained as a result of fire: one at Russia's Progress Station on 5 October 2008, and two at Brazil's Comandante Ferraz Station on 27 February 2012. The first of these fires occurred during construction work, while the second began with an explosion in the machine room.[72] Both necessitated complete rebuilds.

Even when measured in purely material terms, the impact of a base fire can be colossal and, as early as 1961, a fire at the US facility at McMurdo Sound was estimated to have cost £700,000[73] (roughly £11 million today). In more recent times, the price tag of the restoration of the Bonner Marine Laboratory at Rothera was set at £3 million,[74] while damage at the Comandante Ferraz Station was valued at nearly £10 million.[75] Added to these monetary costs must be the value of the science lost – and that remains incalculable, particularly when fires have interrupted studies the importance of which lies, not least, in their longevity. 'If this season is one in which a major trend takes off or is pivotal in some way,' Professor Paul Rodhouse of BAS told reporters after the Rothera fire, 'clearly it would be more difficult to interpret what went on.'[76]

As these more recent incidents show, fire remains an ever-present danger in the Antarctic – and its impacts can be just as profound today as they were seventy or more years ago, particularly at the most remote stations. In 1952, Bernard Stonehouse wrote:

When polar huts become as safe as the normal home it will be possible to relax in them. Until that time, they must be regarded as potential death traps, and a constant vigil must be kept by all who use them.[77]

The time for relaxation on polar bases has still not yet arrived.

2

'STRENGTHENING HIS MAJESTY'S TITLE'

BRITISH DEATHS ON SEA ICE

One of the defining physical characteristics of Antarctica is the great girdle of sea ice which, according to the season, expands, contracts, and expands again, like breath on the face of a mirror. During the fleeting summer months, the sea reaches most parts of the continent's coast but, with the arrival of autumn, the prevailing thermodynamic conditions in the Southern Ocean cause it to freeze, filling the bays and gulfs with ice that can stretch to a point more than 160km to the north. At its maximum extent, Antarctic sea ice covers approximately 20 million square kilometres of ocean and, if combined with the sea ice of the northern hemisphere, it would blanket some 13 per cent of the Earth's surface – an area similar in extent to that of all deserts and tundra combined.[1]

The first visible sign of the onset of the great annual freeze is the appearance of 'frost smoke', the product of cold air streaming outwards from the continental land mass and vaporising as it passes over the warmer ocean. Beneath the airborne frost particles, tiny ice crystals form on the surface of the water and, in periods of calm weather, this 'frazil ice' gradually coalesces to form a brittle skin that can thicken up to 15cm in twenty-four hours. If the wind rises and creates a swell, the paper-thin ice will either crack and 'raft', one sheet of ice riding over another to create a laminar structure, or it will break into distinct plates which, until they are again glued together by the falling temperature, jostle and bump, becoming ever more bruised and dog-eared. This formation is known as 'pancake ice'.

When young and thin, the sea ice is so dark in appearance that it is often known as 'black ice', its transparency revealing the colour of the water on which it floats, but, as it thickens with the fall of snow from above and the growth of more ice below, it becomes opaque and then white. The process continues, slowly but inexorably, with the ice growing in mass until the clingfilm-like frazil ice solidifies into something more akin to concrete, up to 2m thick. Then, as the earth tilts on its axis and Antarctica's mountain ranges flush with the glow of the returning sun, the temperature rises, and a much swifter retreat begins. The speed of the break-up is subject to wind strengths, the depth of the snow blanket, and the warmth and salinity of the ocean currents, but in just a few weeks the solid plate of ice fragments into a chaos of jostling blocks and shards. In some years, a few vestiges may remain close to land, trapped by the islands that sentinel the mouths of sheltered bays and inlets, but the vast majority will break out and float north: the pack ice that presents such a challenge to polar navigators.

In 1914 Professor T.W. Edgeworth David, erstwhile chief scientific officer with Shackleton's *Nimrod* Expedition, estimated that, of Antarctica's 18,000km coastline, less than 6,500km had been 'approximately explored', with only 4,000km of that distance charted 'in very moderate detail'.[2] That so little had been properly surveyed he attributed overwhelmingly to:

> … the fact that old pack ice, ancient fast bay ice, 'schollen-eis' (formed of fleets of grounded bergs with the intervening spaces levelled up with drift snow), coastal ice of the nature of piedmont ice aground or afloat, together with large glacier tongues, fend off ships so far from the true rock coast, that the latter, unless it is formed of high bare rock, is invisible from a ship.[3]

Thirteen years later, Robert Rudmose-Brown, a veteran of Bruce's *Scotia* Expedition and now reader in geography at Manchester University, bemoaned the fact that very little had changed in the intervening period; in his judgement, the 'broad features of the map of Antarctica are not built on ascertained fact so much as on intelligent guesswork'.[4] More positively, he also noted that, with the South Pole no longer a distraction, 'the explorer's energy in the future is more likely to be expended in directions more profitable to the advancement of knowledge'.[5] All, therefore, agreed that there was much for surveyors yet to do. But how to do it?

The rapid development of powered flight during the First World War gave some cause for optimism regarding the role that heavier-than-air machines might play in exploration and, as early as 1921, Frank Debenham opined that it would be worthwhile for any aspiring Antarctic explorer 'to devote a considerable portion of his time to the overcoming of the many technical difficulties which render inadvisable the employment of aircraft for polar exploration without careful previous trial'.[6]

Over the course of the next two decades, the successful Antarctic flights of Hubert Wilkins, Richard Byrd, Hjalmar Riiser-Larsen, Lincoln Ellsworth and John Rymill justified this belief, though the value and accuracy of their geographical discoveries varied enormously. Indeed, so significant did aircraft become that many of those who worked without them came to feel that they were operating at a distinct disadvantage. Andrew Taylor, senior surveyor with Operation Tabarin during 1944, was one such, opining at the end of his arduous survey of Wiencke Island, 'A thousand times more work could be accomplished by a single plane photographing every tortuous sinuosity of the coasts with an amount of detail which cannot be approached by any other method.'[7]

But aircraft remained expensive and their successful operation in Antarctic conditions fraught with danger and difficulty. Nor did aircraft render land parties redundant, as accurate aerial surveys depended upon the triangulation and astronomic observations completed by those on the ground. The great difficulty in accurately judging surface conditions from the air also meant that it was much safer for sledgers, or ships' landing parties, to undertake the collection of geological, botanical and zoological specimens, with pilots landing their machines only on their advice.

Where aircraft were not available, travelling along glaciers and ice cliffs rendered the exact plotting of coastlines very difficult because, as Taylor pointed out:

> One is forced to attempt to plot the position of a shoreline of which one seldom catches a glance; it is to be surmised that it lies vertically below the edge of the ice cliff that verges the course one is following, but it is not always convenient to ascertain this point.[8]

Greater accuracy could only be obtained by travelling on the sea ice abutting the land – but that also presented a number of serious challenges.

Conditions on sea ice vary enormously, according to a number of factors, including the time of year and its precise location in relation to the surrounding geophysical features. Where last winter's ice has been unable to escape northwards, its fragmented remains, when frozen-in again, form a chaos of jagged debris that can be traversed only with enormous difficulty, and with sledges constantly overturning. Where the topography deflects the wind away from the surface, drift snow can collect in such volume that its weight will even push the ice beneath the underlying water, making movement for those on foot not only uncomfortable but dangerous.

Travelling in the lee of James Ross Island, to the east of the Antarctic Peninsula, in the spring of 1945, a survey team of Operation Tabarin met with precisely these conditions. By the beginning of September, temperatures were dipping as low as −40°C, and the soft snow was more than a metre deep; the men sank to their waists with every step and the lead sledge 'acted more like a plough than anything else'.[9] Worst of all, the deepest 30cm of snow had turned to cold, salty slush and the men's feet were soon encased in solid blocks of ice. Inevitably, progress slowed to a snail's pace and frostbite became commonplace.

Conditions were perhaps even worse for a FIDS party traversing the same area in May 1946, and at 'Swamp Camp' the sledgers not only woke to find their sleeping bags in puddles, but were actually forced to abandon a sledge that had become submerged overnight.[10]

The greatest threat of all to those travelling on sea ice, however, is its vulnerability to the action of the wind, which achieves its greatest velocity at the coast. Even apparently thick and stable ice can be broken up if the wind is strong enough, and, once shattered, it will drift northwards to join the pack, almost certainly sealing the fate of anyone unlucky enough to be caught out. For this reason, those choosing to sledge on sea ice are well advised to keep their journeys short, to stay close to land, to take careful note of routes back onto terra firma, to move only in conditions of good visibility, and to observe the weather assiduously. Failure to do so can prove disastrous – as members of Shackleton's Ross Sea party discovered to their cost in May 1916.

★ ★ ★

Conditions at Hut Point, on Ross Island, during the winter of 1916 were enough to depress even the most disciplined of stoics. In two extraordinarily

demanding sledging seasons (24 January–25 March 1915 and 1 September 1915–16 March 1916), parties under the overall command of Merchant Navy officer, Aeneas Mackintosh, had succeeded in laying a series of depots across the Great Barrier to a position 80° South. These depots were intended to sustain the crossing party, which Shackleton planned to lead across the continent from Vahsel Bay during his Imperial Trans-Antarctic Expedition, and they were laid despite a series of major setbacks, including the premature departure of the expedition ship, *Aurora*, with many of the party's supplies, the failure of the Girling motor-sledge, the loss of all but four dogs, and the onset of a crippling – and, for one member of the party, fatal – bout of scurvy.

By the end of the second sledging season, the surviving members of Mackintosh's party were split between two sites, with four located at the Cape Evans hut built by Scott's *Terra Nova* Expedition in January 1911, and the remaining five in the *Discovery* Expedition's old winter quarters at Hut Point. In the *Discovery* hut, Mackintosh, Ernest Joyce, Ernest Wild, Dick Richards and Victor Hayward subsisted on a combination of rations left by previous expeditions and on seal and penguin meat, all of which they cooked on an improvised blubber stove. The stove functioned well enough as a heater, but it emitted dense black smoke that made it difficult to breathe, and left the men and their kit impregnated with a revolting, sticky soot. As Shackleton later wrote, 'Cleanliness was out of the question, and this increased the desire of the men to get across to Cape Evans',[11] where conditions were thought to be much better. The health of those afflicted with scurvy had rapidly improved with their intake of fresh meat, but there could be no question just yet of their attempting the long and extremely arduous overland journey between the two huts; they must wait until the sea ice thickened sufficiently to take their weight.

On 23 April, Joyce, who was by far the most experienced polar traveller in the group, walked 6km north on the freshly formed ice, finding it up to 7cm thick in places. 'Another couple of days' low temperatures,' he thought, 'we then would have been able to travel.'[12] But within hours of his delivery of this verdict to his companions, a fierce blizzard descended from the plateau above and swept all of the fragile ice out to sea, leaving them marooned once again. Joyce was unfazed by this setback, noting in his diary, 'We are jogging along, improving daily … In spite of being cooped up in our blubber hut, the time passes quickly.' Vital occupations included the repair of clothing and equipment, and the daily preparation of food.

Wild and Richards, in particular, also read and reread the few books that had been left by Scott's expedition, though Joyce, who had suffered from snow-blindness, observed that reading 'is not a joy with the flickering wick and smoke from a blubber lamp'.[13]

Mackintosh was altogether less accepting of the status quo, and he made no secret of his wish to cross the ice at the earliest possible opportunity. When the sea again began to freeze at the beginning of May, he quickly decided to test its bearing capacity and, on the 7th, he and Hayward undertook a short exploratory journey to the north, which they completed without incident. Although the two men were only repeating the exercise that he had himself undertaken on 23 April, Joyce was profoundly unimpressed. 'I fail to understand why these people are so anxious to risk their lives again,' he scribbled angrily. 'It seems to me they are inclined to underrate the cruelty of the thin ice, the sticky nature of the surface, and the probability of a blizzard overtaking them.'[14] His patience was about to be tried still further.

At breakfast the following day, Mackintosh announced that he and Hayward intended to walk the 21km to Cape Evans later that morning. In reply, Joyce invited him outside, where, with a soot-blackened finger, he pointed towards Minna Bluff, some 97km to the south. Time and again, the bluff had proved itself an accurate weather gauge and now it lay partially shrouded in cloud – a sure sign of a coming storm, which Joyce predicted would arrive within a couple of hours. Even if the weather did not deteriorate, the journey would be immensely taxing for men who had not walked more than a handful of kilometres since collapsing with severe scurvy, and they could not hope to cover the distance in the three and a half hours that it might take fit men. In Joyce's opinion, 'it would be hell to be caught in a blizzard on the thin ice',[15] and when they returned to the hut, he expressed his views with his usual bluntness. 'You may call me "old cautious" but I would not go to Cape Evans today for all the tea in China.'[16]

Richards, who witnessed the exchange, noted that 'Mackintosh brushed this aside, but I imagined Hayward looked rather doubtful but probably did not like to back out'.[17] Mackintosh's only concession was to agree to turn back if the weather worsened before they reached Glacier Tongue. According to Richards, 'There was not much we could do about this decision. Mackintosh was in charge of the party and short of forcibly restraining him we could only urge them not to go.'[18]

At 11 a.m., Joyce, Richards and Wild climbed to a point close to the memorial cross to George Vince, who had lost his life on the *Discovery* Expedition, and watched their companions depart. 'I can see these two figures now quite clearly in my mind's eye,' Richards wrote forty-six years later:

> They appeared pygmy-like as they grew fainter in the dim light against the vast expanse of sea ice to the north, and we watched them for a while in silence. I think perhaps there was a little bitterness in our hearts that this needless risk should be taken. At that time we were acutely conscious of our recent experience on the ice shelf and the tremendous toil in getting these men back, but as we went slowly back into the hut we hoped for the best.[19]

They hoped in vain. Just half an hour after they waved their friends farewell, the predicted blizzard descended with such ferocity that it confined Joyce and his companions to the hut for nearly four days, and blew all of the young ice out into McMurdo Sound.

When the weather at last moderated, the three men left their refuge and traced Mackintosh and Hayward's footprints, 'raised up in the salty ice',[20] for about 5km to the north, where they came to an abrupt end in the new ice just forming. They would not be absolutely certain of the pair's fate until they themselves managed to cross to Cape Evans on 15 July, but there was really no room for doubt. With the onset of the blizzard, Mackintosh and Hayward had either been drowned almost immediately, as the ice broke up beneath their feet, or they had been blown into the sound on a rapidly disintegrating ice floe. In the latter scenario, the maximum extent of their life expectancy would have been a few hours at most. Even if, by a miracle, they had managed to reach land at some point between Hut Point and Cape Evans, hypothermia would have killed the lightly equipped pair long before they reached a safe haven. 'Such is life,' Joyce noted grimly.[21]

Why did Mackintosh choose to sacrifice his life and that of Hayward in such a foolhardy and unnecessary endeavour? After all, as subsequent events proved, a delay of just a few weeks would have substantially reduced the risks, and an earlier arrival at Cape Evans would have produced no meaningful benefits. In summarising the causes of the tragedy for Shackleton, Richards stated his belief that 'the Skipper' was anxious 'to exchange the quarters at the hut for the greater comfort and better food at Cape Evans',[22] and nearly half a century later he still held to this view, commenting that Mackintosh 'could not put up with the conditions at Hut Point which were primitive indeed'.[23]

Of course, the epicurean delights that they expected to find at the *Terra Nova* hut may have formed part of Mackintosh's motivation, but he was no stranger to physical hardship, having completed a gruelling apprenticeship with the Merchant Navy, which he had joined at 16, as well as serving with the *Nimrod* Expedition, until he was invalided home following the loss of an eye in a shipboard accident. This supposed desire for physical comfort therefore seems uncharacteristic. More probably, as Shackleton suggested, as overall commander of the Ross Sea Party, and in the absence of a wireless link, Mackintosh 'naturally would be anxious to know if the men at Cape Evans were well and had any news of the ship'.[24] In addition, the aristocratic Mackintosh had clashed repeatedly with the humbly born but skilled and highly critical Joyce; perhaps, on this occasion, he determined to assert his authority and independence, no matter what the cost. If this last interpretation is the correct one, then, surely, in the history of Antarctic exploration, there can be no more telling example of pride coming before a fall.

★ ★ ★

In the century since Mackintosh and Hayward's deaths, a further seven British explorers have lost their lives on Antarctic sea ice, meaning that more Britons have died in this fashion than any other nationality. However, this imbalance is due, not to differences in training, equipment, or competence but to a curious and almost certainly unique combination of historic, diplomatic, geographic, economic and political factors.

Although Britain could legitimately claim rights to the South Sandwich Islands, the South Orkneys, the South Shetlands and the Graham Land Peninsula, through their discovery by British sailors at the end of the eighteenth century and in the first half of the nineteenth, for decades her politicians paid scant regard to any portion of these Antarctic and sub-Antarctic territories. After all, with the exception of the Falklands, whose strategic location enabled them to dominate the mouth of the River Plate and the shipping lanes around Cape Horn, of what possible use could they be, with their treacherous wave-whipped shores and barren interiors? They offered no opportunities for trade or agriculture, and if they possessed any mineral wealth their location in such high latitudes made mining impracticable. Admittedly, the Southern Ocean was known to be teeming with whales, especially humpback, fin and blue whales, but the limitations

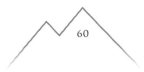

of the available whaling ships and the severity of the prevailing conditions in Antarctic waters made hunting all but impossible.

Despite these difficulties, it was whaling that ultimately brought an end to British indifference. At the beginning of the twentieth century, the demand for whale oil remained insatiable, its uses including tanning, lubrication and the manufacture of soap and margarine. But the depletion of northern whale stocks – a result of three centuries of deplorable profligacy by the Arctic whalers – had brought the industry to the brink of total collapse. If demand was to be met, and the whalers to maintain their livelihoods, new whaling grounds must be identified.

The salvation of the industry at this critical moment can be attributed to one man, the entrepreneurial Norwegian sea captain, Carl Anton Larsen. Crucially, Larsen realised that a number of recent technological innovations at last made exploitation of the southern fisheries a viable proposition. With the new steam-driven whale catchers, factory ships, and explosive harpoons arrayed against them, even the largest and fastest whales would no longer be able to outrun their pursuers. Larsen also had the vision, initiative and funding to test his theory. In December 1904 he built the first whaling station in the Southern Ocean, at Grytviken on South Georgia, and in no time at all the industry swung into full and bloody life. Within a year, the first floating factory sailed into the waters around the South Shetlands and, in less than a decade, a dozen such factories were operating in the region, acting as bases for far-ranging fleets of whale catchers.

Despite their earlier apathy, the British were not slow to appreciate just how important these developments made their sub-Antarctic island groups. In particular, substantial revenue could be generated by leasing land for onshore factories like Larsen's and by issuing whaling licences to those wishing to operate in British territorial waters. Realising, too, that a properly documented territorial claim was now essential if Britain was to benefit from this hugely profitable new income stream, on 21 July 1908, the government issued Letters Patent, in which they asserted that all lands 'situated in the South Atlantic Ocean to the south of the 50th Parallel of South Latitude, and lying between the 20th and 80th degrees of West Longitude, are part of our Dominions'.[25] These territories included the South Orkneys, the South Shetlands, the South Sandwich Islands, South Georgia and the whole of Graham Land.

Although this action seemed decisive, there remained a large and vigorous fly in the British ointment. Worse still, the British had themselves

introduced the fly. Five years earlier, during his Scottish National Antarctic (*Scotia*) Expedition of 1902–04, William Speirs Bruce had established a small meteorological station on Laurie Island, in the South Orkneys. Keen to ensure that his station remained operational, but lacking the necessary funds, towards the end of 1903 Bruce had suggested to the resident British minister in Buenos Aires, William Haggard, that it should be offered to the Argentine Government. Haggard raised no objection, and on 29 December, he personally passed Bruce's suggestion to the Argentine authorities. Four days later, the Argentine Government formalised its acceptance through publication of a Presidential Decree.

When Haggard belatedly notified London of this transaction, and of his own role in facilitating it, some Whitehall mandarins expressed concern that the South Orkneys were uncomfortably close to the Falkland Islands, British possession of which had long been disputed by Argentina. They also appreciated that Argentina might interpret the gift of Bruce's meteorological station as a transfer of jurisdiction over the South Orkneys as a whole. Unfortunately, despite recognition of these risks, no attempt was made to clarify the position to the Argentine Government and, instead, the matter was conveniently forgotten. In this fashion, Britain granted to Argentina a foothold on its sub-Antarctic possessions – just eleven months before the enormous value of those possessions began to be realised.

In the years following their acceptance of Bruce's meteorological station, Argentine ministers repeatedly signalled their desire to formalise their administration of Laurie Island. Moreover, they expressed apparently genuine surprise when Whitehall reminded them that the South Orkneys remained British possessions. Somewhat more reassuringly, when the Letters Patent were issued in 1908, Argentina's Minister for Foreign Affairs asked for a copy but took no further action. Matters only took a turn for the worse in 1927, when Argentine representatives announced to the International Bureau of the Universal Postal Union that their country's overseas territories now included not only the Falkland Islands but also the South Orkneys *and* the South Shetlands. Embarrassingly for the British, whenever the Argentines repeated this claim, they offered as justification the fact that theirs was the only nation permanently occupying and operating a meteorological station in the sub-Antarctic – at Scotia Bay on Laurie Island.

The outbreak of the Second World War gave rise to an altogether more significant escalation. Convinced that Britain's back was to the wall, and

that she was unlikely to possess either the resources or the will to resent an act of trespass, in January 1942 the Argentine Government ordered a naval transport ship, *Primero de Mayo*, to make landings at various points within the Falkland Islands Dependencies: at Deception Island, the Melchior Islands in the Palmer Archipelago, and at Winter Island. During the course of each landing, the Argentine sailors raised their national flag and, at conspicuous points, left a record of their visit, and of their claim to all territory below a latitude of 60°S and lying between longitudes 25°W and 69°34'W. The following year, a similar voyage was made, with landings in the Melchior Islands, and at Port Lockroy, Marguerite Bay and Deception Island.

If Argentine ministers expected that Britain would react to this provocation with a note of protest, but no firm action, they were to be sorely disappointed. As usual, officials at the Foreign Office resisted an escalation, citing the importance of continued good relations with Argentina and the need to maintain imports of Argentine beef, but it was the hawks at the Colonial Office who eventually won the day. As a result of their representations, on 28 January 1943, the War Cabinet ordered an armed merchant cruiser, HMS *Carnarvon Castle*, to make a tour of the Falkland Islands Dependencies. In official communiqués, her voyage was to be described 'as a search for traces of enemy raiders', but this was a rather transparent ruse, not least because, by the beginning of 1943, Germany's South Atlantic commerce raiders all lay rusting at the bottom of the sea. Even more significantly, it was also agreed that, following this action, 'permanent occupation should be established next year on all islands except probably Laurie Island'.[26]

Shortly after the Cabinet meeting, *Carnarvon Castle* dropped anchor at Deception Island where, in line with British Government policy, her crew obliterated all marks of foreign sovereignty, hoisted the Union Flag, and erected four 'British Crown Land' signs. They then sailed to Signy Island in the South Orkneys, where they followed the same protocols, before finally making a cordial visit to the Argentine meteorological station on Laurie Island. Clearly, the Argentine staff reported this visit to Buenos Aires because, just a month later, *Primero de Mayo* returned to Deception Island, where her sailors once again erased the British marks and replaced them with those of Argentina.

Recognising that this rather childish game of tit-for-tat could be played for years with neither side achieving ascendancy, the authorities in London reluctantly accepted that physical occupation of the disputed territory could be put off no longer. An interdepartmental committee again discussed the matter on 27 May 1943, and, under the codename Operation Tabarin, planning for the establishment of manned bases in the Falkland Islands Dependencies began at last.

During the austral summer of 1943–44, the ships and personnel of Operation Tabarin, under the polar veteran, Lieutenant Commander James Marr, established two bases: Base A at Port Lockroy, off the western coast of Graham Land, and Base B, on Deception Island. A third, Base D, at Hope Bay on the northerly tip of the Antarctic Peninsula, was built in February 1945, at which time Andrew Taylor took command.

In terms of scientific and survey work, the expedition achieved a great deal, with a near-continuous meteorological record maintained at its three stations, and much geological, zoological, botanical and glaciological work undertaken. In addition, local surveys were completed at Port Lockroy and Deception Island, while, at Hope Bay, sledging journeys totalling some 1,300km were made between August and December 1945, adding significantly to the maps drawn by Otto Nordenskjöld's Swedish Antarctic Expedition of 1901–04 and the British Graham Land Expedition of 1934–37.

When judged against its primary objective – the curbing of Argentine challenges to British sovereignty – the expedition's results were rather more ambiguous. In fact, the immediate post-war years witnessed a huge resurgence of activity in the region, with *The Times* of 18 December 1946 reporting the preparation or launch of expeditions from Argentina, Chile and the United States. Moreover, the Argentine Government made no secret of its wish 'to reaffirm Argentina's claim to sovereignty over the entire zone lying between the Argentine mainland and the South Pole',[27] and the Chileans proved no less forthright. Argentina and Chile also understood that there was strength in numbers and, on 4 March 1948, their representatives signed an agreement for the joint defence of their rights in the South American Antarctic zone. When asked whether this accord included the potential for military action, the Argentine Foreign Minister, Dr Juan A. Bramuglia, replied that both nations intended to 'exercise all rights derived from sovereignty'.[28]

If, therefore, the British Government had anticipated that Operation Tabarin would bring to an end any challenges to its authority over the Antarctic Peninsula and its outlying island groups, the operation had been a complete failure. In reality, though, while a decisive Argentine volte-face might have been desirable, it had never been the expected outcome. Rather,

the expedition was intended to bolster British sovereignty, which had been weakened by decades of apathy and indecision by successive administrations. In this regard, Operation Tabarin had worked well – but its very success left a complicated and costly legacy. After all, logic dictated that, if British sovereignty had been reinforced by 'boots on the ground', subsequent removal of those boots must reverse the gains achieved by the exercise. It was therefore self-evident, even to a near-bankrupt post-war administration, that a British presence in the Falklands Islands Dependencies must be maintained.

The organisation created by Clement Attlee's post-war government in order to 'fly the flag' in this fashion was the Falkland Islands Dependencies Survey (FIDS) – and its leaders were left in no doubt regarding their most important function. Just as Jimmy Marr had been told in 1943 that his duty was 'to assert and to maintain British Sovereignty over the territory concerned',[29] his successors quickly learned that 'the primary objective of the Survey is to strengthen His Majesty's title to the sector of Antarctica'.[30]

In contrast, their secondary objectives were so poorly defined that Vivian Fuchs, who joined FIDS in 1947, later claimed to have been given 'no directive about the general programme, nor the work to be undertaken',[31] and in the absence of any instructions to the contrary it was assumed that FIDS would continue to pursue the scientific programme originally devised for Operation Tabarin. More important – especially for the adventurous young men recruited to spend one or more winters in the Antarctic – was the general acceptance that every newly mapped kilometre of coastline served to reinforce British hegemony in the region. From the very beginning, therefore, geographic surveying sat at the very core of the FIDS programme, contributing to the sum of human knowledge while also helping to underpin British territorial claims.

The challenges, however, were enormous. In the opinion of Klaus Dodds, one of the leading commentators on the geopolitical history of the Dependencies, 'The preposterous nature of the FIDS's strategic mission was evident every summer season, during which 20–30 men were to map and survey thousands of square miles of ice, rock and water.'[32] And, even if FIDS' resources had been doubled, or even tripled, the physical nature of the Dependencies – renamed the British Antarctic Territory in 1962 – made mapping, and most other work, extraordinarily difficult.

In particular, the Antarctic Peninsula's daunting combination of coastal ice cliffs and mountainous interior meant that, in 1947, six of FIDS' seven

Antarctic bases were located on islands, with Base D at Hope Bay the only exception. While bases have opened and closed in the intervening seventy years, the position remains much the same today, with the British Antarctic Survey's five bases located either on islands or, in the case of Halley VI, on a floating ice shelf. Of course, while the islands offer greater ease of access to ships and more potential for the building of bases, their very nature presents a number of problems, particularly for those tasked with surveying the wider area. Inevitably, the greatest challenge of all remains the need for surveyors and field scientists to use the sea ice as a highway.

★   ★   ★

The FIDS bases located in Marguerite Bay typified many of the problems – and dangers – common to the Survey's stations. The bay itself had been discovered and named in 1909 by Jean-Baptiste Charcot, and both he and subsequent visitors had described in detail the challenging ice conditions along this part of the Graham Land coast. Most problematic of all is the unpredictability of the ice formation.

The first FIDS base to be established in this area, Base E, was built in 1946 on Stonington Island, a small, rocky island in the eastern portion of the bay, but in that first year the sea ice formed so slowly that there was no stable surface even at midwinter. This meant that sledge parties found themselves restricted to the dangerously crevassed Northeast Glacier, which, by way of a steep, drifted snow slope, links the island to the mainland. In other years, the ice, once formed, failed to break up at all, thereby preventing ships from replenishing or relieving expectant shore parties. On one notable occasion, during the austral summer of 1948–49, a belt of fast ice some 64km wide obstinately refused to disintegrate, with the result that five of the eleven-man party then resident at Base E became the first men ever to spend three consecutive winters in the Antarctic. They would not be relieved until February 1950, when a Noorduyn Norseman, dispatched from the RRS *John Biscoe*, at last began the process of evacuation.

The significant logistical problems, and escalating costs, involved in the relief of Stonington Island – to say nothing of the publicity that attended the 'rescue' of the 'Lost Eleven' – convinced the Governor of the Falkland Islands, Sir Miles Clifford, that the base must be closed. Its replacement would be established during the 1954–55 summer season, on Horseshoe Island, roughly 40km to the north. This decision was entirely logical, as ice

conditions were thought to be more predictable in the northern portion of Marguerite Bay. Even so, the residents of the new Base Y quickly discovered that Horseshoe Island presented its own challenges.

In particular, despite long cold periods, gale-force winds continually blew out any newly formed ice, making anything other than very localised sledging quite impossible. In fact, it was not until the winter of 1957 that a party at last managed to undertake any meaningful survey work on the peninsula itself. Surveyors operating from Base W, on Detaille Island, found themselves similarly handicapped, and it became necessary for both bases to establish and stock small refuge huts in case the unexpected break-up of the sea ice left a sledge party stranded.

With their ambitious plans for fieldwork often disrupted or even cancelled altogether because of unsafe sea ice, it was inevitable that the active young scientists and surveyors who manned the bases, and who had volunteered expecting lengthy and invigorating sledging journeys, found extended periods of confinement frustrating. With equal inevitability, in these conditions ice observations often developed into something more closely resembling an obsession than a component of a routine scientific programme, the dominant question in everyone's mind: 'Is the ice thick enough to travel?'

Compared with previous years, the conditions in 1958 appeared fairly benign. At Horseshoe Island, the ice had thickened to 24cm by 29 April, and by 18 May it averaged 50cm. Admittedly, much of the ice around the island had been blown out by a gale on 3 May, but it had been much more fragile then, and between 18 and 21 May, a sledging party travelled all the way to the reopened Stonington Island base without incident. At 6 a.m. on the 27th, the weather was calm, with a temperature of −24°C and visibility of 48km. Overall, in the opinion of John Paisley, the base leader, travelling conditions were 'better than previously experienced and as good as could be expected for the earliness of the season'.[33] It was time to launch the next major sledging expedition of the year.

The purpose of the journey would be to lay a depot on Emperor Islet, one of the Dion group of islands, roughly 60km to the west of Horseshoe Island. Once established, this depot would enable a second party to stay in the area long enough to observe the nesting emperor penguins, and to obtain embryo specimens at various stages of development. As the scientific party would work in the midst of the penguins, it had been decided that they would man-haul, thereby avoiding any risk of a loose dog wreaking havoc among the birds. It therefore made sense for a team with dogs to take the bulk of their supplies to the site before the observations began.

The depot-laying party would consist of three men, all of whom possessed previous Antarctic experience: Dave Statham and Stan Black, both meteorologists, who had served at Signy Island in 1957, and Geoff Stride, a cook and mechanic, who had overwintered at Deception Island during the Falkland Islands Dependencies Aerial Survey Expedition (1955–57) and at Base Y in 1957. Originally, a fourth man, Ray McGowan, the wireless operator, had intended to take part, but at the last minute he decided to stay behind in order to resolve problems with the base transmitter – it was a decision that saved his life.

The three men left the base shortly before lunchtime, taking two sledges and fourteen dogs in two teams of seven. Black, the leader, departed at 11.30 a.m., his sledge loaded with the tent, food and fuel they would need en route. Statham and Stride followed half an hour later, carrying the rations and equipment for the planned depot. By the time they departed, cloud had reduced visibility to 11km, but this was fairly usual and as the conditions appeared stable none of the three men raised any objections to travelling.

When Paisley focused his binoculars on them at 1.15 p.m., both teams seemed to have settled down to their work and they were making good progress. They had already covered a third of the 22.5km to their intended first campsite at the south-western tip of Pourquoi Pas Island, and they would enjoy another three hours of good light in which to complete this stage of their journey. As Paisley boxed his binoculars, he had no obvious cause for anxiety.

From this point, the tragedy unfolded rapidly. Following the calm conditions of the day, during the evening a wind descended on the base from the east, gathering speed throughout the evening until, at midnight, the anemometer at Horseshoe Island indicated an average of 31 knots – a near-gale on the Beaufort Scale. The temperature, too, had risen steeply, with the thermometer registering −12.7°C, a full 10 degrees higher than when the sledgers had departed. In themselves, these changes did not give too much cause for concern because, as David McDowell, the base's senior meteorologist, pointed out, 'In some areas there can be a gale blowing – but that does not mean there is a gale blowing in other parts of the area – the gales can be very localised down there.'[34] Moreover, while the wind at

Horseshoe Island was the strongest for some weeks, the ice on which the three sledgers were travelling was much more robust than it had been at the beginning of the month.

When last seen, they had been moving swiftly over a good surface and they should easily have been able to reach their intended campsite before the wind rose. With the depot stores they were carrying, they would have ample food and fuel even if the ice did blow out and leave them stranded somewhere along the southern coast of Pourquoi Pas Island. And yet, in spite of all these positive factors, Paisley felt deeply, even irrationally, worried, and in his diary he admitted:

> A few minutes after nine I was overcome by an unbelievable feeling of calamity. The force of this was such that contrary to my nature I was compelled to get onto my knees and pray. Such a compulsion has never happened before or since.[35]

For the next two and a half days the weather conditions remained unchanged: the wind continued to howl around the base hut and, worse still, poor surface visibility made it absolutely impossible to ascertain what changes had been wrought on the sea ice. Most troubling of all, though, was the radio silence. The first agreed 'sked' took place at 9 p.m. on 28 May. 'I called them for approximately half an hour,' Ray McGowan reported, 'and frequently told them as I wasn't hearing anything to come up the following night at the same time – which is standard practice.'[36] Although McGowan acknowledged that 'we don't normally worry if a party does not come up on its first schedule,'[37] feelings of normality were beginning to ebb at Base Y, and when they heard nothing on the 29th their anxiety grew still further. Everyone knew that FIDS sledging parties had commonly experienced problems with their field radio sets in the past, but the DWS119 set carried by Black's team was brand new; it had been thoroughly tested prior to departure; all members of the party were familiar with its use; and they would certainly realise that the gales would have caused concern regarding their welfare back at base. There could be no doubt, therefore, that their silence was involuntary.

At last, on the morning of 30 May, the wind began to die away, and with it the drifting snow that had rendered surface visibility so poor. Paisley's worst fears were realised almost immediately:

Paddy woke me early and confirmed a horrible premonition that has been with me since the night of the 27th – the ice has gone. I walked to a good view point along the rocks … All the way I was thinking what I might see, but in spite of that I was totally unprepared for the shock. I was appalled … that ghastly expanse of black water from the ice edge to the horizon. I returned to the hut stunned.[38]

Prior to the gales, Marguerite Bay had been full of ice; now, there was none to be seen beyond a line that ran between Contact Peak on Pourquoi Pas Island to Horseshoe Island, and then down to Camp Point on the mainland. 'As far as it was possible to estimate,' Paisley recorded in his official report, 'there was no ice in Marguerite Bay from that line to the horizon, approximately seventeen miles.'[39]

McDowell also walked to the shoreline to see for himself the effects of the gale. 'We had a look at this huge expanse of water in front of us,' he recalled more than half a century later, 'and I thought, "My God!" It was flat calm when we were there – absolutely, just like a sheet of glass.'[40] Horrified, he and two others stood on the rocks overlooking the fjord that separates Horseshoe Island from Pourquoi Pas Island, 'and we discussed how far sound could travel over still water and so we stood on the edge of the rocks shouting in unison, trying to attract attention … Everyone was very low.'[41]

The situation was far worse than any of them had imagined – but Black and his companions might still be safe and well. In McDowell's opinion, the three men formed 'a sensible party',[42] and they would not have taken needless risks: if the weather conditions had seemed doubtful, they would have remained at their campsite – and it had been impressed upon everybody who left the base that they should, on no account, camp on the sea ice. Nonetheless, Paisley immediately requested a special wireless schedule with the FIDS Secretary at Port Stanley, John Green, and they agreed that an extensive programme of searches should be initiated at once, involving all available personnel from the nearby bases. In addition, all bases were asked to listen for any transmission from the missing men.

Over the next few weeks, and despite treacherous ice conditions and the winter darkness, parties from the bases on Horseshoe Island, Stonington Island and Detaille Island undertook lengthy and often dangerous journeys to every location in the surrounding island groups where it was thought the men might either have camped or possibly landed in the event of having been set adrift on an ice floe. On 6 June, a two-man team from Base W reached the missing men's first possible campsite, at Cape Bongrain on Pourquoi Pas Island. They found no evidence of a campsite, but this was not surprising as, generally, a first bivouac would produce little or no refuse and recent snowfalls would have hidden any disturbance of the surface and covered any small articles that might have been left behind.

The search continued: to Laubeuf Fjord, Adelaide Island and the Dion Islands in the west; to the Debenham Islands and Millerand Island to the south; to the Peninsula coast to the east; and, in the face of high winds and disintegrating ice, to the Faure Islands in the far south-west. Meanwhile, those remaining at Base Y maintained daily watches from Beacon Head, the island's highest point, and, at night, left hurricane lamps burning, their lights visible far out across the bay. All to no avail: Black, Statham and Stride had vanished without a trace.

But not all members of the depot-laying party had disappeared. The hopes of the remaining five Horseshoe islanders soared when, on the night of 5 June, Yana, a bitch from Black's team arrived at the base, clearly exhausted and with her harness, complete except for its clip-hook ring, frozen to the hair of her shoulders. Equipped with lanterns, for hours Paisley and his companions searched the surrounding snow for her tracks, but it wasn't until the following morning that they managed to follow them out into Lystad Bay, the great crescent-shaped feature that first suggested the island's name. They discovered no other footprints and were forced to conclude that Yana had made her way back to the base unaccompanied.

Over the following weeks, another nine dogs were found, either by the search parties or by those manning the bases. All ten dogs appeared fit and healthy – fitter, indeed, than when they left the base on 27 May – and none showed any signs of nervousness or stress. Presumably they had preyed on the available seals. Five of the dogs still wore their harnesses, in various states of repair, but none carried any form of message from the missing men.

In his account of the disaster, published in 1982, Vivian Fuchs makes reference to a number of the harnesses having been cut, giving rise to the theory that some, at least, of the dogs had been freed by the sledgers in a moment of acute danger. Peter Gibbs, who took part in the heroic two-man search journey to the Faure Islands, has remarked:

If your sledge has sunk through the ice and all the dogs and the party are struggling to keep afloat in a tangle of traces, and you are wearing a sheath knife, then it is conceivable that cutting them loose rather than unhooking the clips is preferable.[43]

However, none of the reports or depositions completed at the time of the accident make reference to cuts, all referring instead to the harnesses having been chewed. Unfortunately, Fuchs provides no source for the story of the cuts and, when interviewed in July 2012, McDowell expressed surprise at the suggestion that the dogs had been freed in such a fashion, though he, too, conceded that it was possible.

In the report he prepared at the beginning of September, Paisley observed that the return of so many dogs in such good condition 'led to much speculation from which it was not possible to provide a suitable answer as to the fate of the party'.[44] The consensus of opinion at the time was that they had almost certainly reached their first campsite safely, but that they were then caught out in the open on either 28 or 29 May as they made their way towards their second planned campsite on Jenny Island, off the south-eastern coast of Adelaide Island. In support of this theory, Paisley alluded to the calm weather and good travelling conditions that a party from Detaille Island had encountered in Laubeuf Fjord on the 29th – observations that underpinned McDowell's assertions regarding the localised nature of the weather in Marguerite Bay. The fact that a survey party from Stonington Island had witnessed the ice in Neny Fjord moving out as a single sheet also gave rise to the suggestion that this might have occurred in the northern area of the bay. If so, then perhaps the depot team had been trapped on what amounted to a floating island, which they had been unable to traverse before the channel which separated it from the fast ice, or from land, became too wide for them to cross. Or perhaps, realising the desperate nature of their plight, they had attempted to swim it with the dogs, only to be overcome by the current and the cold.

Given the known dangers of camping on sea ice, and the strict injunctions against doing so, it seems improbable that Black, whom McDowell considered 'very sensible and level-headed',[45] would willingly have taken such a risk. However, Fuchs's experience of sledging in this area during 1949 led him to believe that the party might have met with surface conditions so appalling that they had been slowed down and forced to camp against their will. If this were the case, then it is possible that the ice broke up beneath them as they slept – as happened to the men of the *Endurance* on 9 April 1916, when Stoker Ernest Holness was saved only by the quick thinking of Shackleton, who plucked him, still in his sleeping bag, from the freezing water.

Unfortunately, as Paisley admitted in his deposition to the Falkland Islands Coroner in April the following year, he 'could not tell from the harnesses whether the dogs had been picketed out when they got away from the sledging party or whether they were travelling at the time'.[46]

In the absence of any definitive evidence, either of their campsites or of the point at which they were overtaken by the storm, we can still only speculate as to the precise circumstances in which Black, Statham and Stride met their deaths. 'What happened to the missing party?' David McDowell asked in 2009. 'How did the dogs survive? The truth is no one knows. There can be plenty of theories, but it is all conjecture.'[47]

★ ★ ★

Uncertainty regarding the precise circumstances of the deaths of Black, Statham and Stride led the Falkland Islands Coroner, Aubrey Denton-Thompson, to return a predictable verdict of 'death by misadventure'. Six years later, his successor, Harold Bennett, delivered the same verdict at his inquiry into the loss of Neville Mann, a 23-year-old BAS surveyor, who died on 15 August 1963 when the sea ice close to North Halley Bay Headland broke up during a routine dog training exercise. Neither tragedy was witnessed, but in both cases the men who died were thought to have been acting reasonably in the prevailing conditions, and to have been suitably trained and equipped. There was also no suggestion that either their employers or base leaders had failed in their duty of care. Put simply, all four men had been properly supported and their deaths resulted from misfortune rather than from carelessness or neglect. Moreover, as base leader Maurice Sumner argued in his testimony regarding Mann's disappearance:

If men who are due to spend five months in the field in virtually unknown territory are not allowed to exercise their own judgement 2 miles [3.2km] from base then their chances of making the correct decisions later are less.[48]

Given the known dangers of living and working in the Antarctic, coroners usually delivered non-pejorative verdicts of 'death by misadventure'. Usually, but not always. Two decades later, the conclusions drawn by Coroner Michael Gaiger when he investigated the deaths of Ambrose Morgan, John Coll and Kevin Ockleton were rather more nuanced.

Unlike those of 1958 and 1963, the disastrous field trip of 1982 was driven not by the requirements of a well-defined programme of science and surveying, but by pleasure, pure and simple. There was nothing unusual in this, as BAS had long since accepted that the kind of men they sought to recruit must be allowed to undertake excursions from base if discipline and morale were to be maintained. Ideally, these trips would have an official purpose – but even in the absence of such a purpose, they should still be allowed. As Dick Laws, Director of BAS from 1973, wrote shortly after the accident, such men 'live an isolated and confined life, and they cannot be expected to do so throughout the year without some kind of break'.[49]

According to the plan agreed with Len Airey, commander of BAS's Faraday Station on Galindez Island, the three men would travel on foot across the sea ice to Petermann Island, roughly 8km to the north-east. Using an old Argentine refuge hut as their base, they would explore the island's rocky coastline and icecap, visit the stone cairn left on the summit of the island by Charcot's expedition in 1910, and, if conditions permitted, undertake a journey to the mainland, where they hoped to climb the 880m Mount Scott. Following their assault on the mountain, they would return to Petermann Island before crossing back to Faraday. The whole trip should take only three days but, as a precaution, they would carry with them supplies to last for a much longer stay.

Morgan, whom Airey described as 'keen and able',[50] would lead the expedition, as he was wintering for the second time and had already acquired plenty of field experience. Coll and Ockleton were both in their first year and therefore much less familiar with Antarctic conditions, but Airey thought them both sensible and enthusiastic. He later wrote that all three 'had gained as much sea-ice experience as was possible this winter',[51] and he clearly entertained no doubts regarding their capabilities. Their intended route was also well known, and had been travelled only a few days earlier by both Morgan and Coll.

To all intents and purposes, then, the expedition was a pleasure jaunt undertaken by three men who wished to make the most of their time in

the Antarctic. No such journey could be entirely devoid of danger, but the known risks were deemed to be well within their combined levels of skill and experience and, in the opinion of Graham Hurst, the doctor at Faraday, everyone at the base thought it 'quite natural for them to go'.[52]

The three men departed on 13 July, travelling beneath a dull, overcast sky to reach the rather ramshackle Argentine refuge hut without incident. According to a note they left behind, they made their attempt on Mount Scott the following day, but were forced to abort 'due to fading light and poor condition of Dewsberg Ramp ... Scott south face gully avalanched during afternoon'.[53]

No doubt disappointed that Mount Scott would remain inaccessible for the foreseeable future, the trio spent the 15th walking across the sea ice to explore Girard Bay, a 2km-deep feature that indents the peninsula coastline. By the time they regained the hut late that afternoon the weather was clearly on the turn, and it looked as though their sphere of operations would contract still further. Throughout the evening the wind gathered force, with the American Palmer Station to the north experiencing hurricane-force wind speeds of 80 knots and the Faraday anemometer recording a violent storm of 58 knots. It was now more than three weeks since Midwinter's Day, the temperature had fallen to an unusual seasonal low of −25°C, and the sea ice around Petermann Island was at its thickest. Even so, the next morning Morgan and his companions woke to find themselves stranded, with much of the ice that had bound the islands together, and the islands to the mainland coast, blown far out to sea.

Initially, the men responded to their predicament with unmixed delight. The routine scientific programme at Faraday was complex and time-consuming, including meteorology, seismology, magnetism and observations of the ionosphere and solar radiation. Its maintenance required single-minded dedication from both the scientists and their support staff, and this usually left very little room for recreation. They therefore considered the extension of their sojourn on Petermann Island a boon rather than a trial.

Of course, a long delay in the re-formation of the sea ice might lead to frustration — particularly if local trips became impossible — but even then, they knew that they would have no real cause for anxiety. The Argentine shelter was adequate, if not luxurious, and while its two outhouses had been severely damaged by the storm, this could be viewed as something of a blessing as it meant that they now possessed an ample supply of firewood. Combining their own rations with those stockpiled at the hut, they had sufficient paraffin for ninety days and, even without hunting, food for fifty. They could be confident, therefore, that they would be neither cold nor hungry during their enforced stay. 'No booze and very few fags,' they observed wryly, 'but lots of tea and penguins.'[54]

Their euphoria did not last long. Subject, as ever, to the vagaries of the equipment and the weather, initially Airey maintained daily radio contact with the marooned party and on the 19th, the fourth day after the storm, he noted that they seemed 'well but concerned'.[55] He, too, admitted to some anxiety on their behalf, but this resulted more from their apparent disorganisation than from any real doubts regarding their safety.

Over the next few days, the sea ice continued to tease them, repeatedly re-forming only to break up in the face of the wind and tidal swells. The men themselves vacillated between resignation and apprehension, between boredom and guilt at having left their friends to shoulder the extra burden of work at the base. On 23 July, they 'sounded low over the radio'[56] and inquired about the possibility of a boat from Faraday being dispatched to collect them, but Airey thought this an unjustifiable risk given the uncertain weather and ice conditions. Three days later, he noted that the three men were 'complaining of smelling', leading him again to question their organisation.[57] 'They were not paying attention to personal hygiene,' he recalled. 'The hut apparently stank because of the penguins they ate and the fumes given off by the paraffin lamp and coal fire, I grew more concerned for their well-being.'[58]

His concerns grew still further when, on the 31st, the Petermann party reported that they had been suffering from mild diarrhoea, their symptoms probably a result of their decision to vary their diet by sampling the Argentine food, which was of uncertain age and condition. At Airey's request, Hurst spoke to them and offered advice on basic hygiene, though they assured him that they had already made a full recovery. Overall, the doctor thought that the party seemed reasonably content, though he also noted that they 'complained of boredom and lack of reading material'.[59] From this point onwards base and world news were included in the routine radio schedule and air letters were read out, though doubts about the remaining life of the field radio batteries necessitated a reduction in the frequency of the transmissions.

During the first few days of August the 'pain-in-the-butt weather'[60] continued, with various research stations along the west coast of the peninsula

experiencing a combination of unusually high temperatures and winds so strong that many reported the loss of their aerial masts. When a calm at last settled on 5 August, Penola Strait and French Passage had been swept clear of practically all of the new-formed sea ice, with just a few patches remaining trapped among the Argentine Islands. With the weather suddenly calm and the waterways largely clear, Airey admitted in his diary that he felt tempted to try relieving Morgan's party by boat – but he sensibly decided that caution should be the order of the day:

> The weather has been very unstable over the last few days with winds rising without warning. The air temperature was −10°C, sea temperature −1.6°C and wind speed of 2 knots. A rescue party could soon get into serious problems if the sea froze about them so far from base. I deferred the decision until tomorrow.[61]

Conditions the following day justified his reticence, as the sea again began to freeze in the face of a sudden drop in temperature. Had a boat party reached Petermann Island, they too might have been marooned and forced to await the formation of sea ice sufficiently robust to allow them to walk back, leaving their dinghy for collection at a later date. The temporary absence of three men from Faraday was an inconvenience; the loss of more would have seriously jeopardised the ongoing scientific programme. The wait continued.

By the 12th, the weather had at last stabilised and Airey reported that, with the sea ice continuing to thicken, parties from Faraday had begun to venture further afield. One team, made up of the physicists Pete Salino and Andy Sweetman, almost reached Petermann Island, but were forced to retreat when they encountered a narrow lead running towards the mainland. 'We were very close to Petermann,' Salino recalled, 'but the ice was very suspect near the lead and we turned back.'[62]

The following day, Friday 13 August, the Petermann party could be seen waving cheerfully from the top of the island and during a routine radio schedule that evening they debated their position, options and aspirations, as Airey recorded:

> We discussed their situation at some length. Although the sea ice has formed fairly well, more storms could equally break it up again. If we could not get to Petermann or they could not return to base, then an airdrop would have

to be arranged at some stage. I wanted to know from them if they thought they could cope until the BAS airdrop sometime in October, or would it be necessary to arrange an airdrop from some other source. They wanted time to think about this and would let me know on the next sked. They reported good sea ice conditions at Petermann except for a lead in French Passage blocking a direct route to Faraday. A possible route, they said, may be to head into Penola [Strait] and towards the Jalours [Islands]. They wished to investigate this section of ice on the Saturday or the Sunday as a day trip. I sanctioned the trip, with a few provisos.[63]

Chief among Airey's conditions were that the men should carry full bivouac equipment; they must inform him of any changes to their plans; and they should exercise the greatest caution with regard to weather and sea ice conditions. They also agreed that if, during the reconnaissance, they thought it possible to proceed safely to Faraday, they should do so, leaving any equipment and stores at Petermann Island for collection at a later date. 'With this,' Airey concluded, 'a sked was arranged for Sunday at 1830Z.'[64]

Morgan, Coll and Ockleton were never seen or heard from again. On 15 August, the day on which they were supposed to contact Faraday, storms were reported at the American Palmer Station and at BAS's Rothera Station. Although conditions remained calm at Faraday, a heavy swell had been running for twenty-four hours causing large cracks to appear in the sea ice. Airey could see that the lead in French Passage had widened to roughly 400m and it now extended into Penola Strait and across to the mainland coast. Far more worryingly, at 6.30 p.m. the Petermann party failed to keep the agreed radio schedule, leaving Airey listening to the uninterrupted hiss and crackle of static. 'I became anxious,' he recalled. 'I called for an hour, then on the hour every hour. I knew something was wrong.'[65]

The swell continued to increase in strength throughout the course of the night and on 16 August Palmer Station reported that they had experienced wind speeds of up to 70 knots. 'Today Penola is free of ice,' Airey recorded glumly. The Petermann party were now forty-eight hours overdue. The following day he ordered that dinghies be prepared for a search-and-rescue operation that would commence as soon as sea conditions allowed. At agreed scheduled times, he and his companions also sent flares arcing into the gloom of the winter sky. While they waited, Airey prepared a report for transmission to BAS headquarters in Cambridge. Having described the weather conditions and the plan agreed with Morgan, he outlined the three possible explanations for the prolonged silence of the Petermann party:

> Confusion over the time of the radio sked. This I doubt. I would have thought they would have come up on one of the arranged listening watches. We are also in visual contact, but nothing has been observed.
>
> Radio failure. On the last sked they were extremely weak on VHF but strong on Comcal. I doubt battery failure, but equipment failure is always a possibility.
>
> A heavy swell came in on the Saturday and destroyed much of the sea ice. Storms on the Sunday evening destroyed the remainder of the ice in Penola [Strait] to the extent that there is once again open water between Penguin Point and Penola (excluding brash). It is possible that they were caught out by the ice breaking up.[66]

In reply to this telegram, Dick Laws correctly advised Airey that the decision regarding whether or not to launch a boat must lie with him, as only he could form an accurate judgement regarding the risks. However, he stipulated that the boat 'must not set out unless conditions were ideal and must return to base each night'.[67]

In the event, conditions remained so far from ideal for a boat party that the first serious attempt to locate the missing men was conducted not by the personnel of Faraday Station, but by the Chilean Air Force. With no British aircraft or ships available in the aftermath of the Falklands War, following instructions issued by Cambridge on 19 August, Airey contacted the Chilean base on Fildes Peninsula in the South Shetlands to ask whether they would be willing to participate in a search for the missing personnel. The response was both immediate and, in the words of a later BAS press release, 'in the very best Antarctic tradition of mutual assistance'.[68]

On 20 August, a Lockheed C-130 Hercules of the Chilean Air Force undertook a dangerous 6,000km round trip, flying from Santiago, down the long mountainous spine of Chile to Tierra del Fuego and then south to the Antarctic Peninsula, where it completed a three-hour search of the quadrant defined by Faraday Station, Rasmussen Island, Petermann Ramp and Petermann Island. In near-perfect visibility, the highly experienced Chilean pilot flew low over the peninsula coast, inspected the remnants of sea ice in Penola Strait, circled Petermann Island and the Argentine Islands, and even flew out to sea in a northerly direction – to no avail. 'The Chileans were convinced that our party was not in a survival situation,' Airey reported after speaking with the pilot. 'They offered to return if I could suggest any new locations for them to search. I could not … To my mind there was no reason to search this area again.'[69] In reality, the chances of finding the Petermann trio alive had dwindled to near zero and, if they were dead, their bodies would have been blanketed by recent snowfalls, rendering them invisible to airborne observers.

Petermann Island itself was not reached until 15 October, a full two months after the party's disappearance – and many weeks after any realistic hope of finding them alive had been abandoned. The refuge made a grim spectacle, with its deserted main hut and skeletal outhouses. A large drift had collected against the south wall of the former and a considerable amount of snow had entered the foyer through the outer door that had presumably blown open during the recent storms. In the main living room, tins, packets and items of discarded equipment lay strewn about, along with the butchered remains of three penguins. Despite the concerns that the Petermann party had raised regarding the available rations, Pete Salino, who led the search party, calculated that the remaining stocks of tinned and dried food would have supported the three men for 'several months if supplemented by seal or penguin',[70] and there was also ample fuel, in the form of paraffin, coal and wood from the part-demolished secondary huts.

Given this inventory, it seems clear that, while an airdrop by either BAS or the Chilean Air Force might have made a prolonged stay more comfortable, it would certainly not have been essential for survival. Possibly the three men had painted an unduly bleak picture of their living conditions, perhaps because they feared that efforts to relieve them would not be prioritised if they were thought to be too comfortable and self-sufficient. Tired of the primitive conditions, weary of one another's company and lacking any form of distraction to pass the time, their primary objective had been to escape from their island prison.

Having assessed the equipment left in the hut, Salino believed that the Petermann party had fully complied with Airey's instructions, taking with them everything necessary to bivouac on their reconnaissance journey. With the exception of their cameras, they had deposited all non-essentials in the hut, obviously intending to travel as light as possible. That they had left no note outlining their plans was hardly surprising, as they had discussed these with Airey immediately prior to their departure; the only written records were their entries in the visitors' book, dated 13 July and 1 August, in which they noted their arrival and failed attempt on Mount Scott, and what Salino described as 'a spoof letter telling of their stranding'.[71] This letter was unfinished, apparently because they ran out of ink.

At last, on 18 March 1983, Rex Hunt, Governor of the Falkland Islands, directed the Coroner of the British Antarctic Territory to conduct an inquest into what, even at that late stage, he still called 'the probable deaths' of Morgan, Coll and Ockleton.[72] The inquest itself took place exactly one month later, at Stanley. The only witness to appear in person was Airey, who travelled from Faraday on board the RRS *John Biscoe*, though the coroner received sworn statements from other base personnel, including Hurst and Salino.

As with previous British sea ice fatalities, there can be no certainty regarding the exact time, place and nature of the Petermann party's deaths. The most probable scenario is that they set out from the refuge hut sometime during 14 August, the day after Airey consented to their plans, and that the ice on which they travelled was destroyed by the effects of the heavy swell that rose during the course of the day. Although Morgan had obtained a reasonable degree of sea ice experience during 1981, conditions in that year had been much more stable than in 1982, and the ice much safer. It's possible, therefore, that while he understood some of the dangers of young sea ice in the open passage between Petermann Island and the Argentine Islands, he was less unfamiliar with such phenomena as the tidal scour that can significantly erode sea ice from below, leaving an upper surface that appears firm, but which is actually fragile and unreliable: just the kind of ice that would shatter almost immediately when subjected to a swell. Given that young sea ice usually breaks up into small, slushy pieces incapable of supporting a man, it seems likely that the party found themselves floundering on a disintegrating mosaic of ice, their legs and feet constantly plunging into the freezing water, before they finally lost their balance altogether.

Once in the water, it would have been practically impossible for any of the men to get out again and, fully clothed and booted but without lifejackets, they would almost certainly have drowned in just a few minutes. If, by some miracle, they had been able to clamber back onto the floe, their troubles would have been far from over. Prior to the inquest, Dick Laws had asked Professor J. Nelson Norman, BAS's physiological and medical consultant and himself a Polar Medallist, to provide an expert opinion on the men's possible causes of death. In his view, any man climbing back onto the floe:

... would be in serious trouble unless he could change all his clothing, since the very high thermal conductivity of water, compared to air, would reduce the insulative value of his clothing assembly to 10% of its original value and he would effectively be dressed in something of the value of a swimming costume.[73]

Without immediate re-warming in a hot bath, most men would die in just a few minutes, and certainly within two or three hours at most.

Another possibility is that, instead of plunging through disintegrating ice, the trio found themselves adrift on a larger segment of the floe. The known ice conditions make this appear highly improbable, but if it did occur, the cold, the effects of the freezing sea spray and the men's limited ability to exercise in order to keep warm would have severely limited their life expectancy. In Norman's opinion:

> It would not take more than an hour or so for apathy, clouding of competence and judgement to take place ... I cannot see – even though there are so many variables – that the men would survive the night, even given the best circumstances.[74]

In many respects, the circumstances bore a very close similarity to those surrounding the loss of Black, Statham and Stride in 1958, and of Mann in 1963: in every case the men were properly equipped, but they were overwhelmed by a deadly combination of weather conditions and unstable sea ice. Crucially, however, in other ways, the deaths of the Petermann party more closely resembled those of Mackintosh and Hayward, sixty-six years earlier. In particular, while there is no evidence that either Black or Mann took unnecessary risks – at least when viewed within the context of Antarctic travel – Mackintosh, Hayward, Morgan, Coll and Ockleton all died because they chose to abandon adequately provisioned huts in order to undertake journeys that they knew to be dangerous, and which could have been delayed until such time as the prevailing conditions, including the stability of the sea ice, had improved. Completion of their journeys was highly desirable to all five men (with the possible exception of Hayward), but not essential either to them or to their expeditions – and the decision to avoid the risks of travel at those times, in those places, and on those days, would have produced no dire consequences. All were motivated by an overwhelming desire to reach their destination, and all fell victim to their own flawed decision-making in pursuit of that goal. John Dudeney, who wintered at Faraday in 1967 and 1968, has summed up the opinion of many of those who worked with BAS at the time, 'It was seen as bad judgement on the part of the three themselves, they could have waited, didn't and paid the price.'[75]

Questions must also be asked regarding Airey's role in the tragedy. During the party's month-long stay at Petermann Island, he had repeatedly expressed doubts about their organisation – and yet, when they sought his permission to undertake the sea ice reconnaissance, he left it to Morgan to make the final decision as to whether the journey could be completed safely. In many ways, this approach was sensible as Airey, at a distance of some 8km, could not be expected to accurately assess the condition of the local sea ice; he also instructed them that they should carry all essential equipment and push on towards Faraday only if they could do so 'without risk'.[76] But he knew how ardently they wished to reach Faraday and should perhaps have considered whether the intensity of their desire might override their caution. In retrospect, at least, he also acknowledged that Morgan's knowledge of sea ice, though greater than that of his companions, was still limited. Taking these factors into account, it might certainly be argued that, as base commander, he should have ordered them to remain at the hut until the sea ice had matured and the weather become more settled.

And yet such an assertion fails to take full account of the style of leadership at British Antarctic bases. In Pete Salino's opinion:

> Len could have exerted pressure but as there would be no effective sanction other than return to the UK at the end of the winter, trying to order them would probably have been pointless … a more consensual leadership was required if harmony were to be maintained.[77]

For his own part, Airey made no attempt to eschew responsibility or to place a gloss on the events, and in his introductory remarks to the report on the accident, he wrote that 'I make no pretence that mistakes were not made either on my part or on the part of the field party. Neither, however, will I make any issue of errors made or try to draw any conclusions from them. I leave that, if necessary, to the reader.'[78]

Finally, the coroner must determine whether BAS, as the body ultimately responsible for the safety of all British personnel operating in

Antarctica, should have done anything differently. Was its appraisal of the generic risks of Antarctic travel reasonable, and its standing instructions designed to mitigate those risks adequate? As John Dudeney has suggested, there would also be the broader issues of training, overall command and control:

> … and whether the Argentine refuge was a sensible place to use for a holiday trip – whether it was stocked sufficiently for them to have sat it out until either the ice was sound or there was sufficient open water to allow a boat rescue from base.[79]

Although no record of Coroner Michael Gaiger's deliberations has survived, his verdict indicates that he felt less than entirely satisfied with what he heard during the inquest. When investigating previous sea ice fatalities, his predecessors had all concluded that those deaths had resulted from 'misadventure', meaning that the victims died as a direct result of risks they willingly took, and that the actions and advice of other parties did not unduly influence their decisions or otherwise significantly contribute to their fate. By its very nature, such a verdict leaves no room for further investigation and the case is closed. In contrast, an open verdict – the verdict arrived at by Gaiger in April 1983 – leaves unanswered the question of who was ultimately responsible for a death, or deaths: it suggests that insufficient information has been made available in order for the coroner to reach any alternative verdict, and implies that important questions remain unresolved. While the verdict does not suggest that a misdemeanour has been committed, it leaves open the possibility that blame *could* be attributed, if more evidence were forthcoming.[80] Such a verdict must, therefore, have made uncomfortable reading for Airey, Dick Laws and BAS's parent body, the Natural Environment Research Council (NERC).

Airey, of course, could do nothing. NERC, on the other hand, immediately launched a formal inquiry to investigate the circumstances surrounding the disaster and to 'examine the adequacy of the safety rules and procedures … applying at the time of the accident'.[81] The resulting report emphasised that the Petermann party had been appropriately trained and that they had been fully aware of BAS's instructions regarding travel on sea ice; besides further reinforcing these instructions and taking steps to improve radio communications at Faraday, there was little more that BAS could do.

The Board of Inquiry did criticise Airey on two counts, however. First, he had destroyed the 'spoof' letter discovered by the search party; the board considered that the letter should have been retained and that it might have given 'a possible indication of the state of mind of the party'.[82] Second, he had not made BAS headquarters aware of his doubts regarding the party's organisation and morale. Had he done so, opined the board in phrases that ring with almost ludicrous self-regard, Cambridge 'might have been able by a further suitably reassuring message backed by the authority of the Director to have stiffened their endurance and their morale'.[83] But these criticisms were relatively minor, and in the board's view, the disaster that overtook Morgan and his companions was essentially of their own making:

> In venturing out, the party were taking a risk. Risk can never be totally eliminated in Antarctica: in this case the desire to return to base and re-join their colleagues may have urged them to take an extra chance. Luck cannot be counted upon in Antarctica.[84]

★ ★ ★

Although the Board of Inquiry's criticisms of Airey are too mild to constitute an attempt at scapegoating, its findings still bear all the hallmarks of a bureaucratic whitewash, with blame firmly directed away from the organisation and towards the individuals who died. And yet, despite this desire to erase, unofficially at least, the coroner's inconvenient open verdict and to replace it with the much more palatable – and more usual – 'death by misadventure', the tide was beginning to turn. The early 1980s had proved a particularly disastrous period for BAS, with six individuals lost in three separate incidents between February 1980 and August 1982; worse still, five of the fatalities had been suffered during recreational excursions. Clearly, this state of affairs could not be allowed to continue. If, up to the time of the Petermann tragedy, BAS had been, in the words of one of its senior officers, 'a happy band of amateurs',[85] afterwards, a new professionalism developed, and with it a greater focus on training and safety protocols. This process of transformation began with the influential Logan Report into BAS safety procedures, which was drafted in June 1982 and published in 1983.[86]

Of course, the changes that were introduced over the coming years were not purely the result of BAS maturing as an organisation. On 31 July 1974 – the year following Dick Laws' appointment as Director of BAS – the Health and Safety at Work Act received royal assent, and its provisions constituted a sea change in the way employee safety and employer responsibilities were both viewed and enforced. In July 2008, Lord Grocott told the House of Lords that, in the thirty-four years of the Act's existence, its structures, duties, offences and the approach to safety in the workplace that it established, had 'stood the test of time' and that the 'record of the 1974 Act speaks for itself'.[87]

Between 1974 and 2007, fatal injuries to employees in the UK had fallen by 73 per cent and non-fatal injuries by 70 per cent. In 2003, the most recent year for which statistics were available when Grocott addressed his fellow peers, the number of fatal injuries in the UK was less than half of the average for other European Union nation states (1 per 100,000 workers in the UK, compared with 2.5 per 100,000 in the rest of the EU). Although the location of BAS's field operations required special consideration in terms of the application of the Act, the development of a culture of Health and Safety awareness and of accident prevention and reporting was no less pronounced; indeed, in 1982, NERC was at pains to reassure Logan that 'the standard of safety provided by [the Act] is one we will wish to apply as far as is reasonably practicable in the Antarctic'.[88]

The final piece in the jigsaw is the impact on BAS of events on the wider world stage. Morgan, Coll and Ockleton died exactly two months to the day after General Mario Menéndez, commander of the Argentine garrison at Stanley, surrendered to Major General Jeremy Moore, bringing to an end the short but bloody Falklands War. The effects of that conflict on BAS were profound – but positive. Shortly after Laws took up his post as director, NERC had reduced BAS's operating budget by a tenth. It had applied further pressure in 1979, with the result that BAS cut its representation on the Falkland Islands down to just one member of staff. The Argentine invasion of 2 April 1982 reversed this trend in a remarkable fashion. Just as in January 1943 Churchill's War Cabinet had accepted that 'permanent occupation' constituted the best means by which to underpin Britain's claims to her South Atlantic dependencies, now Margaret Thatcher's government recognised that BAS, as the successor to Operation Tabarin, must receive significant additional funding in order to maintain Britain's geopolitical interests. Thatcher herself took a personal interest and ordered that BAS's operating budget should be doubled. Inevitably, however, greater investment entailed closer scrutiny and this new order must, of itself, bring an end to the happy amateurism of days gone by.

Whatever its primary cause, the fact remains that, following the deaths of the Petermann party, the pace of evolution in BAS increased significantly – and one of the most obvious results of that evolution has been the dramatic reduction in deaths, with the organisation sustaining just one fatality between 1982 and the present day. That Morgan, Coll and Ockleton died unnecessarily is unquestionable, but their deaths contributed to a substantial change in attitudes – and, in this regard, perhaps they did not die entirely in vain.

3

'A Tremendous Asset'

The Advent of Mechanised Transport

After weeks of almost unremitting blizzards, the night of 23 February 1951 was brilliantly clear and frosty along the coast of Queen Maud Land on the eastern edge of the Weddell Sea, the light infused 'with an almost magical brilliance'.[1] Since the departure of their supply ship, *Norsel*, at the end of January, the members of John Giaever's Norwegian-British-Swedish Antarctic Expedition (NBSAE) had been working hard preparing for their second winter. As well as completing all the routine maintenance and meteorological observations, they had dug a new exit tunnel from the expedition's subsurface hut, overhauled the diesel installations and electric generators, repaired and serviced the vehicles, and sorted and catalogued the vast piles of stores that lay strewn around the base site. Sledging parties had also begun to push inland to begin a complex programme of geographic survey and scientific fieldwork, leaving just nine men at the expedition base, Maudheim.

Shortly before midnight, Bertil Ekström, the Swedish mechanical engineer, and his countryman, Stig Hallgren, the expedition's newly arrived photographer, announced that they had completed work on the last of the expedition's rather battered M29C Tracked Cargo Carriers, or 'Weasels', and that they intended to take it for a test drive across the ice shelf while the weather held. Keen not to miss an opportunity for some much-needed recreation, Leslie Quar, the English wireless operator, and John Jelbart, a cosmic ray physicist who had joined the expedition just seven weeks earlier as an ANARE observer, decided to accompany them.

The four men clambered into the small open-topped vehicle in buoyant mood; although the trip would enable them to test the vehicle and provide them with an opportunity to recover some aluminium sheeting from the airstrip and seal meat left at the ice quay during the ship's unloading, in reality they were bent on pleasure. The weather was still brilliantly clear, but within minutes a dense, low fog rolled up from the bay and over the ice, completely obscuring the surface. As they could still see the sky above their heads, the four men continued undeterred – even when they realised that they had lost their bearings. After all, if the fog didn't lift they could find their way back to the base by following their outward tracks in the snow – even if that meant that one of the party must walk in front of the Weasel.

Eventually they located the airstrip and quickly loaded the aluminium sheets, then, more confident now of their whereabouts, they headed towards the quay to collect the seal meat. With Ekström driving, they were motoring down the ramp towards the quay at about 24kph when, suddenly, the fog cleared to reveal the ice edge and, beyond it, the sea. But the ice edge was not where they expected it to be: during the boisterous weather of the last few days, a massive chunk of the shelf, several hundred metres deep and incorporating the quay, had broken off and floated out into the bay.

Charles Swithinbank, the expedition's assistant glaciologist, considered Ekström 'always a fast driver'[2] and by the time he slammed on the brakes it was too late. With clouds of ice particles spewing from its tracks, the 2-tonne Weasel covered the last 15m in a matter of seconds and then toppled over the edge and into the sea. The four men leapt for safety, but all landed in the bitterly cold water and Ekström and Jelbart appeared to injure themselves in the fall.

The Weasel had been intended for amphibious operations – but this plunge was far removed from the kind of controlled launch that its designers had envisaged, and almost immediately it filled and sank. Floundering in the water, the men were now confronted by a sheer wall of ice 4m tall and, with rapidly numbing fingers and the current sucking them beneath the ice front, they had no hope of climbing to safety. Still scrabbling at the ice, one by one Ekström, Jelbart and Quar disappeared, the last calling a plaintive 'goodbye' as he was pulled under.

Shivering violently with the effects of cold and shock, Stig Hallgren swam to a tiny floe about 200m away and, using his sheath knife as an ice axe, managed to climb onto it. He then paddled the fragment of ice to a larger floe and, after another mad scramble, succeeded in transferring to this more stable platform. Once on board, he paced up and down in an attempt to warm himself, shouting all the time in the hope that someone at the base might have noticed the long absence of the vehicle party and followed their tracks to the ice edge. Hallgren was tall and athletic and his superb fitness – coupled with his possession of the sheath knife – had given him the best possible chance of survival. But he also knew that, even if his remaining friends discovered what had happened, it would take hours for them to excavate any of the expedition's boats from the hard snow that covered them – and with every passing minute the current carried his floating sanctuary further and further from aid, out amidst the churning waters of the Weddell Sea.

★   ★   ★

Though not the first to die in a vehicle-related accident in the Antarctic – that dubious privilege went to a US Navy rating mangled by a tractor in 1947 during Operation Highjump – Ekström, Quar and Jelbart had made history of a kind, becoming the first to die while travelling in a motor vehicle. However, when we recall that mechanised transport had been introduced to the continent as early as 1908 – more than four decades before the tragedy at Maudheim and only twenty years after the invention of the modern motor car – in some respects the accident's most surprising feature is that it hadn't happened sooner.

The story of the development of mechanised transport in the Antarctic is long, complicated and, in the opinion of one well-informed observer, demonstrated a 'gallant persistence to develop new ideas, but lacked attention to detail'.[3] It began with Shackleton, who took a four-cylinder Arrol-Johnston motor car on his British Antarctic (*Nimrod*) Expedition of 1907–09. Initially, he intended to use it for hauling supplies from his expedition ship to Hut Point, but he also:

> … thought it possible, from my previous experience, that we might meet with a hard surface on the Great Ice Barrier, over which the first part, at any rate, of the journey towards the south would have to be performed.[4]

If his prediction proved accurate, the car might be able to travel further inland.

Despite its conventional appearance, the Arrol-Johnston boasted a number of modifications intended to render it suitable for polar work. The original water-cooled engine had been replaced with an air-cooled, four-cylinder

unit capable of 12–15hp; it incorporated a Simms-Bosch magneto ignition, and behind the seats a flatbed could be used for carrying cargo, making the car an early form of pick-up truck. Ingeniously, the engineers had diverted exhaust gas both to a jacket fitted around the carburettor to prevent it freezing, and to a foot warmer, intended to provide the two occupants of the open cab with at least a modicum of comfort. They had adapted the four-gear transmission (plus reverse) to provide special low-speed gear ratios, and had strengthened the chassis with wooden beams 'in view of the fact that the car was likely to experience severe strains at low temperature'.[5] Finally, the engineers' confidence in their vehicle could be gauged by the fact that they had fitted a second fuel tank, increasing its range to 480km.

On 1 February 1908, the *Nimrod*'s crew lowered the car onto the sea ice at Cape Royds, ready for its first trial. Bernard Day, a 24-year-old motor engineer appointed by the Arrol-Johnston Company, stood before his charge and, no doubt casting his eyes heavenwards, swung the crank. His prayers were answered: the engine started with ease and 'off the car went with the throbbing sound which has become so familiar in the civilised world, and was now heard for the first time in the Antarctic'.[6]

But the euphoria rapidly evaporated, as Shackleton described:

> The run was but a short one, for within a hundred yards the wheels clogged in the soft snow. With all hands pushing and pulling we managed to get the car across a crack in the ice, which we momentarily expected would open out, and allow the floe to drift away to the north. Once over the crack the engine was started again, and for a short distance the car went ahead under its own power, but it was held up again by the snow. By dint of more pushing and pulling, and with the help of its own engine, the car reached a point about half a mile south of the ship, but our hopes as to the future practical utility of the machine were considerably damped … as there was no prospect of it helping us to reach the land at this time I decided to have it hauled back to the ship and hoisted on board at once, to await a more favourable opportunity for a thorough test … In the morning I had had dreams of mounting the car with Day and gaily overtaking the sledge-party as they toiled over the ice, but these dreams were short-lived.[7]

Although it would have been easy to write off the car after this inauspicious beginning, following completion of further modifications made by Day during the winter months, it did make some useful journeys later in the year, the longest being a 50km round trip to a depot laid on the Erebus Glacier Tongue, halfway between Cape Royds and Hut Point. Crucially, though, all of these trips were made on good windswept surfaces devoid of soft snow: conditions that could not be expected on the Great Barrier as Shackleton pushed south towards the Pole. He later wrote, 'If the car had only been able to travel over the Barrier surface all our difficulties would have been solved, for a hundred miles [161km] a day would not have been too much to have expected of it.'[8] But few people knew the Barrier conditions better than Shackleton and on 29 October, after hitching a ride in the car as far as Erebus Glacier Tongue, he abandoned it in favour of his Manchurian ponies and man-hauling.

Though the knowledge would probably have done very little to assuage their feelings of disappointment, as the very earliest pioneers of mechanical transport in the Antarctic, Shackleton and Day had become the first to encounter a problem that would remain a perennial challenge for all designers of motorised snow vehicles: traction. The expedition had 'secured wheels of several special patterns as well as ordinary wheels with special rubber tyres, and ... wooden runners to be placed under the front wheels for soft surfaces',[9] but their experiences proved that Shackleton and the Arrol-Johnston engineers had devoted far too little time to the problem of how to give their vehicle the necessary grip in variable snow conditions. In fact, the 'special patterns' involved nothing more sophisticated than attaching 'teeth' to otherwise standard rear driving wheels, turning them, to all intents and purposes, into wooden cogs that were intended to grip the surface in the manner of crampons.

The idea was nothing new, as Franz Pfeifer, 'a subject of the King of Württemberg', had sought international patents for a rather more sophisticated embodiment of the same principles as early as December 1905, though his invention seems never to have progressed beyond the drawing board.[10] The idea was also incorporated into three sledges taken by Charcot on his Second French Antarctic Expedition of 1908–10. Charcot tested these on the sea ice of Marguerite Bay, south of Adelaide Island, in January 1909, but he abandoned their further use when he realised that they 'would only be serviceable after a number of trials and changes'.[11]

★ ★ ★

Despite his ill-deserved reputation for being a traditionalist disastrously wedded to the romance of man-hauled sledging, Scott proved to be a champion of motor vehicles in the Antarctic. During the *Discovery* Expedition of 1901–04, his engineer, Reginald Skelton, had suggested that 'a motor car, driven by petroleum, could be constructed to do very good work', though he went on to acknowledge that, 'Of course the design would have to be greatly different from ordinary cars, especially in the matter of wheels'.[12] Scott had become an early convert, and nine years later, watching the tentative progress of his own experimental tractors on the sea ice close to Cape Evans, he admitted to being:

> ... immensely eager that these tractors should succeed ... A small measure of success will be enough to show their possibilities, their ability to revolutionise Polar transport. Seeing the machines at work today, and remembering that every defect so far shown is purely mechanical, it is impossible not to be convinced of their value.[13]

The vehicles he described – and which Skelton had helped to design – were the three Wolseley motor-sledges taken on his *Terra Nova* Expedition. The Wolseleys possessed no steering and no brakes and were powered by four-cylinder, 14hp, air-cooled engines with a top speed of just 5.5kph, compared with the Arrol-Johnston's 26kph.

Perhaps the best contemporary description of these machines was provided by Griffith Taylor, the expedition's Australian geologist:

> The two axles bear two pairs of cogwheels about eighteen inches [46cm] diameter. Around these run two endless bands – one on each side of the sledge – which carry flat square plates. These plates constitute the bearing surface, and each plate is actually stationary on the ground until it comes under the rear cogwheel, when it is caught up and passed forward to the front cogwheel. Hence the car runs on its own platform ... There is a large tool box in front of the engine, and a small elevated padded seat at the back. Otherwise no top hamper obscures the mechanism. When not in use the motor wears a huge quilted hood which keeps the cylinders from freezing.
>
> In work two men are necessary. One drives from the seat, and another holds the end of a rope fastened to a projecting bowsprit. The latter is the helmsman, for at a pull sideways the sledge slews around without the expenditure of much effort.[14]

These tractors, with their 'endless bands', signalled the arrival of the first continuous-tracked vehicles in the Antarctic, making them the direct ancestors not only of the tank, but of the Weasel in which Ekström, Jelbart and Quar met their deaths forty years later.

After successful trials in Norway, on 4 January 1911 two of the three motor-sledges were unloaded from the *Terra Nova* at Cape Evans. Determined to capitalise on the experience gained during Shackleton's *Nimrod* Expedition, Scott had recruited Bernard Day as motor engineer and by the early afternoon both vehicles were in action, towing heavy loads of supplies and equipment 2.5km to the base site.

Lieutenant Teddy Evans was impressed both by Day, whom he considered 'the most undefeated sportsman', and by the tractors, observing that 'the newest motor frequently towed loads of 2,500lb [1,134kg] over the ice at a six mile an hour [10kph] speed. The oldest hauled a ton [1 tonne] and managed six double trips a day.'[15] Another of their functions, 'most fully appreciated', according to Taylor, was that of hauling the man-sledges back to the ship, 'empty except for the wearied pullers who lay back on the sledges and dreamily regarded the clear sky on their welcome rest between pulls'.[16]

The following day, Scott noted that the sledges were 'steadying down to their work' and that Day 'is very pleased and thinks he's going to do wonders'.[17] But his own optimism was clearly on the wane and in private he sounded a note of caution regarding their potential utility, 'fearing that they will not take such heavy loads as we hoped'.[18] He continued in the same vein on the 6th, remarking:

> The motor sledges are working well, but not very well; the small difficulties will be got over, but I rather fear they will never draw the loads we expect of them. Still they promise to be a help, and they are lively and attractive features of our present scene as they drone along over the floe.[19]

Two days later, disaster struck. On arriving at the landing site, Taylor had observed that the sea ice was roughly 66cm thick and 'variable in texture, that near the ship being rather mushy and honeycombed below – while several large cracks traverse it'.[20] This ice had grown increasingly treacherous in the unseasonably warm weather, and many were growing anxious regarding its weight-bearing capability. Nonetheless, during the morning of 8 January, the crew of the *Terra Nova* swung the third and last of the tractors overboard and

lowered it onto the ice. Cherry-Garrard recorded the events of the next few minutes in his diary:

> We were told to tow it on to firm ice as that near the ship was breaking up. All hands started on a long tow line. We got on to the rotten piece, and somebody behind shouted 'You must run'. From that moment everything happened very quickly. [Petty Officer] Williamson fell right in through the ice; immediately afterwards we were all brought up with a jerk. Then the line began to pull us backwards; the stern of the motor had sunk through the ice, and the whole car began to sink. It slowly went right through and disappeared and then the tow line followed it.[21]

The men clung on to the line until the very last moment, letting go only when their feet were within centimetres of the hole through which the tractor had sunk – but there was really no chance of arresting its fall as it plummeted 120 fathoms to the seabed below.

According to Evans, Scott, who had been at the base site when the accident occurred, took the news 'awfully well',[22] but, in the circumstances, he had little option but to put on a brave face – at least to his subordinates. Privately, he noted that he 'stupidly gave permission' for the machine to be unloaded when the condition of the ice was known to be deteriorating and admitted that it was 'a big blow to know that one of the two best motors, on which so much time and trouble have been spent, now lies at the bottom of the sea'.[23] Inevitably, the accident also meant that even more must be expected of the two surviving tractors during the planned polar journey.

On 24 October, the advance guard of the Southern Party, consisting of Day, Evans, Leading Stoker William Lashly and Steward Frederick Hooper, left Cape Evans with the two motor-sledges, each man doing his best to ignore 'the gibes of our friends who came out to speed us on our way'.[24] Besides the party's own equipment, food and fuel, between them the two vehicles towed 3 tonnes of stores, forage and petrol on five 3.5m sledges. By dragging this precious cargo at least as far as 'Corner Camp', a depot positioned on the Barrier some 64km from Hut Point, they would help conserve the energy of the expedition's ponies and reduce the risk to their legs over the difficult sea ice.

If the tractors reached Corner Camp, they would then proceed to 'One Ton Camp' at 79°29'S and further south, if practicable. 'At first there were a good many stops,' Scott observed:

… but on the whole the engines seemed to be improving all the time. They are not by any means working up to full power yet, and so the pace is very slow. The weights seem to me a good deal heavier than we bargained for. Day sets his motor going, climbs off the car, and walks alongside with an occasional finger on the throttle. Lashly hasn't yet quite got the hold of the nice adjustments of his control levers, but I hope will have done so after a day's practice.[25]

In reality, the slow pace was due not to the engines or the weight of the sledges but to that eternal bugbear of polar transportation, traction. On the smooth blue ice in the vicinity of Razorback Island, the wooden soles of the tractor belts failed to gain purchase and it became necessary to throw down old sacks, which functioned much like sand mats for those driving in desert conditions. Despite these difficulties, by the time the party camped at 10 p.m., they had covered a little over 7km and all four 'slept the sleep of tired men'.[26]

The following day, it took a gruelling ten hours to cover less than 5km, with the weary men reduced to what Evans called 'tug-of-war work': pulling the sledges themselves to make any progress at all. Hearing of the problems over the telephone line from Hut Point, on the 26th Scott led a support party of eight men from Cape Evans, but by the time they reached the vehicles' last reported position, there was no sign of them:

Our spirits went up at once, for it was not only evident that the machines were going, but that they were negotiating a very rough surface without difficulty.[27]

When they eventually caught up with the tractors, they found Day so buoyed by their progress that he refused the proffered aid and Scott and his men instead pushed on towards Hut Point. Of course, it was too good to last and a few hours later Lashly and Hooper arrived with the news that Day's tractor had again bogged down and that he and Evans required help after all. Returning to the stalled vehicle, the man-haulers dragged the three huge towed sledges forward in order to reduce the machine's burden. Eventually, they reached Lashly's tractor at Cape Armitage and, after covering the vehicles with their quilted hoods, they walked back to spend the night at Hut Point, exhausted but triumphant.

The vehicles climbed the gentle slope from the sea ice onto the Great Barrier the following afternoon, an event that marked the high point of

their part in the expedition. After the usual stop–start progress caused by recurrent overheating, Day's tractor became the first to complete the ascent. 'One soon saw that the men beside the sledges were running,' observed a delighted Scott:

> To make a long story short, [Day] stopped to hand over lubricating oil, started at a gallop again, and dashed up the slope without a hitch on his top speed – the first man to run a motor on the Great Barrier![28]

The second vehicle made less of a show, but it too completed the climb without trouble. Then, after Lashly and Hooper had received the congratulations and valedictory handshakes of Scott's party, it clattered forward in the tracks of its twin, leaving the man–haulers to return to Cape Evans. 'Lord, sir,' remarked Petty Officer Edgar Evans, watching the motor party surging forward, 'I reckon if them things can go on like that you wouldn't want nothing else!'[29]

Subsequent events proved that the tractors would not be able to 'go on like that', and over the next few days they struggled to complete just a handful of miles, stopping every few minutes to prevent overheating – despite temperatures dropping to −20°. 'Trouble,' wrote Lashly, 'is always staring us in the face, overheating, and the surface is so bad and the pull so heavy and constant that it looks we are in for a rough time.'[30] On the morning of 30 October, they abandoned Day's sledge when the connecting rod broke through the piston, wreaking damage that they could not hope to repair in the field. They managed to cover another 11km before camping, but none now believed that the remaining vehicle could last much longer.

The end came on 2 November. The previous morning, after starting with 'the usual amount of agony',[31] they had advanced 10km before the engine again broke down. Day and Lashly spent much of the rest of the day effecting repairs before limping into Corner Camp, leaving the doubtful honour of hauling the sledges to the men themselves. They unloaded the dog pemmican and three sacks of oats for the ponies and set off once again on the 2nd, heading now for One Ton Camp, the largest of the expedition's depots which had been established the previous February. Before leaving the camp, Lashly articulated what they all knew – that the tractor was nearing its end – and after just 2.5km the phosphor bronze of No. 1 cylinder finally, and catastrophically, disintegrated. 'I can't say I'm sorry,' Lashly observed, philosophically, 'because I am not, and the others are, I think, of the same opinion as myself ... Now comes the man-hauling part of the show.'[32]

'Were [the tractors] to be regarded as a thorough success?' Day asked after the expedition. 'This is not easily answered. The answer, in fact, depends entirely upon what results were expected from the experiment.'[33] To the surprise of many, the most serious and ultimately insurmountable of the mechanical problems was the engines' tendency to overheat. While a fan kept the two front cylinders of each engine sufficiently cool, the two rear cylinders grew so hot that the heat passed down the connecting rods to the phosphor bronze big ends; over time, these crumbled – with devastating results. The second major source of anxiety had been the carburettors. When the engine was running, the bonnet had to be left open in order to reduce the risk of overheating – but this allowed cold air to enter the carburettor, and then the petrol would not vaporise. On the engine missing fire, the bonnet would be shut down, thereafter the engine ran hot. And so the cycle continued. However, on balance, and without attempting to gloss over these failings, Day did consider 'their general performance satisfactory, when the specific difficulties of their task have been duly taken into account'.[34]

Inevitably, not all the explorers were so generous and some, particularly those like Taylor and Herbert Ponting who published accounts in the years immediately after the expedition, capitalised on the comic value of the ill-fated sledges. In his 1921 book, *The Great White South*, the latter admitted that they deserved 'credit for doing a good deal of heavy work in the earlier stages of the adventure' but also stated his conviction that 'their principal achievement was to provoke remarks for which there may be pangs when Gabriel blows his horn'.[35] Such judgements were unfair: certainly the tractors were highly temperamental, but they also completed journeys totalling 80km with payloads of nearly 1,400kg, albeit in very short hops. The judgement of Teddy Evans who, as leader of the motor party, bore much of the brunt of the vehicles' wayward behaviour, is perhaps more balanced. Although he thought the machines 'dreadful', he also recognised:

> We must not omit the great point in their favour: the motors advanced the necessaries for the Southern journey 51 miles [82km] over rough, slippery, and crevassed ice and gave the ponies the chance to march light as far as Corner Camp – this is all that Oates asked for.[36]

One more recent commentator has shrewdly observed that Scott demonstrated 'a curious vacillation between optimism, extreme caution and pessimism' regarding the vehicles.[37] But his vacillation related specifically to his own tractors; so far as the principle of motorised polar travel was concerned, he demonstrated very little doubt. The source of the problems encountered, he believed, lay in insufficient experimentation and he remained confident to the end that mechanised vehicles would one day revolutionise polar travel: 'A little more care and foresight would make them splendid allies. The trouble is that if they fail, no one will ever believe this.'[38]

David Pratt, the senior engineer on Fuchs's Trans-Antarctic Expedition and therefore the man ultimately responsible for the greatest feat of mechanised transport in the history of Antarctic exploration, agreed. In his opinion, Scott's tractors:

> ... were overloaded and under-engined, but it is to their credit that they negotiated 50 miles with a payload of 3,000lb in ½–3-mile hops ... Scott was right in his conjectures and only lacked the experience that has since been gained in the laboratory and in the field.[39]

★　★　★

The next mechanised sledge to be trialled in the Antarctic arrived just two months after the final breakdown of Scott's tractors. Like the Wolseleys, it represented an entirely new departure in the design of motorised vehicles for use in the polar regions. Unlike them, it was the result not of years of painstaking research and development but of a single, near-catastrophic event lasting just a few seconds. Moreover, that accident occurred in circumstances about as far removed from Antarctic conditions as it is possible to imagine: in the skies above, and on the turf of, the Cheltenham Racecourse in Adelaide.

As we will see in a later chapter, it was here, on the morning of 5 October 1911, that Douglas Mawson's hopes of becoming the first man to achieve powered flight in the Antarctic came to a disastrous end when his AAE's newly acquired Vickers REP monoplane crashed to earth during a test flight. Realising that there was no chance of repairing the machine before the expedition's departure from Hobart, an irate and embarrassed Mawson instructed his English engineer, Frank Bickerton, to pack the wreckage in a crate ready for transportation to Antarctica on board the SY *Aurora*.

When it arrived, Bickerton's primary function would be to convert it into a functioning 'air tractor sledge' for the ground haulage of supplies and equipment.

On the voyage south, the Southern Ocean treated the already battered monoplane to yet more rough handling with Bickerton noting, on 5 December, 'a sea came aboard and stove in one end of the case, causing the machine to protrude through the far end some 4ft, driving it through the inch planking and tin lining like a nail'.[40] The same wave passed on to demolish half the ship's bridge and the officer of the watch only narrowly escaped with his life.

Matters did not much improve after the expedition's landfall at Cape Denison on 8 January 1912, when the need to prioritise more essential activities meant that two months passed before the aeroplane could be dragged from a snowdrift and lodged in a rather ramshackle hangar constructed from its packing case and other spare timber. Only then could Bickerton begin the process of converting it into a functional air tractor, straightening its twisted frame and manufacturing brakes from drill bits and pieces of a broken vice.

In the middle of the following October, Mawson outlined his plans for the coming sledging season. There were to be four main expeditions, all would set out in November and all would be 'equipped with all that forethought and experience could devise, to map, examine and record'.[41] Mawson and two companions would take the dogs and, travelling at high speed, head for the far east while two other parties travelled south and east. Finally, Bickerton, Leslie Whetter and Alfie Hodgeman would proceed west with the still untried air tractor. The decision to send the machine west may have been the result of Mawson's increasing scepticism over its reliability. Given its original cost and the labour expended upon its conversion, it must be granted an opportunity to prove itself – but, by sending it in a direction that had already been at least partially surveyed, both by the ship and during an earlier sledging excursion, Mawson wisely minimised the impact its likely failure would have on the overall results of the expedition.

The western sledging journey began on 3 December 1912, Bickerton, Hodgeman and Whetter departing at 4 p.m. 'amidst a spiriting demonstration of goodwill from the six other men then at the hut. Arms were still waving violently as we crept noisily over the brow of the hill, and the hut disappeared from sight.'[42] The engine pulled well, but the load had to be lightened on the steepest stretches of the long snow ramp behind the expedition hut

and Hodgeman and Whetter dismounted to walk on either side. All five cylinders fired evenly and a misfire experienced during an earlier test run seemed to have resolved itself. With 180kg of hauled sledge, supplies and equipment, besides the weight of the three men, they reached Aladdin's Cave, a depot positioned 5km from the base, in about an hour. Here they added three 45kg food bags and 55 litres of oil to the load, along with a sledge stacked with drums of benzine brought up the previous day.

The tractor party had made a good start, but their problems began almost as soon as they left the depot. 'The going was slow,' Bickerton observed, '– too slow – about three miles an hour on ice; this would probably mean no movement at all on snow, which we might expect soon … we did two miles in very bad form.'[43] At 11 p.m., with the wind rising, they decided to camp, 'feeling none too pleased with the first day's results'.

When the aeroplane had crashed in Adelaide, one of the cylinders had been smashed. It had been replaced, but there was a risk of more deep-seated damage, which the conditions of Adélie Land were now making apparent. Such a fault could only be identified by stripping down the engine and, even if the day's calm conditions continued, Bickerton knew that performing such an operation would be a tall order. And then, supposing he could find the cause of the trouble, making suitable repairs was another matter entirely. He decided that it would be best to proceed to Cathedral Grotto, a depot located 18.5km from the main base, and there remove the faulty cylinder. He would only be able to complete the job if the weather held; if it didn't, then they must abandon the machine and continue ignominiously on foot – all the improvements and modifications he had engineered over the preceding months simply so much wasted effort.

By 5 o'clock the next day, they were under way. The motor's pulse remained uneven, with the faulty cylinder spurting oil and giving no compression. Then, after they had covered little more than a kilometre, disaster struck:

> The engine, without any warning, pulling up with such a jerk that the propeller was smashed. On moving the latter something fell into the oil in the crank case and sizzled. The propeller could only be swung through an angle of about 30°. We did not wait to examine any further, but fixed up our man hauling sledge which had not yet touched ground and depoted all except absolute necessities.[44]

It took another forty-five minutes to reach Cathedral Grotto on foot, where they again reduced weight, arranging surplus food bags and other items to make a landmark that would be discernible from the south. Like Scott's motor team, the Western Sledging Party would now be dependent for its success upon a combination of muscle and determination.

Bickerton later asserted that if the prevailing conditions of Adélie Land had been understood before the expedition sailed – it is, after all, the windiest point at sea level on the face of the planet – no one would ever have countenanced the use of an aeroplane:

> It is obvious that a machine which depends on the surrounding air for its traction cannot be tested in the winds we experienced in the winter. One might just as well try the capabilities of a small motor launch on the Niagara rapids.[45]

However, in its incarnation as an air tractor, the primary cause of its failure was mechanical rather than environmental: the legacy of the crash in Adelaide more than a year earlier. In his official account of the expedition, Mawson quickly dismissed the machine, noting that its career 'was mostly associated with misfortune',[46] and even Bickerton admitted that its breakdown 'had not surprised us in an alarming manner'.[47] Forty years later, David Pratt published a more balanced appraisal, observing that its performance 'was astonishing as it was doing 20 mile/h up a 1 in 15 slope against a 15 mile/h headwind'.[48] This achievement would certainly have reassured Shackleton as he planned his next foray into the Antarctic.

★ ★ ★

In March 1914, Shackleton appeared in front of a committee of the Royal Geographical Society to discuss the plans for his Imperial Trans-Antarctic (*Endurance*) Expedition. Among other topics raised by the highly sceptical phalanx of geographical grandees was the subject of the motorised sledges with which he planned to equip both his main crossing party, which would land on the Weddell Sea coast, and the depot-laying party, which would be based on Ross Island. Given the well-known – and oft-repeated – failure of such contraptions, could the explorer seriously place any reliance upon them?

In a spirited, if slightly disingenuous, defence Shackleton replied that his sledges were designed primarily to help conserve the energy of his dogs and if they became a hindrance he would immediately abandon them. Backed into a corner by the determined probing of the committee, he also admitted that the novelty of the machines helped to raise public interest in the expedition, thereby making fundraising considerably easier. None of the vehicles was expected to travel more than 800 out of the 2,900km total, not least because it would be impossible to carry sufficient fuel for a journey of longer duration. 'I am right to think it is worthwhile to try the machines,' he concluded with typical bullishness, 'because if I can do 200 miles [322km] on 500lb [227kg] weight of petrol … it will be a tremendous asset to me.'[49]

The machines in question included two propeller-driven sledges, powered by 30hp Anzani aero engines, and two 'motor-crawlers', powered by 9hp Coventry Simplex engines and driven by Swedish-designed paddle wheels, which were intended to operate much like the modified wheels of the Arrol-Johnston and Charcot's motor-sledges. All had been manufactured by the Dispatch Motor Company of Southwark Bridge Road, the propeller sledges to designs worked up by Thomas Orde-Lees and the motor-crawlers to the plans of Albert Girling, chief engineer at the Royal Aircraft Factory.

In theory at least, the crawlers could tow up to a tonne of equipment, carried on two or three sledges, at a maximum speed of 8kph. The driver stood on hickory runners at the rear of the machine and he steered by operating a lever, whereby 'the desired direction of the tractor [was] attained after the manner in which a plough is steered'.[50] Ingeniously, each crawler had been fitted with a mounting for a Primus stove that could be used for pre-heating the engine, holes for cooking pots that would be warmed by the engine, and a drying cabinet for damp clothes and sleeping bags. Finally, small cisterns would melt snow and provide a constant supply of hot drinking water, negating the need to pitch a tent and light a stove whenever a brew was required.[51]

The propeller-driven sledge bore little relation to the converted Vickers monoplane that Bickerton had laboured over at Cape Denison, and Shackleton had already told his critics, 'It is not an aeroplane; it is a sledge with an aeroplane propeller.'[52] The machine was about 4m long, with the engine positioned at the rear within a tall frame that, in turn, supported the propeller unit and an uncomfortable-looking seat for the 'pilot'. A belt conducted power from the engine to the propeller and the pilot steered by means of pedal-controlled flippers mounted on outriggers.

When tested on a glacier under the Harbangerjokul, near Finse in Norway, the performance of the sledges was mixed. In particular, there could be no doubt that the drive belts needed to be replaced with chains and it would probably be necessary to strengthen the whole design to prevent it shaking itself to pieces. But, if Shackleton felt at all disillusioned, he dissembled well, later telling a correspondent from *The Times* that 'the motor-sledges had worked excellently, both on rising and on falling ground, and the results were quite beyond his expectations'.[53] No doubt his primary concern was to prevent negative reports filtering back to England, where they might dampen the ardour of prospective investors.

At least one member of the Norwegian press who journeyed up the glacier to watch the demonstration was not so easily persuaded:

> Shackleton has constructed a new sledge prototype, characterised by the fact that the sledge is moved by an air-propeller in the same way as an aeroplane ... The propeller achieved an enormous speed ... The sledge, however, did not ... In the enthusiasm of the moment, Shackleton forgot that it was 4–5 degrees above zero when the sledge was tested. It is not certain that the motor will function as well in the Antarctic snow-desert when the mercury will sink to 30 degrees below.[54]

Despite Shackleton's ebullience and Frank Wild's belief that 'the sledge tractors proved satisfactory in their trial runs',[55] some members of their team were as dubious as the Norwegian journalist. George Marston, the expedition artist, glumly predicted, 'Perhaps it will go for twenty min[utes].'[56]

In the event, of course, the propeller sledges failed to run for even twenty minutes in the Antarctic, both sinking to the bottom of the Weddell Sea with the *Endurance* in November 1915, along with the crossing party's Girling motor-crawler. The second crawler, which accompanied Aeneas Mackintosh's Ross Sea party, reached its destination in one piece – but it proved a pitiful failure, hardly able to pull its own weight, let alone a train of heavily laden sledges.

This last machine was unpacked on board the *Aurora* on 18 January 1915, and by 10 p.m. amateur engineer Aubrey Ninnis had the engine running – 'A good achievement!' in Mackintosh's opinion.[57] It was then unloaded onto the sea ice close to Tent Island on 31 January and made ready for its first task: hauling two sledges, weighing a total of 498kg, across 18km to Hut Point. That afternoon, after a brief but successful preliminary trial, the motor party, 'with a jolly good cheer from the ship's company ringing in their ears',[58] set off. They didn't get far.

'A mile out,' Ninnis recorded in his diary, 'I had ignition trouble, wet plugs, snow falling on them from hopper of tank, big job to restart with so much water about.'[59] Closer inspection revealed that the crawler's water tank had been cracked during the process of swinging it out from the ship, allowing water to cascade onto the moving parts of the engine and necessitating constant replenishment of the tank. Uncoupling the heavy sledges, the vehicle party pushed on, but severe vibration caused by the rough ice then loosened the engine's mounting bolts. This allowed the engine to rock and the clutch began to slip and its leather pad to burn. The crawler could still move, sometimes at speed – but not with the heavy sledges attached, prompting Leslie Thomson, *Aurora*'s second officer, to remark derisively, 'The tractor [is] acting as a convenience for keeping Ninnis's feet dry.'[60]

Attempts to repair the damage proved abortive, and the motor-crawler was eventually abandoned close to Hut Point on 7 February. Ninnis would continue to assert that its failure was due to the damage caused by clumsy unloading and to 'entire lack of opportunity to test on actual ice surface',[61] but there could be no denying that it had been an abject failure, completing a single journey of just 20km. In real terms, and after a decade of trial and error, the last motor vehicle tested during the Heroic Age had been the least successful of them all.

★ ★ ★

Given this catalogue of outright failures and, at best, only limited successes, it is not surprising that many polar experts questioned whether motor vehicles could ever make a significant contribution to Antarctic exploration. Typically, in December 1920, Frank Debenham, newly appointed as first director of the Scott Polar Research Institute, told the assembled fellows of the Royal Geographical Society that, in his opinion:

> Mechanical transport will necessarily be confined to comparatively level areas with suitable surface. For travelling over hummocky sea-ice and over crevasses and serac-ed glaciers it appears impossible to design any form of vehicle which can adjust itself to the infinite irregularities of the surface, while the huge snow-covered crevasses of the great Antarctic glaciers will always be a menace to any heavy machine, however long its wheelbase may be.[62]

For Robert Rudmose-Brown, the greatest problem was not the quality of the surfaces but the reliability of the vehicles themselves, 'We live in an age of rapidly increasing mechanical skill. Yet is it ever safe to put absolute trust in a machine? ... Can one ever reduce the risk of the motor-sledge breaking down to reasonable limits?'[63] In essence, he was expressing precisely the kind of scepticism that Scott had anticipated – and feared – sixteen years earlier.

And yet Debenham and Rudmose-Brown were basing their remarks exclusively upon the experiences of the expeditions launched between 1901 and 1914. They could not do otherwise, as the post-war years had witnessed only two forays into the Antarctic, Shackleton's *Quest* Expedition and John Lachlan Cope's British Imperial Expedition, neither of which used motor-sledges. This situation was about to change, and over the coming years one man more than any other would revolutionise opinion regarding the effectiveness of the internal combustion engine in polar conditions. That man was Richard Evelyn Byrd of the United States Navy.

At the time of its launch in 1928, Byrd's first expedition was the most expensive and well equipped ever to cross the Antarctic Circle, taking with it two ships and no fewer than three aeroplanes. Byrd's primary objective was to complete a non-stop return flight to the South Pole – an achievement intended to complement his controversial flight to the North Pole in May 1926 – but he also believed that 'mechanised transport would be the next great step in south polar transport'.[64] To test his theory, he included in his equipment a 'Snowmobile' – a form of hybrid vehicle produced and marketed by an entrepreneurial New Hampshire motor dealer named Virgil D. White.

In appearance, the Snowmobile retained many of the features of a conventional car, but its wheels had been replaced with skis at the front and tracks at the rear, the latter mounted on a horizontal movable axle, with a metal tread running over the idler and rear wheels for traction. Since its release onto the domestic market in 1917, White's design had benefited from a number of further modifications and, by the standards of Antarctic exploration, it was probably the most heavily tested of all mechanised vehicles taken south to that date.

Despite its success in North America, the Snowmobile proved less well suited to travel on the Great Barrier, with its combination of soft, loose snow and sastrugi. As 'Pete' Demas, Byrd's senior engineer, noted, 'Ultimately the differential gave out, due to the sudden gripping of the treads, after the machine had dug itself in, and it had to be abandoned.'[65] Nonetheless, the

Snowmobile completed a journey of 132km and Byrd and Demas remained convinced that 'given the right amount of power, wide treads and length enough to span the average crevasse, motors ought to be able to go places'.[66]

Much more impressive were the vehicles of Byrd's second expedition of 1933–35. These included two Snowmobiles, three Citroën-Kegresse snow cars and one 'Cletrac' tractor. Weighing 5½ tonnes, this last vehicle represented the first move away from the light vehicles favoured by all previous expeditions. During the process of unloading stores, it travelled approximately 370km between the ships and Little America, the base established during Byrd's first expedition, hauling as much as 7 tonnes to a load. It also made a 322km journey to the Bolling Advance Base, though it had to be temporarily abandoned when the crank pin on the driveshaft sheared off.

For this journey, the longest yet undertaken by any mechanical surface vehicle in the Antarctic, a number of important modifications were made to improve safety. The tread was fitted with 61cm plates in order to decrease the bearing load, thereby reducing the risks when crossing snow bridges; the cabin's metal top was replaced with fabric to facilitate an easy exit in case the Cletrac fell into a crevasse; and, most novel of all, a remote control system was devised that enabled the driver to control his vehicle from a towed sledge when traversing heavily crevassed areas. As later events would prove, these were all sensible adaptations that might usefully have been employed more widely.

On the expedition's return, Demas reported:

> For six weeks during the unloading period, the three Citroën Snow Cars and the Cletrac ran continuously twenty-four hours of the day. They were stopped only for minor repairs and periodic fuelling, inspection, lubrication, and greasing.[67]

By the end of 1935, between them the Citroëns had logged more than 18,500km and, while roughly two-thirds of this total had been clocked up during short load-carrying trips from the Bay of Whales to the expedition's base, Little America II, rather than during inland exploratory journeys, by the standards of any previous mechanised polar transport, their record was extraordinary. Byrd thought them 'excellent' and admitted, 'Without them the disembarkation in the Bay of Whales would be a more awful memory of toil and trouble than it is.'[68]

Far less successful were the Snowmobiles. Now based upon the 1932 Model 'A' Ford and with some modifications including a diversion of exhaust fumes to heat the transmission, they still suffered from a tendency to dig themselves into soft surfaces and from a weak differential. Nonetheless, by cannibalising its fellows, the engineers kept one vehicle operational and with careful driving it 'did considerable useful work around the camp'.[69]

Reflecting on his experiences with mechanical transport during Byrd's first and second expeditions, in 1936 Demas published a number of recommendations regarding the design principles for a new vehicle. 'A tractor for the Antarctic,' he wrote:

> ... should be 30–40 feet [9–12m] long, with front and rear drive, built of light material with the weight equally distributed. It should have a wide tread with a maximum bearing load of one pound per square inch of surface. The motors should be inside the body and easily accessible. The load should be carried within the body. Air-cooled engines would be preferable. The fuel should be heated separately for starting, and the exhaust used for heating the fuel while operating.[70]

Some – but, crucially, not all – of these features would be included in the 'Snow Cruiser' designed for Byrd's United States Antarctic Service Expedition of 1939–41. This would be the largest and, visually at least, the most impressive of all overland vehicles ever created for Antarctic travel.

The brainchild of Thomas C. Poulter, a veteran of Byrd's second expedition, the 30-tonne leviathan dwarfed every previous Antarctic vehicle, measuring 16.75m long, 6.10m wide and 4.5m tall. It incorporated sleeping accommodation for four men, a galley, workshop, darkroom, combined chart and radio room, and a platform for the transportation of a light aircraft. Powered by two 112kW diesel engines and equipped with two 75kW electric traction generators, it could also carry 9,500 litres of diesel fuel, 3,800 litres of aviation fuel and 2,800 litres of white gasoline. And yet, in some ways, the most extraordinary feature of this revolutionary new machine was that its traction was provided not by tracks, which had formed the basis of nearly all such vehicles since Scott's Wolseleys, but by four enormous wheels fitted with pneumatic tyres. Ultimately, the decision to rely upon tyres, combined with the Snow Cruiser's colossal weight, would turn this $150,000 'prehistoric land lobster'[71] into an embarrassing white elephant.

As Dean Freitag and Stephen Dibbern have observed:

In designing the vehicle Poulter certainly drew on Antarctic observations. In 1934–5 he had measured gradients of representative slopes, widths of crevasses and (a key element in his calculations) some properties of the snow of the Ross Ice Shelf … These measurements ultimately proved his undoing, for at the time neither he nor anyone else knew how to interpret them.[72]

In particular, Poulter calculated that Antarctic snow could support a load intensity of 30lb per square inch (psi) and that by designing a vehicle that generated just 15psi, he had doubled his safety margin. Of course, Demas, with whom Poulter had worked closely, disagreed – by a factor of fifteen. He believed that such a vehicle should generate no more than 1psi. It would not be long before they discovered who was closer to the truth.

Byrd's ship, *North Star*, reached the Bay of Whales in January 1940 and the Snow Cruiser became one of the first items to be unloaded, Poulter himself driving it down a makeshift ramp. The trouble began as soon as the gigantic wheels touched the snow-covered sea ice. According to Poulter, 'The Cruiser would travel only about three miles an hour [5kph] under full throttle … The tyres were sinking into the snow approximately 8 or 10 inches [20–25cm].'[73]

Worse was to come. With the vehicle struggling to move at all and digging itself ever deeper, the individual wheel motors began to overheat and the Cruiser stalled. After scratching their heads in dismay, the engineers fitted additional wheels to spread the load, placed snow chains on the tyres, which they partially deflated, and then trialled various combinations of gearing and electrical settings in the hope of generating more thrust – all to no avail.

During one of the last attempts to move the Cruiser that summer, it crawled just 1.5km in fifteen hours – an effort that made the man-hauled relays of the Heroic Age look like Olympic sprints. Further attempts during early spring proved no more successful, and Poulter's invention was eventually reduced to the ignominious role of static control tower for the expedition's airstrip, where its well-thought-out facilities made its accommodation some of the most comfortable on the continent. It seems unlikely, however, that Poulter or Byrd found much consolation in this unexpected benefit.

The total failure of the Snow Cruiser was no doubt influential when the time came to choose the vehicles for Byrd's fourth Antarctic expedition,

Operation Highjump (1946–47). Designed to test military personnel and equipment in 'frigid zone' conditions, this mammoth government expedition took a number of jeeps for light local work, but the vast majority of its vehicles were tracked. These included tractors, bulldozers and Weasels. As well as testing the Weasel in Antarctic conditions for the first time, the expedition made history in a rather less fortunate fashion, becoming the first to suffer a fatality as a result of a vehicle accident.

On 21 January 1947, a young sailor named Vance Woodall was involved in unloading operations close to the planned site of the expedition's primary base, Little America IV. Also engaged in this work were a number of 16-tonne Caterpillar D6 tractors. Experience had shown that, once loaded, the D6 was simply too heavy to move on the snow-covered ice and that, in order to gain sufficient traction, it was first necessary to let the tracks grind their way down to the underlying ice. Inevitably, one track would strike the ice before the other and this would cause the tractor to rock violently from side to side until both gained purchase. On this occasion, it appears that Woodall was, quite simply, in the wrong place at the wrong time: presumably he was attempting to assist in rocking the D6 because, just as its tracks gripped the ice and allowed the tractor to move, his right arm and head became snagged in the slats of the roller. Before the driver realised what had happened, the vehicle surged forward and the young sailor was killed instantly, his spinal column being severed 'high in the neck'.[74]

Woodall became the first to die in a freakish vehicle accident – but he would not be the last. On 7 July 1959, for instance, Hartley Robinson, an Australian diesel mechanic, was crushed to death by his own Caterpillar 'Traxcavator' when its handbrake slipped after he dismounted. 'I thought he might have been pressed into the snow,' recalled eyewitness John Williams, 'but it was ice ... We buried poor old Robbie up on the ridge overlooking Wilkes.'[75]

★ ★ ★

For some years after Operation Highjump, the Weasel would be the mainstay of mechanised transportation in the Antarctic. Whereas Dr Poulter's Snow Cruiser had been designed for peacetime use by a nation that would be at war in less than two years, the Weasel had been designed and built in wartime and, quite specifically, for combat use. Conceived in 1940 by an English intellectual named Geoffrey Pyke, originally it was intended to transport commandos throughout occupied Norway, thereby tying down German troops who might otherwise have been sent to different theatres of war.

Pyke realised that the Germans actually controlled only a fraction of Norway, focusing almost all of their attention, quite naturally, on the centres of population. In contrast, the country's vast tracts of sparsely populated mountain, snowfield and forest remained almost completely unoccupied. Always supposing that it was possible to provide them with suitable means for covering large areas of such difficult terrain, troops trained in winter warfare techniques could use these tracts as both highways and hiding places: launching surprise attacks on military and industrial installations and then disappearing back into the wilderness. He succeeded in convincing both Lord Louis Mountbatten, Commander of Combined Operations, and Churchill of the merits of his plan and they, in turn, persuaded their US allies that Operation Plough could shorten the war by years and that some portion of America's industrial might should be dedicated to the development of the required vehicle.

As a result, on 1 July 1942, the US Government's Office of Scientific Research and Development was instructed to:

> Design, develop, build and test one or more pilot models of a track-laying, airborne, amphibious snow vehicle, to carry a payload of 1,200lbs [544kg] up a 25 degree slope in deep snow, and have a maximum speed on level packed snow of 35 mph [56kph].[76]

The product of this research was the Wessel. By the war's end 12,000 had been built by the Studebaker Automobile Company of South Bend and they would play significant roles in helping to keep the Nijmegen bridgehead open in September 1944 and during the Battle of the Bulge, between December 1944 and January 1945. However, their use in the theatre for which they had originally been intended was limited to the liberation of Finnmark in north-eastern Norway late in 1944.[77]

Despite its wartime success, many viewed the Weasel with suspicion, if not downright hostility. According to one veteran, in Finnmark 'they were a perpetual source of anxiety for the transport officers. The fan belts broke and the tracks broke.'[78] Paul-Émile Victor's French Greenland Expedition of 1949–51 had also discovered that they wore out an endless supply of tracks; they must be handled with extreme caution; and they could not be relied upon to pull more than about 1½ tonnes.

The experiences of Giaever's NBSAE proved altogether more satisfactory: although its three vehicles required substantial refurbishment after being immersed in saltwater during their outward voyage, they covered a combined total distance of approximately 10,500km during the expedition, requiring repairs and replacements 'only as a result of fair wear and tear'.[79] Inevitably, much of the distance was covered during unloading operations, but in November 1950 the Weasels were used to establish an advance base 300km to the south-east of Maudheim, and in October 1951 two completed a seismic ice-depth profile to a point 600km from the base. Overall, and despite its dubious reputation before the expedition, Charles Swithinbank thought the Weasel 'proved a most excellent vehicle for use in the Antarctic … Provided that a Weasel is driven and maintained with care, the possibility of an irreparable breakdown in the field is remote.'[80] Of course, the operative word in Swithinbank's analysis is 'care'.

There can be very little doubt that the tragedy of 24 February 1951 was entirely due to human error compounded by adverse environmental conditions. Given that it had just undergone a complete overhaul, it seems highly improbable that Ekström's Weasel suffered mechanical failure, and in his account of the accident, Hallgren – who was rescued by small boat after thirteen hours on the ice floe – made no reference to any problems with the vehicle; rather its brakes could not take effect when it was driven at such speed on the sloping surface of the ice shelf. Ekström had driven recklessly – and he, Jelbart and Quar had paid the ultimate price.

★ ★ ★

After four accident-free decades, in the years following the NBSAE motor vehicle-related deaths in the Antarctic accelerated alarmingly, with three fatal accidents in 1956 alone, and more in 1957 and 1959. Of course, the primary factor influencing this increase was the huge growth in Antarctic operations by the nations preparing for, and participating in, the International Geophysical Year (IGY) of 1957–58. During this short period, the summertime population of the continent multiplied by a factor of twenty-eight, with the 1955 population of just 179 rising to roughly 5,000. Inevitably, this colossal influx of men – most of whom would possess, at best, only a very limited understanding of the environment in which they would be operating – resulted in an equally rapid rise in the number of accidents.

Given the scale of the government-funded Antarctic Service Expedition and Operation Highjump, it is unsurprising that the nation with the most ambitious IGY programme in the Antarctic was the USA. In the first phase of Operation Deep Freeze I, again under the command of Byrd, US Navy Task Force 43 would build two bases: one close to Captain Scott's old headquarters at Hut Point, on Ross Island, and the other, known as Little America V, at the eastern extremity of the Ross Ice Shelf, some 725km around the coast of McMurdo Sound. Once this second base had been constructed, tractors would push into the interior of Marie Byrd Land to establish a third, Byrd Station, late in 1956. The base at Hut Point, meanwhile, would become the key to the most logistically challenging of all IGY operations in the Antarctic: the erection of the expedition's fourth base, the Amundsen–Scott Station at the South Pole.

In order to avoid the gruelling 1,368km overland journey from the coast to the pole, last completed by Scott on 17 January 1912, it had been decided that the Amundsen–Scott Station would be established by air – a task that would involve flying in all the personnel and nearly 700 tonnes of supplies and equipment, including tractors, furnishings, food, medicine, power plants and prefabricated huts. This airlift could not be completed by non-stop flights from New Zealand, so a vital component of the new logistics hub on Ross Island would be a hard ice runway where, prior to heading inland, incoming C-124 Globemaster cargo planes could refuel and embark the material brought in by sea.

Construction began with the arrival of the task force in the austral summer of 1955–56 and it was on 6 January 1956 that the first fatal vehicle accident occurred. On that day, Richard T. Williams, a driver with the Construction Battalion, or 'Seabees', was engaged in unloading the task-force ships and hauling cargo across the sea ice towards Cape Evans in readiness for the planned construction of the airstrip. Prior to being shipped south, his D8 Caterpillar tractor had been fitted with 137cm-wide tracks in order to reduce ground pressure, but this modification did not prevent the collapse of a snow bridge spanning a wide crack in the ice, and the 34-tonne tractor sank so swiftly that Williams was unable to escape, the small cabin doorway and surrounding safety frame of his D8 making a quick exit all but impossible. The tractor and its unfortunate driver plunged to the seabed 100 fathoms below, their last resting place located just a few kilometres from the rusting wreckage of Scott's Wolseley, which had sunk in similar circumstances forty-five years earlier.

Later in the same month, Williams' fate was shared by Ivan Kharma, a driver mechanic at Mirny, the Soviet IGY base in Queen Mary Land. When a tractor driven by a colleague became stuck in a hole in the fast ice, Kharma volunteered to recover the stricken vehicle. The early stages of the collapse had been slow enough to enable the first driver to leap to safety. Kharma was not so lucky: hardly had he climbed aboard when his additional weight caused the tractor to complete its dive, taking the unlucky volunteer with it – the whole terrible sequence being caught on film by a Soviet cameraman.

Once away from the obvious, if often underestimated, risks of travelling on sea ice, the greatest danger faced by drivers was the crevasse. These fissures, caused by the gradual seawards flow of the ice sheets and by their collisions with underlying surface inequalities, mountain ranges and each other, can vary from a few centimetres in width to a few metres, and they often run for kilometres, frequently forming just one strand in a vast web of interlinking cracks. Sometimes they are rendered completely invisible by the accumulation of snow and tricks of the light; at others, their presence is indicated by gaping holes or by telltale depressions in the surface, where warmer temperatures have caused the snow bridges to sag.

Generally, a man travelling on skis or on a dog sledge is safest, with his weight well spread; travelling on foot, with his weight bearing down on a smaller surface area, he will be at much greater risk. Dogs on a fan trace will also scatter if one of their fellows drops into a crevasse, usually bringing their sledge to a safe halt – though whole teams, their sledges and their drivers have been lost when a wide bridge collapses without warning – as happened to Belgrave Ninnis during Mawson's AAE. The dangers for men driving relatively slow-moving vehicles, sometimes weighing many tonnes, and all too often with poorly designed and cramped cabins, are obvious.

Two months after Williams's death, another Seabee, 22-year-old 'Fat Max' Kiel, became the first driver to die in a crevasse accident. On 5 March 1956, Kiel was involved in laying fuel depots between Little America V and the intended location of the new Byrd Station. Aerial reconnaissance had revealed that the junction between the floating ice shelf and the land-borne ice sheet was riddled with crevasses, but no viable alternative route to the target site had been identified. Over this minefield, Kiel's convoy of 34-tonne D8s, each towing fuel sledges weighing a further 20 tonnes, must wend its cautious way. Walter Sullivan, the chief science writer for *The New York Times*, made a journey along this route slightly later in the operation and, according to his report, the pounding of the tractors:

... made the ice tremble for miles around and their smoke trailed off in parallel plumes, like those of a ship convoy. The throb of their great diesel engines seemed to say that the twentieth century was on the march – that nothing could stop it. Nothing, that is, except a crevasse.[81]

At a point approximately 177km from Little America V, Kiel's party noticed that the vibration of the vehicles was causing some of the snow bridges to crumble. Like many D8s, Kiel's tractor had been fitted with a bulldozer blade, so he began using this to push large masses of snow into one of the more dangerous-looking crevasses in order to create a man-made 'plug'. But, as Kiel reversed in order to collect more snow, another hole opened directly beneath the rear section of his vehicle. Without warning, the massive D8 toppled backwards into a 30m-deep, V-shaped chasm, its superstructure flattening between the ice walls as it fell. Two of Kiel's fellow drivers attempted to recover his body but, as is so often the case when a vehicle is compressed by a narrowing crevasse, it proved impossible to separate it from the twisted wreckage. 'We felt so badly about it,' Kiel's commanding officer reported, 'that we just sat down next to that hole and cried.'[82]

★ ★ ★

The efforts, and sacrifices, of explorers engaged in pushing the boundaries of geographic and scientific knowledge will always give rise to the invention of new tools and systems designed both to further those efforts, and to minimise the sacrifices involved. Following this long tradition, in April 1957 John C. Cook of the Southwest Research Institute, in San Antonio, Texas, patented what he described as an 'electrical crevasse detector'.[83] In an earlier paper on the same subject, Cook noted that he had developed his invention for the US Department of Defense in 'response to an urgent need for rapid and reliable means of crevasse detection'.[84] It had been tested successfully in Greenland and Antarctica at surface speeds of up to 32kph and 'pronounced and distinctive electrical anomalies have been obtained at every crevasse tested to date'.[85]

Walter Sullivan saw Cook's device in action – indeed, while travelling with a convoy en route to Byrd Station he had relied upon its accuracy – and in his opinion, while it 'was not infallible, its use on the exploratory journeys helped prevent further loss of life'.[86] However, the real problem with Cook's invention had less to do with its fallibility and more to do with its newness and the resulting lack of availability; in essence, it was the same problem that beset maritime navigators after the invention of John Harrison's remarkable marine chronometers in the eighteenth century. Until Cook's device, or something similar, could be perfected, manufactured in sufficient numbers and widely distributed, crevasses would remain one of the most dangerous features of the polar landscape. When inexperience and errors of judgement were added to the mix, the risks were multiplied tenfold – as a New Zealand party discovered to its cost at the beginning of the austral summer of 1959.

On 19 November, a large New Zealand survey party consisting of eight men, three dog teams of nine dogs each, and two bright orange Sno-Cats were camped on the Ross Ice Shelf, about 24km south of Cape Selborne, a prominent projection of the Victoria Land coast that forms the southern entrance to Barne Inlet. Led by geologist Bernie Gunn, and tasked with extending the detailed survey of the Ross Dependency begun by Scott and Shackleton, the party had set out from their base on Ross Island during the first week of the month. Initially they had made good progress, covering 290km in a fortnight, but when they closed on Cape Selborne a combination of sastrugi and wide crevasses blocked their path, forcing them to turn inland onto smoother and apparently crevasse-free land ice.

That morning Gunn, fellow geologist Jim Lowery, and Lieutenant Tom Couzens of the Royal New Zealand Armoured Corps decided to undertake a gravimetric survey in the direction of a rock outcrop roughly 8km from their campsite. 'The ice we stood on was undoubtedly aground, not part of the ice-shelf,' Gunn later reported. 'It seemed flat and we had not seen a single crevasse. There was no major ice-flow coming off the land to cause crevassing nor could I see any suspicious humps and hollows.'[87] Gunn knew what he was talking about, having undertaken a significant amount of sledging while serving with Ed Hillary's contingent of the Commonwealth Trans-Antarctic Expedition. But he also knew that appearances could be deceptive. His real mistake, as he freely admitted, was in being persuaded by his less experienced companions to undertake the survey with a Sno-Cat instead of one of the dog teams.

Designed and manufactured by the Tucker Sno-Cat Corporation of Medford, Oregon, this vehicle had originally been built to facilitate the repair and maintenance of telephone lines in northern Canada and Alaska. Powered by a 200hp Chrysler V8 petrol engine and capable of 24kph, its greatest advantage lay in its unique traction system, consisting of four tracks, one for each of its four pontoons, located at the vehicle's four corners in much the same manner as the wheels of a standard car. When the front pontoons were turned to the right, the rear pontoons turned to the left, so that the Cat turned on its own axis, thereby reducing friction and preventing the vehicle from ploughing a trough for itself when it turned – a common fault in more conventional tracked vehicles like the Weasel. Crucially, this system not only generated a mere 0.75psi of ground pressure (0.25psi less than Pete Demas had considered desirable) but also provided almost 100 per cent traction, even when turning in soft snow.

Taken in the round, these features made the Cat highly innovative and, on paper at least, much safer to drive in Antarctic conditions. But it also weighed over 3 tonnes and, as Vivian Fuchs had discovered during his epic continental traverse in 1957–58, it too could fall victim to crevasses. *County of Kent*, the Cat that the New Zealanders now mounted, had taken part in Fuchs' crossing and Gunn had once sworn never to ride in one, 'especially after seeing the horrific pictures taken by the crossing party of this same machine suspended over gaping chasms'.[88]

The flat surface over which the Cat now trundled showed no obvious signs of disturbance – but the overlying snow proved to be at least 30cm deep, thick enough to conceal the kind of telltale inequalities that might indicate the presence of a crevasse. 'We laughed and joked in a carefree way,' Gunn recalled:

> And then suddenly appeared to be precipitated into another dimension. We were falling, upside down, iron clanging off walls of ice. I had the slightest impression of seeing the right front drive pontoon shoot up in the air, of a roll to the right and a crunch of snow against the Sno-Cat body and a long fall. I had time to think, 'Must be a crevasse!' and then, 'If we survive this one, we will be lucky!'[89]

Couzens was not lucky: the Cat's fall ended with a 'monumental crash' and impact with the vehicle's steering wheel killed the 28-year-old ex-Korean War tank commander instantly. Gunn and Lowery were not much better off. When he regained consciousness, Gunn found himself upside down, pinned in a tiny space between the seats and the instrument panel, with his knees just inches from his face. Lowery was even more tightly wedged.

It was clear that the Cat had partially crossed an invisible snow bridge, which had then collapsed, precipitating the vehicle backwards into a 30m crevasse. It ended its fall with its pontoons pointing skywards and its cabin roof flattened to within a few centimetres of the seats. Both survivors had suffered broken backs and Lowery's jaw was smashed. Neither could move. With their radio out of action, and with the temperature plummeting as the heat of the engine faded away, they could only wait in hope of rescue. Their situation worsened still further when snowflakes began to filter down into the crevasse, indicating a deterioration in surface visibility; in these conditions, their comrades at the campsite would simply assume that any delay in their return was due to poor visibility.

The two geologists spent twenty-two hours down the crevasse before their rescuers arrived, the bitter cold seeping into their immobile limbs. By 8 a.m. on the 20th, the more badly injured Lowery could no longer feel his feet, and he was drifting in and out of consciousness. Gunn, meanwhile, believed that he kept his ears only because he had been able to wriggle his head sufficiently to replace his dislodged hat: 'lucky that'.[90] In Gunn's opinion, by the time they were cut free, both men were close to death. 'Lowery had sunk to a point where his life expectancy was measured in a handful of hours and ... brave talk aside, I didn't have many hours left in me either.'[91]

Neither man would walk again for many months, and the cold damage to Lowery's feet eventually necessitated a double amputation. Nonetheless, they had fallen 30m into a crevasse with 3 tonnes of machinery and they had lived to tell the tale. By the standards of most such accidents, they had been very fortunate indeed.

★ ★ ★

On 12 October 1965, and in circumstances in many ways similar to those of the New Zealand tragedy, the British Antarctic Survey suffered the worst vehicle accident in the long history of British Antarctic exploration. Indeed, along with the NBSAE catastrophe of February 1951 and a Chilean disaster that occurred at the Bernardo O'Higgins Station on 28 September 2005, it ranks equally as one of the three worst vehicle accidents in the annals of international Antarctic exploration.

On 11 October a four-man contingent from BAS's Halley Bay Station separated from a larger survey party camped at the Pyramid Rocks in the Tottan Mountains (Tottanfjella), intending to lay a depot close to the Milorgknausane nunataks. The leader of this small group, David 'Dai'

Wild, had travelled in the area the previous season and he believed that, with their single Muskeg tractor and dog team, they would be able to reach a point 48km south of the nunataks without encountering any serious crevassing.

A poor surface slowed their progress during the first day, but conditions improved during the morning of the 12th and, with the dog team running with the sledges, they made good time. To aid navigation, they placed flags every 3km as route markers, took regular prismatic compass bearings on the Tottan and Central mountain ranges, and used the driving mirror to align their course with their own tracks and with the mountains to the rear. 'Although not entirely satisfactory,' reported Ian Ross, the party's geologist, 'this was the only feasible method available ... The aircraft compass fixed in the vehicle was worse than useless, giving a consistent reading (usually about 20–30° off) only if vehicle and engine were both stopped.'[92]

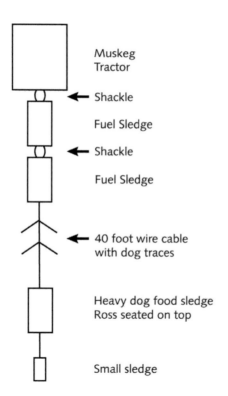

Muskeg
Tractor

Shackle

Fuel Sledge

Shackle

Fuel Sledge

40 foot wire cable
with dog traces

Heavy dog food sledge
Ross seated on top

Small sledge

Configuration of BAS Muskeg and Sledges,
12 October 1965.

Towards evening, a combination of low surface drift and a rolling landscape rendered navigation more difficult, with Mount Cathedral, the most prominent of the landmarks, often disappearing altogether from view. Nonetheless, at a point roughly 55km from the Pyramid Rocks, they caught their first distant view of the planned location for their depot. 'I had been talking to Wild about our route,' wrote Ross:

Wild stated that quite a lot of crevasses were to be found in the large, shallow, basin-like depression stretching from the bottom of the hill over which we were travelling, as far as the Stella Group; also, that as long as we kept out of the above depression, we should not meet any crevasses for at least another 25 miles [40km].[93]

Shortly after this conversation, Ross, who had been riding in the Muskeg with Wild and Jeremy Bailey, surrendered his place to Dr John Wilson, who had been riding on one of the Maudheim sledges, in order to let him 'thaw out'.

A few minutes later, at around 7.45 p.m., the tractor train came to a halt, but without, Ross noted, any 'shocks or jars'. At that instant he had been looking towards the mountains at the rear and, with all sound deadened by his balaclava and by the hoods of his windproof and anorak, he had heard nothing. When he turned to find out why they had stopped, the Muskeg was nowhere to be seen; the leading 'tanker' sledge, however, sat tilted in the mouth of a crevasse. 'I ran forward to the edge of the crevasse,' Ross reported, 'and saw that the Keg had broken loose from the tanker sledge which was held only by its A-bar sticking into the far side of the crevasse nearly 6 feet [1.8m] down. There was no reply to my shouts and no sound at all was heard.'[94]

Running back to the sledges, Ross grabbed skis, a medical bag and a climbing rope, and then edged forward until he could see about 15m into the crevasse – but still there was no sign of the vehicle, or its occupants. He drove a pole into what appeared to be a more stable area of snow, lashed himself to it with the climbing rope and leaned over the gaping hole. At last he could see it, about 30m down, with its tracks jammed against the north wall and its cabin, 'flattened beyond recognition', against the south wall. 'I again shouted several times but there was no reply and I was wondering what to do when I heard shouts coming from the Keg. This was about 20 to 30 minutes after the accident occurred.'[95] Ross subsequently made a verbatim record of the conversation:

'Dai? … Dai?'
    'Dai's dead. It's me.'
    'Is that John or Jerry?'
    'Jerry.'
    'How is John?'

'He's a goner, mate.'

'What about yourself?'

'I'm all smashed up.'

'Can you move about at all or tie a rope round yourself?'

'I'm all smashed up.'

Ross then told Bailey that he could do nothing from his position on the south side of the crevasse because of an overhang, but that he would work his way round to the north side to see what he could do from there. 'Okay', replied Bailey, 'but watch yourself.'

Having collected spare poles and ropes, Ross made his way to the other side of the chasm, anchored the rope and threw the loose end into the hole, though the failing light made it impossible for him to see whether it reached the vehicle. The conversation continued:

'Jerry, can you see the rope at all?'

'Look, Ian, I'm all smashed up. You'll never get me out of this. Save yourself. Get back to the others.'

'Take it easy, Jerry. I'll get you out.'

'I'm a goner, mate. I'm all smashed up.'

'Take it easy, Jerry, I'll get you out. I won't be long.'

According to Ross, 'Bailey then said something about Omnipon,[96] but I could not make it out. He then screamed (a loud, fast groaning) for about two minutes and did not reply to my shouts. The screaming stopped suddenly with a "bubbling cough" and nothing further was heard.'[97]

Phillip Law has remarked that 'An accident in which members of a party lose their lives can have a shattering effect upon morale. The protective illusion of "it can't happen to me" is violently dispelled by death striking in the very midst of the small closely-knit group, and all feel suddenly naked and vulnerable.'[98] Surely, no one could have felt more naked and vulnerable than Ian Ross at that moment. Convinced that all three of his companions had died in the crevasse fall, he nonetheless made repeated attempts to reach them, thwarted each time by the rope's tendency to cut into the overhang of snow. In these conditions he knew that, if he descended, he would never be able to climb back out. Eventually, accepting the inevitable, and realising, too, that his own survival now hung in the balance, he decided that he must use the dog team to return to the campsite at Pyramid Rocks.

Accordingly, on the morning of 13 October, he harnessed the dogs and broke camp – but his own inexperience, the bad weather, the dogs' poor condition and, no doubt, his own acute shock, all militated against him and after many hours of futile effort he again pitched camp. To make matters worse, the failure of his party's radio meant that he could not call for help, advice or reassurance. The following day, he tried again and 'eventually got the dogs to pull an empty sledge'. Restricting himself to the bare essentials, he loaded the sledge and managed to cover 9.5km in four hours. On the 15th, they travelled 18km in eight hours, and, during the 16th, a further 29km in nine hours. The last 16km were covered on the 17th and, at 2.45 p.m., Ross finally reached safety, having led the dogs on foot for all but 9.5km of the whole tortuous journey.

Once again, the disaster that overwhelmed the party led by Dai Wild did not result from any failings in their vehicle. Built by the Canadian Bombardier Company, the Muskeg relied upon twin continuous tracks, much like those of the Weasel. However, it was slightly lighter than the Weasel and generated a ground pressure of just 0.75psi, equal to that of the Sno-Cat and less than half of the Weasel's 1.9psi. The Commonwealth Trans-Antarctic Expedition had taken just one Muskeg, but had found it 'easy to drive and sturdy' and, when used around the base and on firm surfaces, 'excellent and extremely fast'.[99] Gordon Bowra, medical officer at Halley Bay during the season prior to the accident, opined that the Muskegs had 'no down side … It was a question of what you did with the tractors and how you used them.'[100]

Given that no one inside the Muskeg's cab survived the accident for more than a few minutes, there can be no certainty regarding its exact causes. The poor light would have made crevasses more difficult to spot, but for his part, Bill Bellchambers, who served at Halley Bay during 1957–58 and again in 1964–65, believed that the fatalities were caused primarily by an error of judgement. When interviewed in 2011, he stated:

> This was not a big crevasse … It was a work of art to get a tractor down it … When you get onto a crevasse, there is only one way out and if you don't take it, you are a goner, and I think … they detected the crevasse, put the brakes on – nosedived.[101]

If Bellchambers' assessment is correct – and this explanation has been widely accepted – then it might be that the 24-year-old Bailey, the driver

at the time of the accident, acted instinctively and pressed the brake rather than the accelerator when the snow bridge began to collapse. However, we can only speculate on the events of those last few seconds and Rod Rhys Jones, a member of the larger survey party from which Wild and his companions separated on 11 October, has also pointed out that Bailey was not a novice driver: 'Jerry had experience of polar travel with Americans in Alaska and it was generally agreed that, if slipping backwards on sea ice, to press the accelerator – oh and jump out of the open door.'[102]

In the opinion of Willoughby Thompson, the Colonial Secretary to the Falkland Islands, who chaired the accident inquiry, the factor that contributed most to the scale of the disaster was 'the practice at Halley Bay to ride "three-up" in a Muskeg tractor'.[103] This was a practice that Ray Adie, the Deputy Director of BAS and a highly experienced sledger, considered 'extremely unsafe' – though he also admitted that there were no standing orders forbidding it.[104]

★ ★ ★

In the half-century since the accident near the Tottan Mountains, at least fourteen more individuals have died in vehicle-related accidents in the Antarctic, including three South Africans, three Chileans, three Argentines, three Americans and two Britons. Of these deaths, nine resulted from crevasse falls, four from other vehicle rolls or crashes, and one from a tractor plunging through sea ice. The only significant variant in these fatalities is that five involved the latest and, in some ways, the most innovative of polar vehicles: the Snowmobile, or, as it is often known, the 'Skidoo'.

As its generic name suggests, the Snowmobile is a direct descendant of the rather less successful vehicle first tested in the Antarctic by Byrd during his 1928 expedition; indeed, variants continue to be manufactured by some of Virgil D. White's original, but longer-lived, competitors. In its most recognisable guise, the Snowmobile now consists of a small open vehicle driven by a single continuous track, which the rider straddles, and is steered with handlebars connected to two skis at the front. In design and appearance, it is closer to a motorcycle than to a car and, in the words of one casualty report, driving it is 'an art akin to riding a motorcycle, requiring good balance and control'.[105]

In 1962, Charles Swithinbank, who in 1951 had become the first man to ride a motorcycle in the Antarctic, trialled Eliason and Polaris models along the western margin of the Ross Ice Shelf. On terrain that ranged from level shelf ice to steep mountain glaciers, and from smooth snow to giant sastrugi, the expedition's five Eliasons covered between 930km and 1,100km each, while the single Polaris achieved 1,164km. Moreover, as an impressed Swithinbank later reported, 'In terms of the number of breakdowns per thousand traverse miles, the motor sledge has already proved superior to the Sno-Cat.'[106]

Other advantages included lightweight spares, the potential to operate remotely, and the fact that a party running four Snowmobiles, each hauling 680kg, could afford an irreparable breakdown to one vehicle, as its load could be distributed between the remaining three. Finally, as the machines weighed less than 300kg, they could be loaded easily into an aeroplane or helicopter by just three men. Later trials did nothing to contradict Swithinbank's positive assessment and in just a few short years, Snowmobiles had become, according to a report published in the United States in 1979, 'the main form of land transportation for field parties in Antarctica'.[107]

In some circumstances, however, the Snowmobile's advantages – its lightness, cheapness, speed and versatility – could contribute to its undoing. On the one hand, the machine naturally lends itself to recreational use; on the other, as the US study observed, 'climate, topography, and crevasse dangers in Antarctica require specialised Snowmobile techniques not required in other regions'.[108] A limited appreciation of these localised dangers, when combined with a poor understanding of the specialised techniques required, could have fatal consequences.

This lack of experience almost certainly contributed to the death of Dewald Voight, a 25-year-old South African antennae specialist, who died on 22 December 2006 when he drove his Snowmobile off the edge of Vesleskarvet Nunatak in Queen Maud Land. He had arrived on the SA *Agulhas* that very day.

But experience does not always lead to safe practices. On 16 May 1981, two Britons – one an experienced 'general assistant' – were killed when their Snowmobile plummeted into an unseen crevasse on the Shambles Glacier during a recreational journey from BAS's Rothera Station. In this instance, one, and possibly both, fatalities could have been avoided if the party's two Snowmobiles had been roped together and if the weight of the two men had been divided between the Snowmobile and a towed sledge instead of being combined on the vehicle. In the words of the subsequent inquiry, this accident demonstrated 'the danger of having two people on a skidoo in an area where crevasses may exist, and the practice in such areas should be firmly discouraged'.[109] Essentially, John Anderson and Robert Atkinson had died because they had travelled on the same vehicle – just as Bailey, Wilson and Wild had done fifteen and a half years earlier. And, once again, BAS found itself in the acutely embarrassing situation of having to explain to an inquest that, while detailed instructions on the operation of Snowmobiles had been drafted, these 'were not available at the time of the accident'.[110]

★ ★ ★

Inevitably – and as we have seen throughout this survey – every vehicle introduced to the Antarctic has had its limitations. However, when operated within those limitations few, if any, have failed in such a fashion as to cause the deaths of those responsible for their use. Ironically, in the years immediately following their introduction, when the vehicles were at their most primitive and unreliable, no fatalities occurred. This was because they were incapable of travelling far from the immediate environs of the expedition bases – and because their operators placed very little reliance upon them. As the technology improved, they were pushed harder and further, being driven in poor visibility, on sea ice and into crevasse fields. Expeditions relied upon them to complete a range of tasks, from unloading to field surveys, and their usage increased exponentially. In the last decades of the twentieth century they even bridged the gap between pure utility and recreation. As a result, accidents became, if not commonplace, then far from uncommon.

In the eyes of some shrewd observers, disasters such as those that overwhelmed the BAS parties in 1965 and 1981 have served to highlight the dangers, not only of polar exploration by motor vehicle but of exploration as a whole. 'Exploration anywhere has its hazards,' opined Willoughby Thompson, 'and in the Antarctic, much of which is still uncharted and where the climate is extraordinarily severe, these hazards must always be expected and accidents will happen.'[111] Moreover, in some respects, the characteristics that make certain men not only fit for exploration, but keen to pursue it, are the very same characteristics that make them willing to take the kind of risks that, in certain circumstances, increase the likelihood of accidents. By and large, they are young and happy to 'serve one or two years in Antarctica before (as so many of them put it) "settling down"'. Most significant of all, in Thompson's opinion, there is:

> ... and must be, a certain amount of devil-may-care in their attitude to life. They are ... young enough to be explorers, young enough not to want to bother too much with written instructions, and on a contract short enough to be disregarded if the weight of instruction and discipline becomes too heavy.[112]

By the mid-1960s, BAS's policy of recruiting such men had proved extremely successful when measured in terms both of results and of the harmony that prevailed at most of its bases – but the continuation of that success demanded that discipline be applied with a light touch, and that regulations remained flexible and open to the interpretation of those operating in the field.

Sir Donald Logan, a career diplomat responsible for reviewing BAS safety protocols, supported this view. 'I assume,' he wrote in 1982:

> ... that any young man volunteering for such a period in Antarctica would be prompted by a spirit of adventure.
>
> Most will be – and are – self-reliant, confident types who would be unlikely to remain for two years within an area no bigger than a medium-sized field, with tempting scenery all around them, even if recreational journeys off-base were prohibited. We would find them adopting some scientific justification for getting about.[113]

Although there is no empirical evidence to suggest that these adventurous 'types' are any more prone to the kind of 'positive bias' demonstrated by many young men when rating their abilities behind the wheel, or to the feelings of invulnerability that directly contribute to the dangerous behaviours of many drivers, there is ample evidence that obvious safety protocols, such as not travelling in the same vehicle together and the roping-up of snowmobiles, have been wilfully ignored because they are considered, in the words of one accident survivor, 'a pain in the neck'.[114] This, then, is the danger inherent in the decision not to rigorously apply the kind of 'heavyweight' instruction and discipline alluded to by Thompson.

Whatever its dangers, there can be no doubt that motorised exploration is here to stay. In some areas of the Antarctic and sub-Antarctic, such as Macquarie Island, motor vehicles are banned for ecological reasons.

In others, a better understanding of the risks has resulted in their use being made seasonal. Nonetheless, except in extreme sports, where a test of human endurance is the aim rather than an unavoidable consequence of the exercise, the internal combustion engine has replaced muscle as the primary motive power of fieldwork in the Antarctic. The revolution in polar transport that Scott envisaged at the beginning of the last century has become an irrefutable and irreversible reality.

4

'A PECULIAR MADNESS'

MENTAL ILLNESS AND SUICIDE IN ANTARCTICA

When, in 1921, Raymond Priestley suggested that polar exploration would make 'a fruitful field for the trained psychologist', he was stating what had long been accepted, at least by those with Antarctic experience, as a self-evident truth.[1] From the very beginning of the Heroic Age, with chapped fingers and freezing ink, expedition surgeons had recorded their observations of the often profound effects of the prevailing conditions on both their companions and themselves, and many had concluded that the physiological and psychological demands of Antarctic exploration constituted some of its greatest challenges. Recognising the potential of such a field of study, Priestley's editor remarked that psychology 'derives its material largely from observing the reactions of abnormal individuals in ordinary environments, but the behaviour of normal individuals under exceptional conditions is not less instructive'.[2] Where better to conduct a study of ordinary men in extraordinary conditions than Antarctica?

The study began on Adrien de Gerlache's *Belgica* Expedition of 1897–98 – the first to overwinter in Antarctic waters – and in his book, *Through the First Antarctic Night*, the *Belgica*'s surgeon, Frederick A. Cook, provided one of the earliest descriptions of the effects of the austral winter:

> The men were incapable of concentration, and unable to continue prolonged thought. One sailor was forced to the verge of insanity, but he recovered with the returning sun …

The human system accommodates itself sluggishly and poorly to the strange conditions of the polar seasons, and we, too, are slow in adapting ourselves to the awful despondency of the long winter night. It is possible to close your eyes and befog your brain after a time, when all the world is enveloped in prolonged darkness, but this is not physiological adaptation; it is abnormal education. We have all felt the effects of the night severely.[3]

Henryk Arçtowski, the expedition's Polish meteorologist, also thought the polar night 'of great interest from a psychological point of view … Some became nervous, excitable, and sleepless, with the imagination continually wandering and dreaming' and he candidly admitted that he 'was one of these'.[4] Similarly, Erik Ekelöf, 'medical member' of Otto Nordenskjöld's Swedish Antarctic Expedition of 1901–04, noted, 'As regards psychical [*sic*] conditions we have to note a certain degree of depression and increased irritability, exhibited by the greater part of the members of the three wintering parties, especially during the dark season', though he observed that these symptoms never developed into 'melancholia or any other mental disease'.[5]

Writing of his experiences during Scott's National Antarctic Expedition of 1901–04, Edward Wilson struck a rather different note, claiming that 'to everyone the winter months came as a most welcome time of rest and recruiting'.[6] But Wilson was guilty of a retrospective application of the British stiff upper lip; at the time, locked in his cabin on the icebound *Discovery*, he thought differently, admitting in his diary, 'If one couldn't work and hadn't more than one can get through, this life would be quite unbearable.'[7] His shipmate, Lieutenant Charles Royds, noted, 'the absence of the sun has, and must have, a depressing effect on the best of men',[8] though he expressed disgust at what he saw as the distinctly 'un-English' excesses committed by the men of the *Belgica* during their incarceration, their excesses including a propensity to tearfulness and a willingness to let their hair grow long.[9] Priestley, who served on both the *Nimrod* and *Terra Nova* expeditions, certainly believed in the existence of a 'peculiar madness which has played a major or a minor part in most expeditions', but he thought the madness restricted to those expeditions 'that have undergone hard times'.[10] As a member of Scott's Northern Party, few men had undergone harder times and lived to tell the tale, so it seems reasonable to assume that he, too, had either witnessed this 'peculiar madness' among his companions or experienced it himself.

Almost without exception, then, the early explorers had come to realise that the 'long winter night' posed one of Antarctica's greatest challenges. With every degree of southern latitude, the period of winter darkness increases until, at 90° S, it lasts for a full six months, with the sun setting on 21 March and not rising again until 21 September. Deprivation of daylight can have profound effects, and expedition diaries and medical reports are filled with references to symptoms including insomnia, depression, irritability, reduced motivation, poor cognition and even a fugue-like state, often referred to as the 'Antarctic stare', or the '20-foot stare in the 10-foot room'. The severity of the symptoms varies from individual to individual and, crucially, it is also all but impossible to predict which members of an expedition might prove most susceptible.

★ ★ ★

At South Ice, the forward base of Bunny Fuchs' Commonwealth Trans-Antarctic Expedition (CTAE), all of these symptoms were encountered. Established by air approximately 440km inland from the expedition's main base on the Filchner Ice Shelf, South Ice was both a glaciological research station and the first milestone in Fuchs' planned land traverse of the continent.

After the last supply flight on 25 March 1957, the three-man team, consisting of Hal Lister (base leader and senior glaciologist), Ken Blaiklock (surveyor) and Jon Stephenson (geologist and assistant glaciologist), was left to its own devices. For the next eight months, this triumvirate would eat, sleep and work in a tiny subsurface hut on the edge of the Polar Plateau, linked by wireless to the larger bases but, in all other respects, completely isolated and, during the winter months, far beyond the reach of external aid.

Within days of the hut's completion, swirling drift had buried it up to its chimneys, and when the men ventured outside to visit drift-recording or meteorological apparatus they had to make their way down a 27m tunnel before exiting via a trapdoor to the surface. At an altitude of 1,350m above sea level, and so far inland, South Ice generally experienced fewer blizzards than the expedition's main winter quarters but, with the temperature sometimes dropping as low as −52°C, the hut's inhabitants quickly began to refer to the comparatively temperate Weddell Sea coastal area as 'the banana belt'.

At first the work went well. Blaiklock concentrated on meteorological observations, while also taking star sights to fix South Ice's precise location and plotting the results of the previous season's aerial surveys. Stephenson worked in a 15m vertical shaft sunk into the ice sheet, drawing and analysing ice core samples, which he studied microscopically to establish how snow gradually turns to ice without first melting. Finally, Lister prepared a detailed record of drift densities at various wind speeds – onerous work that necessitated daily trips to an array of photocells and specially designed drift cylinders mounted on a Dexion mast some distance from the trapdoor. But then, in the midst of the winter darkness, Stephenson, whom Blaiklock described as 'a tough, stocky Aussie',[11] began to exhibit worrying mood swings. Sometimes he would be snappish and inclined to 'screaming defiance about results',[12] at others he became taciturn and gloomy, spending long hours every day huddled in the eerie depths of the glaciological pit.

On 17 August, after nearly five months of troglodyte existence, an increasingly anxious Lister described the young Australian's condition:

> Jon terribly depressed, saying nothing unless asked a direct question and even then, only answering in a very quiet strained voice. Head in hands much of time and looking extremely miserable but says he is OK. Frequently much of day in bunk and nights spent working … These periods of depression have become more frequent and this one is the most intense and alarming. Medical opinion at base could probably do little to help so best not asked for. Even Ken somewhat alarmed by Jon and asked me if I thought there was anything seriously wrong with Jon.[13]

With the benefit of more than a century of Antarctic exploration and the results of a series of scientific experiments and observations, we now know that the symptoms described by Lister constitute a near-perfect textbook example of a condition described by medical science as 'winter-over syndrome', but which is better known by its colloquial name, 'cabin fever'. Its cause is reduced exposure to daylight and a consequent acceleration in the pineal gland's secretion of melatonin. Although recent research has suggested that these symptoms can also be caused, or exacerbated, by other factors, including a reduction in concentrations of the hormone T3 (polar T3 syndrome) and, in severe cases, the psychiatric disease of subsyndromal seasonal affective disorder (SAD), to non-clinical observers the effects on an individual appear almost indistinguishable, with the only difference being one of degree. In the majority of cases, too, the symptoms disappear with the arrival of spring and the return of the sun – though in a small isolated community this positive prognosis is unlikely to reduce the impact of one or more team members being affected by the condition. Typically, Stephenson made a full recovery, and when discussing cabin fever in later years he blithely stated his conviction that 'at South Ice we experienced little of this'.[14]

★ ★ ★

Although its most easily recognised symptoms are behavioural, winter–over syndrome is a physiological condition caused, primarily, by the absence of daylight. Equally unavoidable aspects of Antarctic exploration – including, to name but a few, the absence of privacy, sex, thick moist air to breathe and any vegetation larger than lichen – all have the potential to generate or exacerbate a range of other problems that are more appropriately categorised as psychological or psychosocial in nature. Chief among these factors are isolation and confinement. Some base sites are extremely difficult to access even during the summer, particularly those on the Weddell Sea coast, and most are impossible to reach during the winter. Expedition diaries are full both of the frustration of men concerned at being baulked of their ambition to reach the continent by seemingly impenetrable belts of pack ice and euphoria at being able to break through the girdle. Unfortunately, the immense challenge of overcoming this first obstacle can also serve to reinforce the feelings of isolation once land, or shelf ice, is reached: of a door slamming shut behind them. In the words of Phillip Law, Director of ANARE from 1949 to 1966, 'It is the irrevocability of their exile which oppresses them.'[15]

Not surprisingly, those with families feel the separation most keenly, and research undertaken at US Antarctic bases has indicated that married personnel are much more prone to winter depression. Derek Williams, a cameraman who accompanied the CTAE's Advance Party on the expedition ship *Theron*, recalled the unmistakeable stress visible on the faces of the eight explorers left on the edge of the Filchner Ice Shelf as the vessel began its retreat to civilisation on 7 February 1956. He recognised, moreover, that they were much more concerned with their families than with the immense and daunting task before them:

They were all looking at my camera and they were waving and they had, I'm afraid, very forced smiles: they were obviously upset and perhaps frightened. They were thinking, I believe, 'I'm not looking at Williams and his camera, and I'm not looking at Bunny and David Pratt and David Stratton, I'm looking at my wife through that lens – I'm looking at my mother and father through that lens – I'm looking at my girlfriend through that lens: they are the ones who will see me left here and I'm trying to force a smile and wave goodbye to them'. I'm sure that's what they were thinking.[16]

From the very earliest expeditions to the most recent, it's doubtful that anything could alleviate the raw emotion at the actual moment of separation – but once that moment has passed and base routine has been established it might seem probable that improved communications between polar bases and home would do much to mitigate the painful intensity of such feelings, particularly as the American study identified 'real or imagined unpleasant events at home' as one of the major causes of stress.[17] The reality is far more complex.

In 1967 Hugh Simpson, a FIDS medical officer between 1956 and 1957, published the results of his investigations into stress reactions in both the Arctic and Antarctic. During his field research, he completed an eighty-three-day dog sledge journey up onto the Graham Land Plateau; made a 380km man-haul trek around James Ross Island and, on the other side of the world, skied 644km across the Greenland ice cap. Crucially, he also measured stress reactions to various events at the base at Hope Bay.

Here, he discovered that wireless signals from home, far from reducing stress, actually increased it. According to Simpson:

Most men hated the summer shipping season because of the frequent signals and disruption of base routine … The majority were in fact attuned to the isolated Antarctic environment and preferred to have as little contact with the outside as possible.[18]

Inevitably, the levels of stress caused by such contact varied enormously. During Operation Tabarin, for instance, the first British party to overwinter at Hope Bay listened, in real time, to the sounds of a German air raid on London, courtesy of the BBC's Overseas Service – an experience hardly likely to reassure them regarding the well-being of their loved ones at home. Similarly, in September 1957, the occupants of South Ice could hear reports of the disappearance of one of the expedition's Auster aircraft with its two-man crew, but their inability to take part in the search-and-rescue operations left them feeling utterly impotent and dejected. 'We don't contribute,' raged Lister, 'we just waste time and express ourselves. How puerile! … we must take a back seat and only listen, and not talk, for Gordon and Allan are first on the priorities, poor devils.'[19]

Even in the absence of such dramatic events, many explorers have found that the advent of technology like the radio-telephone actually served to emphasise the gulf, both geographic and emotional, separating them from those at home. Richard Brooke, an English naval officer serving as surveyor with Ed Hillary's CTAE party at McMurdo Sound, certainly felt uncomfortable with the medium. 'I know the others took a lot of advantage of [it],' he recalled. 'I think I spoke, I don't know, once or twice at the most – I couldn't think what on Earth I could say!'[20] For his part, Bob Miller, Hillary's overworked second in command, found that the immediacy of the contact removed the ability to filter emotions. 'Fear I may have given a doleful account of life,' he wrote, after one call to his wife and children, 'but that is how toll calls go.'[21]

Of course, many explorers feel no such reservations and have found, instead, immense solace in their ability to speak with their families. Hillary, for instance, thought the radio-telephone a tremendous boon, his only concern being that, at 4s 6d for a three-minute call, he risked 'wasting a packet of money on phone calls'.[22]

The fact that ease of communication with home has been identified as a potential cause of stress and some explorers have evidenced a clear preference for 'radio silence' perhaps makes it less surprising that depression is comparatively uncommon at the most remote and physically demanding bases. The men and women who encounter the very worst that Antarctica can throw at them have generally volunteered to do so: they have actively sought its dangers and remoteness and, as a result, are more likely to benefit psychologically from mastering these difficulties.[23] While the same might be said of polar explorers as a whole, there are differences in degree, and these differences can go a long way towards explaining the variations in explorers' responses to their environment.

In considering the benefits of embracing and ultimately overcoming challenges, both physical and mental, the Hungarian-born psychologist Mihaly Csikszentmihalyi has developed a theory of 'flow': a state of concentration so intense – and fulfilling – that the individual experiencing it becomes totally immersed in what he is doing, even to the point of sublimating the most basic motivations, such as hunger and thirst.[24] In relation to polar exploration, it has been argued that personnel operating in the most extreme environments are more likely to experience this 'flow' because 'there was a greater correspondence between their expectations ... and their actual experiences than was the case among personnel at stations located in less severe physical settings'.[25] In other words, by deliberately placing themselves *in extremis*, these explorers experience enhanced satisfaction and self-esteem because they achieve their goals against the odds.

Given that a physically demanding environment can produce such a positive reaction, it is less surprising that much easier conditions sometimes result in feelings of disappointment and regret. Approaching the American base at Hut Point on Ross Island in January 1957, Richard Brooke's imagination was filled with stories and pictures of the Heroic Age expeditions of Scott and Shackleton. The reality appalled him. Established as part of Operation Deep Freeze I during the austral summer of 1955–56 and boasting two airstrips, the facility had grown into an ugly shantytown of orange prefabricated huts and fuel dumps. 'I wasn't very enchanted,' Brooke recalled:

> ... with ... the close proximity of the American base, which is so big and, in my view, so out of keeping with the polar regions, or the magic of the polar regions. It's a pity ... it was so out of keeping.[26]

He was equally horrified by the attitude of many of the US servicemen who occupied this eyesore, and frequented its cinema, bars and chapel: 'Most of the people there didn't want to be there. They hoped that all their normal creature comforts had been imported to the Antarctic – which was pretty largely true.'

At the earliest opportunity, Brooke harnessed his dog team and set off to discover the Antarctic of his imaginings. He wouldn't return to Ross Island for 127 days, by which time he and his team had sledged well over 1,600km, collecting sufficient data in the process to complete, for the first time, a detailed topographic and geological survey of the 32,187 square kilometres of the mountain country between the Mulock and Mawson glaciers.

★ ★ ★

In 2004, a group of American academics concluded that, in Antarctica, 'the social environment may be a more powerful determinant than the physical environment of psychiatric disorders'.[27] Four decades earlier, Phillip Law had drawn the same conclusion. In his analysis of the psychological and psychosocial stresses inseparable from Antarctic exploration, he argued that by far the greatest were the stresses between individuals, between groups and, perhaps most damaging of all, between the leader and his men:

> In a large city a man with peculiar characteristics, strange prejudices or embarrassing weaknesses can often escape from stress situations merely by avoiding them. If he does not like his job he can change it; if he does not get on well with one type of person he can choose another type as his acquaintance. If he likes company he can live gregariously, but if he is a solitary type he can be anti-social without attracting too much attention. He can bolster his confidence by joining ego-protecting associations and clubs, and shelter behind their conformist activities. Even gross weaknesses in character can be reasonably well hidden by frequent changes of job and domicile.[28]

This is not the case at a remote station where 'a man's avenues of escape are considerably restricted, and his chances of hiding his weaknesses are almost nil'. Richard Byrd agreed, remarking:

> It doesn't take two men long to find each other out. And, inevitably, this is what they do whether they will or not, if only because once the simple tasks of the day are finished there is little else to do but take each other's measure.[29]

Moreover, in Law's opinion, acceptance of the impossibility of hiding one's idiosyncrasies can result in their more overt expression. In the words of one ANARE doctor, 'Life on such stations definitely shows people in their true colours, if only for the reason that there is so little point in keeping up pretences under such circumstances.'[30]

Usually, the mutual dependence that forms an essential part of life on any polar base will engender a healthy and fairly forgiving atmosphere in which an individual's professional competence compensates for any number of peccadilloes. His companions recognise the importance of adopting a 'live and let live' philosophy and character traits and personality defects

that might not be tolerated in 'civilised' life will be ignored or glossed over for the benefit – and potentially for the survival – of the community as a whole. Most men, but not all; most of the time, but not always – and the annals of polar exploration are littered with examples of sometimes bitter strife where there is no suggestion of psychiatric illness. However, where such illness does exist, the potential for discord increases exponentially, particularly during the depths of the polar winter when the inmates of a small expedition ship or hut are denied the outlet of sledging journeys and face, instead, months of unavoidable intimacy and relative inactivity. Likewise, the inescapable strains of life in the Antarctic have the potential to force into the open the symptoms of what, up to that point, has been only a latent condition.

The expedition that suffered perhaps the most extreme example of internal conflict resulting from mental illness must surely be the AAE of 1911–14. Although Douglas Mawson originally intended to spend just one year in the Antarctic, the loss of his two companions, an entire dog team, and most of his supplies and equipment during the Far Eastern Sledging Journey significantly delayed his return to winter quarters. Faced with the risk of his ship becoming iced in, John King Davis, the expedition's second in command, was then forced to retreat to Hobart leaving a team of six men to search for the missing party and to overwinter for a second time. Only one member of this relief party was new to the Antarctic: Sydney Jeffryes, the ship's wireless officer, who volunteered to trade places with the homesick Walter Hannam.

Jeffryes had been extremely keen to join the expedition and initially he performed well, demonstrating a good understanding of the Telefunken wireless set and a high degree of competence in its use. But at the beginning of July 1913 his behaviour turned increasingly paranoid. On the 8th, Cecil Madigan, the expedition's meteorologist, recorded one of the earliest of his outbursts: 'Jeffryes seems to have had enough of me, but to our horror, this evening he went up to Bickerton and asked him if he would be his second if he did any shooting. Bick tried to pacify him.'[31] The next day, Madigan and Bickerton, the mechanical engineer, 'put away all the cartridges ... Jeffryes has no firearms and can't get any now.' Innocent conversations which in no way bore upon the wireless operator were interpreted as insults and slights, resulting in uncontrolled ravings and accusations, and on the 11th Archie McLean, the expedition surgeon, admitted in his journal that there were 'undoubted signs of delusive insanity'.[32]

At Cape Denison, which has been identified as the windiest location at
sea level on the face of the planet, opportunities for winter excursions are
perhaps more limited than at practically any other site on the Antarctic
mainland and, with very few opportunities for either exercise or distraction,
the impact of Jeffryes' malaise upon his companions – none of whom had
either planned or desired to spend a second year in the Antarctic – was
profound. In later years, Bickerton described another outburst. Typically,
it had started with Jeffryes accusing him of plotting his murder:

> He accused [me] at breakfast before them all. The Doctor had a talk with
> him and advised [me] to argue with him as though he were sane and try and
> prove calmly that [I] had not made any attempt to kill him. There was a long
> argument and then the madman asked, 'Would you swear on the Bible that
> you did not and will not try to kill me?'
>
> [I] of course said 'yes, bring me a Bible'.
>
> 'Would you swear on your mother's Bible?'
>
> 'Yes, if I had it.'
>
> 'Swear by all you ever held truest and dearest?'
>
> 'Certainly I would.'
>
> 'Well even if you did all that I wouldn't believe you.'[33]

One day, Jeffryes even threatened to resign from the expedition and Mawson
only succeeded in defusing the situation by half-humorously pointing out
that such an act would necessarily result in his relinquishing all claim upon
the expedition's accommodation and supplies. Jeffryes also refused to attend
to his personal hygiene and the other explorers were reduced to washing
his soiled garments and bed linen while the deranged man sat scowling and
muttering to himself on his bunk.

No one was immune to the impact of this catastrophic decline in Jeffryes'
condition and normal intercourse became practically impossible through
nervousness and the dread of sparking another outburst. The fluctuations in
his mood – his rants were interspersed with periods of apparent rationality
– initially encouraged Mawson to allow Jeffryes to remain in charge of the
wireless. But when they discovered that he was sending reports claiming
that his companions had run mad, he was relieved of his responsibilities and
kept under close watch.

Although it has been suggested that Jeffryes might have benefited from
the care of a more imaginative doctor than McLean appears to have been,[34]

he did not experience any remission of his symptoms once he returned to Australia and was placed in the hands of physicians presumably better versed in the treatment of mental illness. Instead, he spent the remainder of his life in asylums, eventually dying, as delusional as ever, in an institution in Ararat, Victoria, in October 1942.

Initially, Mawson had ascribed Jeffryes' behaviour to a particularly extreme bout of winter-over syndrome, noting in his diary, 'His touchy temperament is being very hard tested with bad weather and indoor life. A case of polar depression.'[35] It is more probable that, while the Antarctic winter served as a trigger, his psychosis was longstanding, though sufficiently well hidden – from others and, perhaps, from himself – to allow him to hold down the job of ship's wireless officer with the Australian United Steam Navigation Company. Certainly, his sister, Norma, seems to have been completely unaware of any problems prior to his breakdown in the Antarctic. In the words of Philip Ayres, Mawson's biographer, Jeffryes chose to sail south and, in doing so, let 'the Furies loose'.[36] Had he chosen otherwise, is it possible that his illness might never have been triggered and that he might have lived a normal, happy life? We will never know.[37]

★ ★ ★

While Jeffryes' paranoid schizophrenia ranks as perhaps the most extreme example of mental illness encountered during any Antarctic expedition, even less florid cases have the potential to be both damaging and highly disruptive. One such occurred on board Scott's old ship *Discovery*, during the now largely forgotten National Oceanographic Expedition of 1925–27. This expedition, which would evolve into the better-known *Discovery* Investigations, was intended to support the economy of the Falkland Islands, more specifically the southern whaling industry, by undertaking detailed research into the ecosystem of the waters around Antarctica, from the microscopic animal and plant life known as plankton, through the tiny shrimp-like crustaceans collectively called krill, up to the great whales themselves.

Command of the expedition was divided between Stanley Kemp, the scientific director, and Joseph Stenhouse, captain of the *Discovery*. They would prove to be a very ill-matched pair. Tall, lean and balding, the 42-year-old Kemp was the *beau idéal* of the ascetic, dedicated and self-effacing man of science. Although one of his team later wrote,

'No finer leader and no better companion for a long and lonely voyage in sub-Antarctic waters could be imagined',[38] he possessed little or no ability to inspire any but those who were already members of the scientific fraternity and showed very little interest in even attempting to do so.

In contrast, the 37-year-old Stenhouse was equally tall, but broad-shouldered, barrel-chested and firm-jawed. A Merchant Navy officer by training, he had served with great distinction as chief officer and then temporary captain of the *Aurora* during Shackleton's *Endurance* Expedition, bringing his badly damaged ship safely back to port after an extraordinary and punishing ten-month drift trapped in the pack ice of the Ross Sea. His war record had been equally distinguished, resulting in the award of a DSC for his role in sinking *UC-33* on 26 September 1917 and a DSO for his work with the Allied Expeditionary Force to North Russia during 1918–19. When added to the Polar Medal and OBE that he had received for his contribution to Shackleton's expedition, these medals made him one of the most highly decorated of all British Heroic Age explorers.

What would not have been obvious to anyone looking at Stenhouse's burly frame and medal ribbons was his history of mental illness. In fact, he had decided to join Shackleton's expedition while on sick leave from the British India Steam Navigation Company, whose doctors had described his ailment as a nervous breakdown. In reality, it was almost certainly a prolonged and serious bout of depression, a malady that would dog him throughout his career. He had fought his demons throughout the drift of the *Aurora*, constantly trying to bolster the morale of his men while he himself was tortured with anxiety, doubt and, all too often, loathing for everyone and everything around him. Typically, on 24 October 1915, he had written in his diary:

> Have been suffering from severe dose of Blues due, not to the surroundings, but the opportunity to think; I think happiness is a myth; whenever I have leisure the old, old curse comes back to me … I think and brood over the use of anything and am worked into thinking that all is chaos.[39]

When *Discovery* sailed from Dartmouth on 24 September 1925, it seemed to many of those on board that they had embarked on a great adventure: an opportunity to study nature at her harshest, among towering seas and on the edges of a mysterious and beautiful land of ice.

Stenhouse, whose character was essentially romantic in nature, shared their enthusiasm and he admitted to one journalist that he found 'a peculiar and poetic interest in the *Discovery* going into the very latitude where her first commander perished'.[40] Kemp thought differently. As far as he was concerned, the expedition would be undertaken on rigidly scientific lines, with little or no place for the kind of muscular exploration which Stenhouse loved and which his old leader, Shackleton, had come to epitomise. Moreover, the science was driven by hard-nosed economic reality. The accumulation of knowledge for the broader benefit of mankind would be countenanced only where such activities complemented the purpose of the expedition, and of exploration for exploration's sake there would be none. 'Our work will be in connection with whaling,' he told polar historian Hugh Mill, 'in all probability we shall not cross the Antarctic Circle and I fear we may have little opportunity for coastal surveys.'[41]

Despite this marked difference in outlook, the initial cause of tension between the two men was *Discovery* herself. Like many ships designed for work in the ice, she rolled abominably in open water; so abominably, indeed, that Henry Herdman, the expedition's hydrologist, thought 'she'd roll in the lake at Wembley!'[42] Such a tendency made the ship fundamentally unsuited to the work of the expedition, which required the frequent completion of 'stations', each station consisting of a detailed observation on a vertical line into the ocean's depths. With *Discovery* constantly rolling and pitching even in moderate seas, the lines were continually dragged from the vertical, making the critical assessment of the depth from which the samples were taken quite impossible. As a result, a significant proportion of the results were compromised.

Stenhouse quickly recognised that the old ship was unsuited to the work, but to him, whatever her faults, *Discovery* remained a thing of legend and the feelings of nostalgia when he trod her decks, particularly in an ice-strewn seascape, were strong. Kemp, on the other hand, had little time for such emotions and he felt no compunction in sharing his disappointment and frustration with the expedition committee. 'It is ... to the unsuitability of the ship,' he told them, 'that our lack of success is mainly to be attributed.'[43] In his professional judgement, *Discovery* had failed and should be replaced as quickly as possible with a vessel better suited to the task in hand. Relations between the two men remained cordial, but the seeds for future discord had been sown.

The pressure mounted. In June 1926, when *Discovery* reached Simonstown Naval Dockyard for an essential refit, Stenhouse admitted to his wife, 'I have had quite a lot of worry and trouble through breaches of discipline and I get rather tired of it.'[44] Two months later he was forced to dismiss his first officer, Lieutenant Commander W.H. O'Connor, whom he believed guilty of causing 'suspicion and general discontent not only between the officers but also between the officers and ship's company'.[45] We know that this was not paranoia on Stenhouse's part because his decision to sack O'Connor had, to some degree, been forced by a petition from his other officers, who threatened to resign en masse if the first officer remained in post.

Unfortunately, the matter did not end there. On reaching South Georgia on 5 December 1926, after an extremely difficult voyage through ice-choked waters, Stenhouse learned that O'Connor had lost no time in laying his very biased account of recent events before the members of the *Discovery* Committee in London. Naively, they took O'Connor's word and addressed a stinging rebuke to Stenhouse. Once the facts had been investigated, Stenhouse regained the committee's full confidence. But the damage had been done.

By the end of 1926, Edward Marshall, *Discovery*'s surgeon, was observing signs of intense nervous strain in Stenhouse's behaviour. Discord between himself and Kemp, the difficulties inherent in performing the duties that he had been set, the sacking of O'Connor and the criticisms of the committee had all served to fray his temper. According to Marshall, he had become 'unapproachable on the ship, morose, and irritable at table'.[46] Perhaps in an unconscious attempt to convince himself of his own value to the expedition, he had also begun to push himself forward among men such as the whalers of South Georgia, to seek 'the limelight, to do all the honours and to relegate Dr Kemp to a subordinate position'.[47]

The storm that had been gathering for so many months finally broke on the expedition's arrival in England. Almost as soon as he set foot on shore, Kemp wrote to the *Discovery* Committee categorically refusing any suggestion that he should ever again serve with Stenhouse:

> In my opinion Captain Stenhouse does not possess the right temperament for the post he holds: he is very nervy, subject to prolonged fits of depression, and being by nature egotistical, the fact that he was not in full command of the expedition has always been very distasteful to him. I do not feel that I have had

from him that loyal co-operation which I had a right to expect, and except as a safe navigator I have scarcely a shred of confidence left in him.[48]

Having learned the lessons of the O'Connor debacle, the committee decided to seek the opinions of other members of the expedition and, on 2 December 1927, Lieutenant Commander John Chaplin, the replacement first officer, Alister Hardy, the chief zoologist, and Dr Marshall gave their evidence to an extraordinary meeting held at the Colonial Office.

The first two witnesses equivocated; while they painted a picture of a ship rendered deeply unhappy by a divided command, neither would attribute blame. Marshall was altogether more forthright. He told the committee that he had become increasingly concerned over Stenhouse's state of mind. On ship and shore the captain became two different men: hearty and companionable by land, morose, irritable and intensely nervy by sea and prone to question everybody else's judgement. 'Captain Stenhouse "cried for ice" at South Georgia in 1926,' he told the committee, 'but when he got it in 1927 was very nervous.' All the symptoms, the surgeon opined, were indicative of an imminent and 'definite breakdown in the Captain's health … Captain Stenhouse's condition was almost pathological and … probably he could not change'.[49] Faced with such a weight of professional opinion, the committee had little option but to dismiss Stenhouse, a task they performed with sensitivity, providing a generous financial package and an excellent reference.

By the time Stenhouse took command of *Discovery* he had already spent more than twenty years in some of the most physically and mentally demanding situations imaginable, convinced that only work would allow him to stay one step ahead of his black dog. A decade at sea as an apprentice and then as an officer had been followed by two years with the Imperial Trans-Antarctic Expedition, during which he had fought against enormous odds to bring a badly damaged ship back to safe harbour after a drift of ten months in pack ice. Moreover, during this entire period he had felt wholly responsible not only for the men aboard his ship but also for the shore party that he had been forced to abandon, unprepared and ill equipped. He had then joined the war effort, commanding Q-ships in a continuous duel with marauding U-boats, before being transferred to fight both Germans and Bolsheviks in the snowbound wastes of the Kola Peninsula. Individually, each of these episodes had included moments of high exhilaration and enjoyment; they had brought him into close companionship with men he both liked and respected; and they had been rewarding, if not financially then at least in terms of fame and decorations. But it was inevitable that two decades of often extreme pressure and responsibility for other men's lives must exact a physical and mental toll. With the benefit of hindsight, we can now conclude that, by 1926, Stenhouse was almost certainly suffering from post-traumatic stress disorder – and there is equally little doubt that his condition was rendered even more debilitating by his recurrent bouts of severe depression. What is more surprising is that he continued to function as well as he did for so long.

★   ★   ★

Writing in 1937 of the psychological challenges of polar exploration, Teddy Evans noted, 'During the winter darkness one has to be constantly watching one's subordinates.'[50] While it is easy for us to smile at Evans' implicit suggestion that officers and gentlemen were less prone to the onset of psychological problems than foremast hands, Phillip Law, with almost twenty years of continuous Antarctic service under his belt, would have understood Evans' point of view. He was convinced that much trouble could be avoided at polar stations if only men with 'a reasonable measure' of intelligence and education were selected for service:

> Such men seem to have more flexible minds and fewer rigid prejudices. They have wider interests and are not easily bored. Their inner resources are greater, and they are more self-sufficient. Above all, they have the sense to analyse situations, and to use their minds to control their reactions.[51]

He also believed that a team member with a lower level of education was far more likely to develop a social or intellectual inferiority complex and that such a man might:

> ... tend to be aggressive and difficult in his relations with other men, and therefore become unpopular. This increases his sense of inferiority and the size of the chip on his shoulder, which makes him even more unpopular. There is thus a descending spiral of deterioration in his morale, often accompanied by a developing persecution complex.[52]

This observation, based on extensive experience, makes the case of Andrew Taylor all the more interesting.

As an engineering graduate, senior surveyor and, during its second year, overall field commander of Operation Tabarin, Taylor would not appear to have been an obvious candidate for social or intellectual inferiority complexes, but his diaries and memoranda make it very clear that he suffered just the kind of 'descending spiral' described by Law. Whereas Jimmy Marr, the expedition's first commander, had shown a willingness to give his men the benefit of the doubt and to overlook even their more irritating peccadilloes, Taylor made copious and often highly critical notes on the expedition's personnel, beginning long before he assumed command.

Few of the men would have felt flattered by the vignettes that he committed to paper, but by far the most damning remarks were reserved for Tom Berry, the cook: 'His addiction to liquor is such that he cannot be trusted with its charge … His inquisitiveness knows no bounds, and his knowledge of manners stops at the table.'[53] At a disciplinary interview held on 24 May 1945, Taylor advised Berry that, henceforth, all alcohol would be removed from his control; that he would be denied access to the radio cabin in order to prevent his reading confidential messages; and that any further instances of indiscipline would be considered 'tantamount to mutinous behaviour' and be reported to the governor, whose intervention 'might delay his return to England for some time'.[54] While many expeditions have suffered interpersonal conflict, Taylor's references to mutiny and jail are quite exceptional.

Perhaps the individual most affected by this discord was Taylor himself, as he made clear in the autobiographical element of his Private Report on Personnel:

> When I took on this job, I thought it would be an easy one as long as one treated the men fairly: but as someone has remarked, 'There are some horses to whom you cannot feed oats' – and there are some people who look upon fairness and decency as weakness. I had not run against any of that particular stripe before, and it is obvious that my tactics with them must alter … Moods of depression seem to be settling over me with increasing frequency, and though largely due to my physical condition being not quite what it should be, they are also due to the sense of frustration I feel in having pleased neither party concerned. However, one can but do one's best.[55]

Throughout his two years with Operation Tabarin, Taylor spent long hours at the typewriter, working on the expedition's official diary during the day and on his personal journal in the evenings 'by way of recreation'.[56] 'His style is very readable,' noted David James, the assistant surveyor, 'and this *magnum opus* is now beginning to assume the dimensions of *Gone with the Wind*.'[57] But Eric Back, the medical officer, believed that Taylor's commitment to recording the expedition's activities resulted from something more complex than a simple love of writing:

> He was known as 'Quadruplicate Andy' ... his doctrine was, 'If you put it down in writing and in quadruplicate, nobody can lose it' and, therefore, that if you've done anything, you'll get the credit for it. If you don't write it down, somebody else will get the credit for it.[58]

It seems, therefore, that over time the stress of Taylor's responsibilities, his feelings of insecurity regarding his own position, and the strain of a divided command festered to become something akin to the kind of persecution complex alluded to by Law.

The passage of time did nothing to heal his wounds, whether real or imagined. If anything, his resentment grew and later disappointments, including his failure to qualify for an army pension, increased his anger still further – a trend revealed in the fact that many of his more acerbic remarks regarding Operation Tabarin were uttered decades after the end of the expedition, including his cry, made in 1987, that he had been treated like 'a dog on that tour'.[59]

Depressed and disillusioned, he became more and more embittered, and he would go on to develop a firm conviction that his services in the Antarctic had not been properly recognised. In private, he would also belittle his predecessor's work, accuse him of alcoholism[60] and bemoan the fact that, in his eyes at least, rewards had been lavished upon Marr while he had been completely neglected. In fact, besides the Polar Medal, which was also awarded to Taylor, Marr received no distinction of any kind for his leadership of Operation Tabarin or for his many years of work in the Antarctic. Taylor, on the other hand, was decorated with the Order of Canada – one of his nation's highest honours – albeit not until 1986.

★ ★ ★

Given the hardships inseparable from life in the Antarctic and the range of physiological, psychological and psychosocial conditions that it can give rise to, we might anticipate that suicide constitutes a high risk among Antarctic explorers. In fact, the opposite appears to be true. If we discount the death of Captain Lawrence Oates, the circumstances of which are so well known and which did not result from any form of mental illness, in the years since the first Heroic Age British expedition crossed the Antarctic Circle on 23 January 1899, only one member of a British expedition has deliberately taken his own life while serving in the Antarctic or sub-Antarctic. Between the launch of Mawson's expedition in 1911 and the present day, only one Australian has committed suicide and no New Zealanders have done so in the sixty or so years since their nation became active in the region.

An obvious explanation for this seeming anomaly is the fact that, for the vast majority of those who volunteer to undertake it, exploration is a deeply pleasurable and satisfying experience. According to Henry Guly, who served with the BAS Medical Unit and who has written extensively on the medical aspects of Heroic Age exploration, 'Despite the horrendous events that undoubtedly occurred, the majority of experiences were probably good, and the number of explorers who returned a second or third time speaks for itself.'[61] Mawson, himself a serial explorer, described the lure of Antarctica very well in his preface to *The Home of the Blizzard*:

> Once more a man in the world of men, lulled in the easy repose of routine, and performing the ordinary duties of a workaday world, old emotions awakened, the grand sweet days returned in irresistible glamour, far away 'voices' called.[62]

If, then, the challenges of Antarctica are manifold, so too are its attractions – and these attractions take different forms for different people. For some, as we have seen, it is the challenges themselves – and, crucially, the ability of the individual to overcome them – that appeal most powerfully. Indeed, if the obstacles turn out to be less demanding than expected, the disappointment can weigh very heavily. For others, it is the prospect of becoming the first human being to see and set foot within a virgin landscape. Looking into the distance from the 396m summit of Cape Longing, on the eastern edge of the Graham Land Peninsula, Andrew Taylor noted, 'On so beautiful a day, it was an inspiring view, none the less so from the knowledge that it was one which no one else had ever enjoyed since time began.[63] On the same day, and just a handful of miles to the north of Taylor's position, David James described a similar experience, remarking, 'It was a strange feeling on such a warm and sunny day to approach this cliff so remote and yet so like any cliff at home, to reflect that its peace had never been broken before.'[64]

Linked to what, in many cases, is undoubtedly a highly charged reaction to the privilege of precedence, is what Ron Roberts has described as the 'cosmic perspective' of Antarctic exploration.[65] This perspective is expressed through the 'reflections on the beauty, spiritual significance and grandness of nature' that are to be found in the personal accounts of many explorers: it is their version of Wordsworth's 'emotion recollected in tranquillity'. On first setting foot on the continent in the company of Ernest Joyce, Stenhouse noted that they 'were rewarded by a sight which Joyce admitted as being the grandest he had ever witnessed ... Looking down into that wonderful picture one realised, a little, the "Eternalness" of things.'[66] Shackleton expressed something similar, though his effusion was a response not only to the sublime beauties that he had witnessed, but also to the fact that he and his men had survived seemingly insurmountable odds:

> In memories we were rich. We had pierced the veneer of outside things. We had 'suffered, starved and triumphed, grovelled down yet grasped at glory, grown bigger in the bigness of the whole'. We had seen God in His splendours, heard the text that Nature renders. We had reached the naked soul of man.[67]

Nor should we undervalue the more prosaic pleasures of exploration – as Phillip Law recognised:

> The existence of an expedition member is socially uncomplicated. No such simplified existence is possible in a civilised community. There is no money, and therefore no financial anxiety. One has no concern about social status – the Joneses have been left far behind – and any petty inferiorities of dress, possessions and social graces cease to have significance. Nor does one have to balance delicately the rival obligations to one's wife, one's children, one's job, one's garden and one's sporting acquaintances.[68]

Law believed that this lack of distractions can be beneficial, not only because it means that more work can be achieved – an obvious concern for a director of research expeditions – but also because the results of that work, and the effort involved in completing it, are more immediately observable to the community as a whole:

A good man thus experiences a double sense of accomplishment – the realisation of having done his job well, and the gratification of knowing that his competence has been appreciated by his fellows (a gratification not always forthcoming in an urban community).[69]

Naturally, there are cases where the opposite has been true. For instance, there is clear evidence that Jimmy Marr, a highly experienced marine zoologist and already a holder of the Polar Medal when he was appointed to the command of Operation Tabarin, tortured himself for not having fulfilled the brief given to him by his expedition committee. Instructed to build Base A at Hope Bay, ice conditions and the caution of the ships' captains made this impossible and he was forced to locate it instead at Port Lockroy, off the western edge of the peninsula. This circumstance, which he had very little ability to influence, rendered much of the planned exploratory and scientific work of the expedition impossible to achieve. Unable to accept what he saw increasingly as a personal failure, Marr grew ever more anxious and depressed. By February 1945 his condition had deteriorated to such a degree that Dr Eric Back expressed serious concern at the risk of self-harm:

Lt-Cdr Marr is suffering from mental and physical exhaustion associated with depression. He requires very careful observation and treatment since suicide is not unknown in such cases … He has a marked tremor, cannot sleep and worries a great deal. He is the type of man who will not give in but keeps on and on until he is exhausted. Under the circumstances I feel it is essential that he should leave the Antarctic at once.[70]

Andrew Taylor also admitted to being 'extremely concerned'[71] and it was fortunate that good shipping links with the Falkland Islands made it possible for Marr to be evacuated. Having voluntarily resigned his command, he left the Antarctic on board HMS *William Scoresby* on 9 February, never to return.

Although details are fairly scanty, Arthur Farrant seems to have experienced feelings similar to those of both Marr and Taylor: of failure on the one hand, and isolation and distrust on the other. Worse still, he appears to have lacked the self-belief that enabled Taylor to function effectively even in the face of widespread disunity.

Originally appointed as diesel electric mechanic at FIDS Base B on Deception Island, the 38-year-old Farrant was described by his interviewer in November 1951 as an 'excellent type and with his 5 years' Naval experience should do well. K.I.V. [Keep in View] as potential Base Leader.'[72] A little over eight months later, the outgoing leader, Captain Edward Dacre Stroud of the Royal Marines, agreed that Farrant would be 'above suitable', but added the worrying caveat that this would be the case only 'with new staff. I have found him entirely satisfactory but he does not fit in with majority here.'[73] Ray Berry, the meteorological officer at Deception Island, thought this inability to integrate a result, primarily, of the disparity in the ages of the personnel: while Farrant was nearly 40, all his companions were in their early twenties. But he also noticed that, over time, the mechanic's withdrawal became somewhat paranoid, evidenced through his habit of jotting down the dots and dashes of outgoing Morse transmissions in case they contained any disparaging remarks about himself – dots and dashes that Berry believed would have been incomprehensible to Farrant, who possessed only the most rudimentary understanding of Morse.[74]

Stroud's recommendations were followed, at least in part, and certain members of the base personnel were transferred to other stations before Farrant was confirmed as the new base leader. But these changes produced only limited benefits and he continued to encounter serious problems. By the end of March 1953, he felt unable to cope any longer and, in a telegram dated the 26th, he asked the FIDS Secretary at Port Stanley to 'Please arrange my resignation as Base Leader here. Am unable to get co-operation from other members [on the] Base.'[75] The answer he received the following day was an unequivocal negative: 'Am not, repeat not, prepared to accept your resignation. Please discuss with Captain Johnston and Assistant Secretary.'[76]

It is curious to speculate on the conversation that ensued between Farrant and Captain Bill Johnston, master of the RRS *John Biscoe*, when the FIDS supply vessel touched at Deception Island shortly after this exchange. Remembered by one shipmate as 'a very cool character held in some esteem and also a certain amount of awe',[77] and by another as 'one of the calmest of people in emergencies',[78] what advice did the unflappable ice captain offer to the clearly emotional and testy Farrant? We will probably never know. What we do know is that after a further exchange of telegrams between Johnston and Port Stanley, Farrant was offered a change of scene in the form of a temporary sojourn at FIDS Base G, a small meteorological station at Admiralty Bay. But the respite was only temporary, and in April Farrant returned to Base B, this time as deputy base leader, with Ian Clarke as senior officer. The decision to send him back would prove to be tragically misguided.

Whatever his other flaws, in the preceding months Farrant had shown himself to be a highly competent and conscientious mechanic, working hard to bring the base's trio of decrepit diesel generators into a state approximating efficiency. However, on his return he found that, Sisyphus-like, he must start again from scratch. None of the generators worked and two had been completely dismantled in the period of his absence. According to Clarke, 'He set about, and within a week had one diesel generator operating, and a few weeks later a second was operative.' Clarke continued:

> Throughout the remainder of the year he has constantly maintained these two units which have needed a great deal of attention because of extremely worn parts and lack of replacement parts. He has always been most willing and co-operative in the normal activities of the Base and was the type of person who, on seeing a job needing to be done, would go ahead and do it. At times he seemed to prefer doing work on his own rather than ask for the assistance of the other Base members, and would always occupy his time with actual work rather than relax in some other form of occupation or pursuit ... He felt his responsibility as diesel mechanic very keenly and was not prone normally to so much as allow other Base members to start them up in case something went wrong.[79]

This obsessive nursing of the temperamental generators continued, day in, day out, for the next seven months. More importantly, it became clear that Farrant had begun to blame himself for the poor condition of the machinery. 'I knew that he was worried about the diesel engines and about spare parts that he had neglected to order,' recalled Frank Hall, the assistant meteorologist:

On my suggesting that he had done a good job and had nothing to worry about, he said that I would see when the *John Biscoe* came in. I imagined that he was implying that he would be reprimanded for the state of the engines.[80]

Despite the reassurance of his companions, guilt and anxiety continued to gnaw at Farrant's peace of mind, worsening as the day of the *Biscoe*'s next visit grew ever closer. By 16 November, he could take no more and, approaching Clarke, he 'asked me to send through his resignation … The matter was discussed and he agreed to await the arrival of the *John Biscoe* and discuss it with the Master.'[81]

But Farrant would not wait for the reprimand that he had by now convinced himself was inevitable. On the evening of the 17th, as the *John Biscoe* again tied up in Whalers Bay, he helped to push out a dinghy heading to the ship to collect the long-awaited mail. Rather than clamber into the boat, he cheerfully waved it off and then returned to the base hut. When the boat returned he assisted in carrying the postbags up to the base. According to Arthur Lewis, the relief meteorological officer:

> We all chatted for a while in the Meteorological Office in the Base Hut whilst the mail was being sorted out, then all of us except Farrant went to the kitchen for a cup of tea. On returning to the Met. Office, I met Farrant coming out carrying his mail and I asked if he had all the letters he wanted. He replied that he had. This was the last time I saw Farrant.[82]

At 7.50 p.m., Bernard Taylor, the radio operator, was surprised to find that the normally efficient Farrant had failed to start the generators in time for the routine wireless transmission to Port Stanley. During a quick search of the base, he reported hearing what he thought to be 'the back door slamming to',[83] but then proceeded to the radio room to make the transmission using the emergency set. Although no one felt any particular cause for concern, at about 8.30 p.m. Douglas Mumford, the new radio operator, decided to make a more comprehensive search for Farrant. He spent around fifty minutes walking round the hut, the outbuildings and the oil tanks before taking a last look behind the main building. It was there that he found the missing mechanic, 'lying there on his back with one arm across his chest and the other flung out on the ground'.[84]

The next morning, the Governor of the Falkland Islands, Sir Miles Clifford – the man who had interviewed Farrant two years earlier – received a terse telegram from Johnston: 'Urgent. Farrant shot himself through head shortly after our arrival last night and died instantaneously. Please instruct.'[85] Clifford ordered the captain to conduct an immediate inquest and to then bury Farrant's body in the small whalers' cemetery on the island. Meanwhile, he forwarded the news to the Secretary of State for the Colonies and, ultimately, to Farrant's family. In the circumstances, the result of the inquest was never in doubt: 'Verdict suicide while of unsound mind. Weapon used was .45 Webley Service Revolver, shot through mouth which penetrated brain and skull.'[86]

A note found in Farrant's left hand consisted of nothing more than a briefly worded apology that shed no light on the reasons for his actions, and when he wrote to the Secretary of State on 30 December Clifford could only 'emphasise that no complaint had or has been made of his work which was satisfactory in every respect and that the cause of his death remains a complete mystery'.[87] Of course, the governor was not being entirely candid, as he knew full well that Farrant had experienced a series of problems – or, perhaps more accurately, repeated instances of the same problem – throughout his period of service with FIDS. Unable to cope, he had twice attempted to resign and on both occasions, he had been dissuaded. It seems probable, therefore, that in his report Clifford decided to be economical with the truth in order to avoid potentially awkward questions regarding the manner in which he and his subordinates had handled Farrant's case. Perhaps, too, he wondered whether the tragedy could have been averted had he accepted Farrant's resignation, as his predecessor, Sir Allan Cardinall, had accepted Marr's in February 1945.[88]

★ ★ ★

Even those for whom exploration turns out to be an overwhelmingly positive experience can suffer from feelings of anti-climax, frustration and even depression – particularly on their return home. While many Heroic Age veterans such as Priestley, Mawson, Frank Debenham and Teddy Evans went on to distinguished careers in their chosen fields, an equal number seemed to lose their way entirely. Shackleton burst his heart chasing a dream with sad, despairing tenacity; Frank Wild, the veteran of more Antarctic expeditions than any man of his generation, ended his life as a drunk; and Frank Bickerton, when not serving with the RFC and later the RAF, wandered from job to job, apparently directionless.

Of course, Bickerton was in no way unique and most veterans served in the armed forces soon after returning from the Antarctic, often in combat roles and sometimes with great distinction, and it seems probable that these experiences further complicated their relationship with everyday life. As Guly has remarked, 'To have achieved so much by a young age and to feel that nothing else you do will have the same excitement or interest must be dispiriting.'[89] This being the case, it seems reasonable to assume that, for some, their desire to return to the Antarctic was as much a product of their need to once again feel the gratification and accomplishment referred to by Law as it was the result of a love for the place itself.

This certainly appears to have been the case with Bertram Armytage, who experienced intense feelings of anti-climax and futility on his return from the *Nimrod* Expedition. On 12 March 1910, he donned his full dinner dress, lay down on a counterpane removed from his bed, placed two pillows beneath his head and then blew out his brains with a Colt patent automatic revolver. Like Farrant, he seems not to have particularly enjoyed his period in the Antarctic – he, too, found it difficult to integrate – but the fact that he placed his Polar Medal and his South African campaign medals where he could see them when he pulled the trigger appears to indicate that he counted these episodes as the highlights of his career. 'I have little or no doubt,' Raymond Priestley wrote shortly after hearing the news:

> … that if any of us had seen him and had pointed him out some way in which he could do useful exploring even in a small way it would have made all the difference to him. He was plainly much oppressed by the idea that he was no use in the world. He was a peculiar chap, very introspective but one of the best.[90]

Given the array of mental illnesses that Antarctic explorers have suffered – and that have been described in detail from the very earliest expeditions onwards – it seems obvious that expedition organisers will ask whether there are types of personality that are particularly well suited to the life of an explorer and, contrariwise, whether there are character traits that can and should be identified as key indicators of risk. Are there individuals who, when placed in such extreme circumstances, are much more likely to suffer what Cherry-Garrard described, in his own case, as 'an inevitable breakdown'?[91]

When it came to judging an applicant's character and overall fitness for exploratory work, for many years expedition leaders really had little choice but to rely on their own shrewdness and insight. Of course, this need for self-reliance did not necessarily pose a problem. Shackleton, for instance, was so confident in his ability to gauge a man's qualities that some candidates found themselves appointed or rejected on the basis of interviews lasting no more than a few minutes. Like his illustrious predecessor, Bunny Fuchs eschewed any form of psychological profiling and he even asserted that the 'idea of taking a psychiatrist on a polar expedition hardly bears thinking about'.[92] To some medical professionals like Rainer Goldsmith, the man recruited as medical officer and physiologist for the Advance Party of the CTAE, this refusal to adopt more objective means of assessing character seemed both extraordinarily old-fashioned and short-sighted. According to Goldsmith:

> [Fuchs] took people, generally, who wanted to go and that was his only criterion. He didn't ask anything about whether you got on with people or whether you had schizophrenia or depressions … We suggested to him that it might be a good idea to have some sort of psychological profile or something to help select people. But he was dead against this – dead against it! He knew exactly who to choose: 'I know who to choose! If I like somebody then I'll choose him'.[93]

In fact, Fuchs was far from being oblivious to the need for understanding a man's psychological fitness for exploration, stating, 'Emotional stability governs both the physical and mental factors brought into play during any tests of endurance.'[94] But while he considered psychology to be important, 'it did not mean that the men should be subjected to analysis'.

Derek Williams remembered discussing with Fuchs the type of man that he thought best suited to expedition work:

> He sought to choose, and he told me this, calm equable people – people who were undramatic, phlegmatic and, it goes without saying, unimaginative and less critical – didn't think too much, didn't brood. And people who didn't

brood were optimistic, cheerful and above all steady, stable people … they were phlegmatic, optimistic and remained as cheerful as they could under the circumstances.[95]

Such views would have chimed well with those of many expedition leaders from all periods. Mawson, for instance, believed that the 'first consideration in the choice of men for a polar campaign should be the moral quality',[96] while Shackleton asserted that the most important qualities for exploration included optimism, patience, physical endurance, idealism, courage and good fellowship.[97] In more recent years, Phillip Law, Fuchs's contemporary, also argued that, in the selection of personnel, 'Character, "guts" and "stickability" are basically essential'.[98]

Although Goldsmith was highly critical of what he considered to be Fuchs's amateurish and anachronistic approach to recruitment, in fairness to Fuchs, the kind of profiling that Goldsmith advocated was still in its infancy in the early 1950s, and its application to the selection of personnel for the polar regions practically unheard of. This began to change only in 1956, when the US Navy trialled a new screening programme for the selection of the thirty-nine men who would overwinter at its planned IGY Scientific Station at Gould Bay on the Weddell Sea coast. This exercise would mark the commencement of a long-term programme of personality testing intended to 'screen in' and 'screen out' those individuals most suitable and least suitable for the challenges of Antarctic exploration. It would also take on a new relevance when consideration began to be given to the challenges of space exploration. These studies found that the 'ideal candidates for long-duration missions in isolated and confined extreme environments have the following characteristics: military service, low levels of neuroticism, extraversion and conscientiousness, and a low desire for affection from others'.[99] The similarities between these traits and those identified by the expedition leaders could hardly be more marked.

Given that Fuchs served as Director of FIDS and its replacement, BAS, from 1958 to 1973, it's not terribly surprising that the organisation has continued to reject psychological testing when recruiting personnel, relying instead upon the expertise and judgement of its staff to determine the fitness of candidates. And perhaps it is no coincidence that it was not until 1999, the year of Fuchs's death, that BAS launched its Selection of Antarctic Personnel (SOAP) project in order to:

... investigate whether standard psychological tests can predict how people actually will adapt to and cope with winter life in Antarctica, and to determine whether the SOAP battery of psychological tests improves the validity of the selection process.[100]

Although the published findings suggested that 'in the future, the tests in the SOAP battery and perhaps other, similar measures, may contribute to improvements in selecting out and selecting in candidates for appointments at Antarctic stations',[101] these recommendations were not adopted and no further work has been commissioned. In the words of Peter Marquis, one of the report's authors, BAS 'did not go ahead and use such things ... [as] present procedures [are] deemed as good as other nations' success, failure rates etc'.[102]

While it is tempting to laugh at the arbitrary recruitment techniques of the Heroic Age – and, indeed, to dismiss BAS's rejection of psychological testing as some kind of misguided homage to its first director – the marked similarities in the 'ideal characteristics' identified by everyone from Shackleton and Scott at the beginning of the twentieth century to the US Antarctic Program's psychologists at its end must lend credibility to the idea that individuals with certain personality traits are more suited to Antarctic exploration than those without. Nor should the failure of those traits to act as a talisman against psychological breakdown be allowed to undermine that credibility. As Lawrence A. Palinkas and Peter Suedfeld have pointed out, while the vast majority of individuals who volunteer for polar exploration are highly motivated and enthusiastic, these traits constitute:

... weak prospective predictors of behaviour and performance during the winter because such performance is affected more by the situational characteristics of isolation, confinement, and extreme environments than by stable traits of individuals.[103]

Put more simply, the unique combination of social and environmental factors at play on any Antarctic base are likely to test even the most well-balanced individual in ways he or she could never imagine and there exists no mechanism capable of predicting their reactions accurately.

BAS's selection processes would not seem alien to the Heroic Age leaders – but those processes have been very largely successful, with the personnel at

British bases tending to cohere to a remarkable degree. As Phillip Law once remarked of the interview process, 'Once settled in a chair with a cigarette, and lulled with small talk until his nervousness subsides, the average man will blithely bring out all you want to know and keep on talking, often to his considerable disadvantage.'[104] It is up to the skilled interviewer to take advantage of this frankness.

Crucially, Law also recognised the need for pragmatism in the selection process, 'When the only healthy, qualified and capable applicant is of doubtful emotional stability, we sometimes have no alternative but to send the man, warn his leader, and keep our fingers crossed.'[105] Given the unpredictability of living and working in the Antarctic, it is not very surprising that the fingers of every expedition leader have remained firmly crossed from the time of the very earliest expeditions to the present day.

The most iconic of all Antarctic monuments: the cross erected to the memory of Scott's Polar Party on Observation Hill, 22 January 1913. (Photo by Chris Arcus © Antarctica New Zealand Pictorial Collection, Image 25356, 2001–02)

'Eagle House', the Falkland Islands Dependencies Survey's base at Hope Bay. Deep snow drifts have often made escape from burning buildings particularly difficult. Two men died when Eagle House was destroyed by fire in November 1948. (Courtesy of Justin Marshall)

The surviving members of the Eagle House Party on board the RRS *John Biscoe*. Left to right: Frank Elliott, John O'Hare, Brian Jefford, Stephen O'Neill, Bill Sladen. (British Antarctic Survey Archives Service, ref. AD6/19/2/BM14. © Natural Environment Research Council. Photo by R.S. Moss)

Crew from the *John Biscoe* erect permanent memorials to Oliver Burd and Mike Green, Hope Bay, 1949. The temporary crosses made by John O'Hare can be seen on the grave to the left. (British Antarctic Survey Archives Service, ref. AD6/19/2/BM183. © Natural Environment Research Council. Photo by R.S. Moss)

Depot laying during the austral summer of 1915–16. The figure in the foreground is Aeneas Mackintosh, who lost his life on 8 May 1916 during a premature attempt to cross the sea ice between Hut Point and Cape Evans. (Courtesy of Sarah Mantell)

The survivors of the Ross Sea Party and their rescuers on board the SY *Aurora*, January 1917. Left to right: Jack, Stevens, Richards, Wild, Gaze, Joyce, Cope, Shackleton and J.K. Davis. (Courtesy of Sarah Mantell)

A particularly gloomy (or particularly tongue-in-cheek) Midwinter's Day party at Signy base, 1957. Left to right: Gene Donnelly, Doug Bridger, Dave Statham, unknown (obscured), Derek Skilling, Robin Sherman and Stan Black. Statham and Black would die the following year. (British Antarctic Survey Archives Service, ref. AD6/19/3/D21. © Natural Environment Research Council. Photo by C.D. Scotland)

Base Y, Horseshoe Island, as it looked in 1958. (British Antarctic Survey Archives Service, ref. AD6/19/3/C/Y4. © Natural Environment Research Council. Photo by C.D. Scotland)

Memorial cross to Dave Statham, Stan Black and Geoff Stride on Beacon Head, Horseshoe Island. (British Antarctic Survey Archives Service, ref. AD6/19/2/Y10/1. © Natural Environment Research Council. Photo by E.R. McGowan)

Faraday Base personnel, 1982. Back row: John Coll, Len Airey (looking right), Graham Hurst, Martin Herbert (with flat cap), Roy Whitfield and Colin Morrell (off to right). Middle: Pete Salino (in checked shirt). Front row: Davey Burke, Kevin Ockleton, Ian Davies, Ambrose Morgan, Justin Koprowski and Andy Sweetman. (Courtesy of Pete Salino)

John Coll, Kevin Ockleton and Ambrose Morgan depart from Faraday on 13 July 1982, bound for Petermann Island. (Courtesy of Pete Salino)

The Argentine refuge hut on Petermann Island with the Graham Land coast in the background, photographed in October 1983, two months after the disappearance of Morgan, Ockleton and Coll. (Courtesy of Pete Salino)

Ironically, the least successful of all Heroic Age motorised vehicles is the only survivor. The motor-crawler used by Shackleton's Ross Sea Party is lifted aboard HMNZS *Endeavour* in 1957, ready for transportation to the Canterbury Museum in Christchurch. (Photo by F. Davidson © Antarctica New Zealand Pictorial Collection, Image 9238, 1957–58)

Seabee Max Kiel aboard his 34-tonne D8 Caterpillar tractor – a photograph taken shortly before both plunged into a crevasse while depot laying in Marie Byrd Land on 5 March 1956.

A D8 tractor disappears through the sea ice at Hut Point, 1956. Seabee Richard T. Williams died in a similar accident on 6 January 1956. (Photo by Kim Westerskov © Antarctica New Zealand Pictorial Collection, Image 53, 1956–58)

Sno-Cats of the New Zealand field parties, 1959–60. The ex-Commonwealth Trans-Antarctic Expedition vehicle *County of Kent* is parked facing away from the photographer. (Photo by Jim Lowery ©Antarctica New Zealand Pictorial Collection, Image 45, 1960–61)

County of Kent upside down in a crevasse near Cape Selborne, 19 November 1959. The driver, Tom Couzens, was killed instantly. (Courtesy of Derek Gunn)

The Cape Selborne crevasse in which Couzens died. The trench in the foreground was cut to enable rescuers to lift the injured personnel and Couzens' body. (© Antarctica New Zealand Pictorial Collection, Image 39631, 1959–60)

A survivor of the New Zealand Sno-Cat accident being evacuated, 20 November 1959. Bernie Gunn and Jim Lowery both sustained broken backs; Lowery also lost his feet to frostbite. (Courtesy of Derek Gunn)

New Zealand geologist
Bernie Gunn, who spent
twenty-two hours in
the mangled wreckage
of *County of Kent*.
(Courtesy of Derek
Gunn)

Unveiling a memorial to
Tom Couzens at Scott
Base on Ross Island
during the 1961–62
season. (© Antarctica
New Zealand Pictorial
Collection, Image
10009, 1961–62)

British survey party in front of a Studebaker Weasel at the Pyramid Rocks in the Tottan Mountains, October 1965. Left to right: Rod Rhys Jones, George Beebe, Patrick Haynes, Dai Wild, Lewes Juckes, Jeremy Bailey, Ian Ross, Geoff Lovegrove, Brian Porter, John Wilson. (Courtesy of Roderick Rhys Jones)

A Weasel, sledges and dogs in a configuration similar to that adopted by the ill-fated depot-laying party on 11 October 1965. (British Antarctic Survey Archives Service, ref. AD6/19/3/Tv14. © Natural Environment Research Council. Photo by Dai Wild)

Jeremy Bailey asks the way south. Bailey was driver of the Bombardier Muskeg on 11 October 1965. (Courtesy of Brian Dorsett-Bailey)

The wreckage of the Muskeg, pinned between the walls of a crevasse near the Milorgknausane nunataks on 11 October 1965. All three occupants died. (British Antarctic Survey Archives Service, ref. AD6/2Z/1965/H. © Natural Environment Research Council. Photo by D. Beebe)

A Muskeg with the roll cage fitted to British vehicles after the disaster of October 1965. (British Antarctic Survey Archives Service, ref. AD6/19/3/ Tv17. © Natural Environment Research Council. Photo by Alistair MacQuarrie)

McCallum Pass and the Shambles Glacier, where John Anderson and Robert Atkinson were killed on 16 May 1981 when their snowmobile fell into a hidden crevasse. (British Antarctic Survey Archives Service, ref. AD6/19/5/11/1. © Natural Environment Research Council. Photo by Stephen Hinde)

Commander J.R. Stenhouse on the bridge of the RRS *Discovery* during the National Oceanographic Expedition of 1925–27. A highly decorated war hero, Stenhouse eventually came close to a complete mental breakdown as a result of the accumulated pressures of his Antarctic and wartime service. (Courtesy of Sarah Mantell)

FIDS base hut on Deception Island in the South Shetland Islands. Arthur Farrant shot himself behind this hut on 17 November 1953. (British Antarctic Survey Archives Service, ref. AD6/19/2/B64/19. © Natural Environment Research Council. Photo by Edward Dacre Stroud)

A rare photograph of the Vickers REP monoplane purchased by Douglas Mawson for use during his Australasian Antarctic Expedition. On 5 October 1911, Frank Wild and Hugh Watkins came close to becoming the first casualties of Antarctic aviation when the monoplane crashed to Earth during a test flight in Adelaide. (Author's collection)

On 26 December 1929 Norwegian pilot Leif Lier (pictured) and his observer, Dr Ingvald Schreiner, became the first men to die in an aircraft accident in the Antarctic. Their aeroplane disappeared during a flight from the whaling factory ship, *Kosmos*.

Three of the survivors of *George I*, in the sickbay of USS *Pine Island*, 13 January 1947. Left to right: M.A. Long, chief pharmacist's mate (not in the crash); Owen McCarty, chief photographer's mate; James M. 'Robbie' Robbins, aviation radioman; William Warr, aviation machinist's mate. (Official US Navy photograph)

A stamp issued to commemorate the life and death of André Prud'homme, an experienced meteorologist who disappeared on 7 January 1959 while undertaking routine observations at France's Dumont D'Urville Station on Petrel Island.

The last known photograph of Shin Fukushima, whose frozen corpse was discovered eight years after he disappeared during a blizzard at Japan's Syowa Station on East Ongul Island in October 1960. (Photo by Murakoshi © National Institute of Polar Research, Japan)

Each year the personnel at Syowa Station gather at Fukushima's memorial cairn to pray that that they will avoid his fate. (© National Institute of Polar Research, Japan)

Top left: The first of the Heard Island party to die, Richard Hoseason drowned during an attempt to cross a beach at the foot of the Challenger Glacier, 26 May 1952. (Photo by Alan Campbell-Drury © Australian Antarctic Division, RS51967)

Top right: Alastair 'Jock' Forbes, who died of hypothermia when trying to traverse the Baudissen Glacier during the night of 26–27 May 1952. (Photo by Alan Campbell-Drury © Australian Antarctic Division, RS51965)

Left: The sole survivor: Lawrie Atkinson who, despite cold and shock, managed to live through a night in the open before walking and swimming back to the Australian winter quarters at Atlas Cove. (Photo by Alan Campbell-Drury © Australian Antarctic Division, RS51970)

Peter Lancaster Brown, an experienced outdoorsman, was highly critical of what he saw as the foolhardiness of Forbes' party. (Photo by Alan Campbell-Drury © Australian Antarctic Division, RS51971)

Unusually for an Antarctic memorial, during the summer months the concrete cross to Alastair Forbes and Richard Hoseason is surrounded not by snow and ice, but by the lush green cushion plant *Azorella selago*. (Courtesy of Bob Schmieder)

5

'SPECTACULAR DARING'

THE BIRTH OF ANTARCTIC AVIATION

On 24 June 1954, in a smoke-filled room on Queen Anne's Gate in London, Air Marshal Sir John Slessor took the chair at the inaugural meeting of the General Management Committee of the Commonwealth Trans-Antarctic Expedition. On the table in front of Slessor and his fellow committee members lay the embryonic plans for perhaps the most audacious of all British polar expeditions; plans that would require three ships, four aircraft, thirteen motor vehicles, and more than thirty men of four nations, excluding ships' crews. They would necessitate the establishment of three bases over the course of two full years in the Antarctic and would culminate in a gruelling journey of some 3,200km, from the Filchner Ice Shelf on the southern shores of the Weddell Sea, through uncharted mountain ranges and crevasse fields, across the 4,270m Polar Plateau via the South Pole, and then down the Ferrar Glacier to the sea ice of McMurdo Sound. And yet, despite the colossal logistical challenges that the fulfilment of such a plan would entail, Slessor declared that the most pressing problems to be faced by the expedition 'were not operational but financial'.[1]

It was an assertion that would have resonated with every aspiring polar explorer of the previous half-century, from the days immediately following the Sixth International Geographical Congress of 1895 to the beginning of the Second World War. In this period, practically all expeditions to the Antarctic were private enterprises, wholly reliant upon the generosity of learned bodies, such as the Royal Geographical Society and the Royal Society, whose geographical and scientific interests were self-evident, and upon the backing of private companies and individuals,

whose motivations were more varied and complex. Some sought personal aggrandisement through reflected glory and the naming of topographical features in their honour; some valued the advertising generated by corporate sponsorship; others anticipated profits generated more directly, perhaps by the exploitation of mineral deposits; and a few were driven by altruism or a frustrated sense of adventure that they now saw the opportunity to sate, albeit vicariously.

The success with which the various expeditions were able to tap these rich veins varied according to the personality and experience of the explorers themselves. Most effective of all was Shackleton, a self-publicist and fundraiser *sans pareil*. When seeking backing for his expeditions, the charming Anglo-Irishman excelled at playing on the egos and sensibilities of wealthy backers such as William Beardmore and Janet Stancomb-Wills; at obtaining sponsorship from companies who saw the potential of advertising through association; at drumming up popular support through the shrewd manipulation of the press; and at coercing a reluctant establishment to cough up additional funds through methods little short of moral blackmail.

His imaginative and occasionally morally ambivalent approach to fundraising was perhaps nowhere more apparent than in his use of technology. In the lead-up to the *Nimrod* Expedition, for example, his lightly modified Arrol-Johnston motor car probably did more to stir the interest of the newspapermen than any other single initiative, and the fact that the car failed almost completely in the Antarctic made no difference either to the enthusiasm of the general public or to Shackleton's willingness to make extravagant claims for the equally untried vehicles that he took on his *Endurance* Expedition.

One man who had noted with particular interest the publicity generated by Shackleton's motor car was Douglas Mawson. Mawson had served as physicist on the *Nimrod* Expedition and, when developing ideas for his own AAE, he had sought Shackleton's advice and help. Naturally, 'The Boss' had impressed upon him the value of novelty when seeking to capture the public imagination – and, in response, Mawson decided that his expedition would be the first to attempt powered flight in the Antarctic. His inspiration almost certainly came from the Antarctic balloon flights made during Scott's *Discovery* Expedition on 4 February 1902 and during Erich von Drygalski's *Gauss* Expedition two months later. Scott's balloon – quaintly named the *Eva* – had cost an extravagant £1,300 and, at the edge of the Great Ice Barrier, it had made two flights, reaching a maximum altitude of 244m. But the balloon had leaked and its further use was abandoned. Drygalski's ascent had been rather more successful, reaching 488m.

Given that the Wright brothers' first-ever powered flight had taken place only in December 1903 and that Louis Blériot had not succeeded in flying across the English Channel until July 1909, any experiment in aeronautics remained extremely dangerous, with early aviators routinely falling from the skies, either as a result of mechanical failure or lack of knowledge and experience. And, inevitably, flight in the polar regions was subject to even greater risks – as had been amply demonstrated in 1897 when, in an attempt to cross the North Pole in a balloon called the *Ornan*, the Swedish aeronaut Salomon Andrée and his two companions had died in miserable circumstances after they crash-landed on the sea ice, not far from Kvitøya. But no expedition to the Antarctic was devoid of danger and Mawson remained convinced that the benefits of a successful flight would more than outweigh the risks.

An obvious use for an aeroplane in the Antarctic would be spotting leads, or channels, in the sea ice wide enough for the expedition ship to push through but, since Mawson's machine would have to be transported in a crate, there would be little chance of utilising it in that way. Besides, the problems of launching an aeroplane from a ship wouldn't be seriously addressed until the exigencies of war led to systematic research under the auspices of the Royal Naval Air Service. Once assembled at the spot chosen for the expedition's winter quarters, however, it could be used for reconnaissance and survey work. According to *Flight* magazine, it might even be employed in a dramatic 'final dash for the pole',[2] though such a claim hardly fitted with the determinedly scientific objectives of the expedition.

The AAE's expedition staff of thirty was to be made up almost entirely of graduates from the universities of Adelaide, Sydney and Melbourne, but Mawson recognised that in Australia – a country that had not witnessed its first powered flight until Colin Defries' brief exploit at Sydney's Victoria Park Racecourse on 9 December 1909 – aviators were likely to prove rather thin on the ground. In making up the shortfall, he demonstrated a willingness to listen to the advice of friends and colleagues in England.

Kathleen Scott, wife of Captain Scott and herself an aviation enthusiast, assisted him not only in the choice of an aeroplane – an REP monoplane, which he purchased from Vickers for £955 4s 6d – but also in the selection of a pilot: Lieutenant Hugh Evelyn Watkins of the 3rd Battalion, Essex Regiment. Although a competent mechanic, Watkins would need the assistance of another engineer to maintain the machine in Antarctic conditions and the man selected for this role was Frank Bickerton, treasure hunter, friend of Aeneas Mackintosh of the *Nimrod* Expedition, and a recent graduate of London's City and Guilds (Technical) College, where he had been one of the first students to attend a series of lectures on the new science of aeronautics.[3]

The machine and its attendants arrived in Australia during September 1911, and preparations began immediately for a series of exhibition flights intended to thrill the pounds, shillings and pence out of the pockets of the crowds of spectators – just the kind of publicity-attracting spectacles that Shackleton advocated. The first flight was scheduled to take place at Cheltenham Racecourse in Adelaide on 5 October, with the Governor of South Australia as Watkins' volunteer passenger. Thereafter, daring members of the public could venture into the skies upon payment of a not inconsiderable £5, all proceeds dropping into the expedition's still disturbingly empty kitty.

Bickerton, Watkins and Frank Wild, the veteran English explorer, spent three days preparing the machine and Watkins took it up for the first time on 4 October. The monoplane performed well but, on landing, a wing struck a post and Bickerton spent much of the remainder of the day repairing the damage. At 6 a.m. on the 5th, Watkins decided to try one last preliminary ascent before the arrival of the fee-paying public. This time Wild occupied the front seat and, in a letter to a friend, he described what happened next:

> We got away beautifully and had got up to about 100ft [30.5m] when the left wing was caught in an air eddy and we came down like greased lightning, and struck the earth at over seventy miles an hour [113kph], the aeroplane turning over and pinning us both under it. It seemed a devil of a time before anybody came to help us, but really it was only about two minutes when Bickerton and half a dozen more lifted the wreck up and dragged us out.[4]

Clearly, Wild was not aware that Watkins had begun to experience difficulties almost as soon as they had taken off. To the spectators on the ground it had been obvious that the monoplane had side-slipped, rapidly losing altitude. It seemed that Watkins had recovered the situation, because

the aeroplane then climbed to around 46m before it struck the fatal eddies that Wild noted. In its aeronautics column, *The Times* regularly reported accidents like this: planes dropping from the clouds, folding up in mid-air or colliding, and all too often the pilots and their passengers were killed outright. Here, amazingly, both men survived. Badly bruised and shaken, Wild managed to walk to the jockeys' hospital unaided. Watkins's injuries were more serious but not life-threatening, the worst being a cracked sternum.

The aeroplane itself suffered the most devastating damage. The fragile wings had crumpled with the impact; the nose was bent; the tail section lay in pieces and, on closer inspection, Bickerton discovered that one of the engine's five cylinders had cracked. With the necessary spare parts and time, it might have been put back into 'flying order', but neither parts nor time were available. Although he made light of the accident when discussing it with reporters, calling it 'a small matter',[5] in reality Mawson was furious. Any hope of recouping the costs of the machine by exhibition flights had been forfeited as no one would pay £5 to see it trundle disconsolately along the ground. Worse still, if news of the accident were not handled skilfully, the expedition could become the butt of journalistic humour. Lastly, any hope of a pioneering Antarctic flight had now been permanently dashed.

Just one ray of hope penetrated the prevailing gloom. Ignorance regarding surface and wind conditions at the expedition's eventual landing point meant that it had never been certain that an Antarctic flight would be feasible and, in June, Mawson had ordered special runners and attachments from Vickers in order to facilitate conversion of the machine for the ground haulage of heavy supplies and equipment.[6] Now he decided that Bickerton should turn the mass of bent wreckage into a functioning 'air tractor sledge', the bulk of the work to be completed in the Antarctic. Watkins, meanwhile, would return to England, any dream he might have entertained of becoming the first man to fly in the Antarctic even more thoroughly wrecked than the monoplane itself.[7]

Whatever his disappointment, however, he and Wild could count themselves lucky – they had, after all, missed by the merest whisker the rather more dubious distinction of becoming Antarctic aviation's very first casualties.

★   ★   ★

In the years following the crash on Adelaide Racecourse, the aeroplane evolved rapidly, largely due to its ever-expanding role during the war. The Royal Flying Corps, for example, possessed fewer than 100 aircraft when war broke out in August 1914; by November 1918 it had more than 30,000. Moreover, despite the initial scepticism of senior military commanders – in 1910, Field Marshal Sir William Nicholson, Chief of the Imperial General Staff, had dismissed military aviation as 'a useless and expensive fad'[8] – the RFC's functions had swelled to include artillery spotting, long-range bombing, ground strafing, massed aerial combat and even night patrols. By the war's end, aircraft could confidently be expected to take to the air in all ordinary weather conditions and to cover previously unimaginable distances without the need to land for refuelling or maintenance. In this particular set of circumstances, the aeroplane had, Frank Debenham told the Royal Geographical Society in December 1920, 'speedily reached a standard of efficiency that renders it available already for certain types of work in high latitudes'.[9] Unfortunately, he continued, the improved reliability, robustness and range of modern aircraft 'by themselves are not nearly enough to satisfy the polar traveller'.

The challenges facing any aspiring Antarctic aviator – then or now – can be divided into three main categories: topographical, navigational and meteorological. Of these, Debenham, who was not a pilot, considered the topographical to be the most problematic, in particular, the scarcity of suitable landing grounds. With the support of ship- or land-based reconnaissance parties, he believed it might be possible to identify, or even engineer, a sufficiently level area for take-offs and landings using wheels or skis. Ignoring for a moment the dangers resulting from localised changes in wind and visibility, a pilot setting off from such an airstrip could feel reasonably confident that he would be able to return to it and land safely 'after the lapse of the time taken up by any ordinary non-stop flight'.[10] However, the return to a landing site after a much longer period of absence, when surface conditions might have changed substantially, or an attempt to land in an area that had not previously been surveyed, would be very different propositions. 'I can state definitely,' Debenham told his audience:

The surface of snow- and ice-fields can never be relied upon to remain constant for a long period. The ground is normally covered with a patchwork of hard, medium, and soft drifts, comparable ... to a landing-ground consisting of alternate bands of hard rock, soft mud, and shifting sand. It would be impossible to distinguish the components of such a snow surface from above with any certainty, for the appearance presented would depend almost entirely upon the lighting up of the individual snowdrifts, and therefore upon the lie of crest and hollow with reference to the incident rays from the sun.[11]

It was a conclusion with which few experienced Antarctic aviators would argue – least of all those who have swept in to land on what they believed to be a smooth snowfield, only to discover on closer inspection that a trick of the light has hidden from view the serrated crests of iron-hard sastrugi or the gaping mouth of a crevasse.

Given the prevalence of these hazards, Debenham observed presciently that 'promiscuous landing upon the Antarctic land surfaces can only become safe when some device, such as the helicopter perhaps, enables the speed of landing to be radically decreased'.[12] In the meantime, in the interests of safety, wheeled and skied aircraft should only be operated between known landing grounds where ground personnel could maintain the surface, and indicate its suitability (or unsuitability) through the use of flares or other signals.

Where Debenham felt much less sceptical was in the use of seaplanes. These, he believed, would be invaluable as an auxiliary for plotting coastlines and, if included in the equipment of an oceanographic expedition, 'might add considerably, not only to speed of manoeuvre in pack-infested waters, but to the chances of survival of a beset ship'.[13]

For his part, and despite the near destruction of his de Havilland Beaver when he descended onto a field of sastrugi during the Commonwealth Trans-Antarctic Expedition,[14] Squadron Leader John Claydon believed that successful polar aviation 'depends primarily on navigation'.[15] Unfortunately, successful aerial navigation is perhaps nowhere more difficult than in the skies above Antarctica, where its three key elements – identification of the desired direction, steering and the determination of position at any given moment – are all made particularly difficult by the unique phenomena to be found at high latitudes and by the fact that, until late in the twentieth century, the maps of Antarctica were both incomplete and unreliable, with major features such as coastlines, glaciers and mountain ranges either unmarked or marked inaccurately.

The close proximity of the Magnetic Pole, and the fact that the pole does not remain permanently fixed, render magnetic compasses highly unreliable, with the result that, until the advent of satellite navigation, the polar pilot was forced to rely to an extraordinary degree on dead reckoning and the use of the sextant. Prior to the development of lightweight gyroscopic compasses, he might also use the 'directional gyro', an instrument that is immune to the influences that so affect the magnetic compass and reads the exact heading of the aeroplane, following it without lag no matter what the speed of the turns made. Although the directional gyro must initially be set by the magnetic compass, and requires checking every twenty minutes or so in order to correct the small errors to which it is prone, it was still, in the opinion of pioneering Arctic pilot and historian of polar aviation, John Grierson, 'the most valuable instrument produced since the science of "blind flying", of piloting without a visible horizon, began'.[16]

In the second half of the twentieth century, increased confidence could be placed in gyro compasses – but, while gyro compasses are not affected by magnetism, they are influenced by friction, air resistance and the effects of the Earth's rotation. Aviators could make corrections using astro and radio navigation, but here, too, they faced serious problems, as astro navigation is rendered impossible by dense cloud cover (a common phenomenon in Antarctica, particularly during the spring and early summer when most flying takes place), and radio signals are interrupted by equally common magnetic storms. The time-consuming and skilled process of plotting a position through the use of astronomical observations also required that pilots be accompanied by an experienced navigator – a requirement that many expeditions struggled to meet.

So far as meteorology is concerned, the Antarctic pilot faces a range of hazards, many of which interact with each other to create an extraordinarily dynamic environment in which to operate. Antarctic winds, for instance, are the strongest surface winds to be encountered anywhere in the world, often travelling at immense speed and carrying vast amounts of drift snow blown from the surface of the Polar Plateau. These blizzards can start with remarkably little warning and then last for anything between a few hours and a few days, though they are most frequent during winter and spring.

Most dangerous of all, though, are the white-outs, which occur when surface features are completely covered with snow and the sun is obscured. In these conditions, light rays bounce backwards and forward between the snow surface and the clouds, eliminating all shadow and creating an intense glare; the horizon disappears, and the landscape and sky blend to form an unbroken and utterly disorienting expanse of white. It becomes impossible to distinguish landmarks or contours, or to determine distance or height from the ground – an experience that Richard E. Byrd memorably likened to 'flying in a bowl of milk'.[17] Visibility can also be diminished by the effects of the low temperatures, with any airborne moisture freezing on contact with the glass or Plexiglas of cockpit windscreens. Taken in the round, Lincoln Ellsworth thought 'the weather problem was the greatest to be faced in relation to the use of aeroplanes in the Antarctic'.[18]

★ ★ ★

The discoveries of the expeditions launched during the first quarter of the twentieth century meant that many of these challenges were understood long before Antarctic aviation became, in terms of suitable machines, a viable proposition. And yet it was, in the opinion of Robert Rudmose-Brown, 'inevitable that aviation should be tried in high latitudes, if for no other reason than its spectacular daring'.[19] The purposes of such aviation would be threefold: exploratory, commercial and logistical.

Exploratory and commercial flying began almost simultaneously. In 1920, John Lachlan Cope, a veteran of Shackleton's Ross Sea party of 1914–17, launched his grandly named British Imperial Antarctic Expedition, which included in its objectives a circumnavigation of Antarctica (using Scott's old ship, *Terra Nova*); a continuation of Nordenskjöld's survey of the eastern coastline and outlying islands of the Antarctic Peninsula; and, most ambitious of all, not only the first powered flight in the Antarctic but also the first flight over the Geographic South Pole. According to the expedition's Australian second in command, Captain Hubert Wilkins MC, for this last exploit, 'We had ... twelve airplanes – a gift from the Royal Air Force Disposal Board, old wartime stock which we intended to use in relays, abandoning more than half of them en route.'[20]

Given the utter chaos and incompetence that seemed to be inherent parts of the expedition, Cope's abject failure to raise the necessary £100,000 almost certainly saved lives, and his wildly ambitious venture eventually dwindled to little more than a largely forgotten but fascinating footnote to the history of Antarctic exploration.[21]

Despite the thinly veiled contempt with which certain of Cope's men viewed Wilkins – one tersely remarked that, at a crucial moment in the expedition, he 'declared that his intention had been and still was to return home by a whaler if by chance a catcher called to see us before leaving at the end of the whaling season'[22] – the Australian's interest in Antarctic aviation never wavered. On returning to New York after his ignominious

retreat from Graham Land, he planned to accompany Norwegian whalers to Port Lockroy on the western side of the Antarctic Peninsula, and from there to use two Junker mono-wing seaplanes to make flights 'as far as possible with the machines available' during the 1921–22 whaling season.[23]

When this scheme, too, came to nothing, he instead opted to join Shackleton's *Quest* Expedition, with the intention of making flights along the peninsula and down the Weddell Sea coast. But once again his plans went awry and the aeroplane that had been transported by mail steamer as far as Cape Town was eventually abandoned there as a result of alterations to the *Quest*'s route south.

This sorry saga did nothing to dampen Wilkins's enthusiasm, and he would later state that his 'experience throughout the three months [January–March 1922] in the Antarctic served to confirm my belief that airplanes could be used successfully throughout an Antarctic summer'.[24] For the next few years, his attention would be diverted to the Arctic, where he made his name and earned a knighthood for his pioneering trans-Arctic flight of 15–16 April 1928, but Antarctic aviation clearly remained 'unfinished business'.

The success of his Point Barrow to Spitsbergen flight meant that, by the late spring of 1928, Wilkins was very well placed in terms of attracting sponsors. With the support of the American Geographical Society, the Detroit Aviation Society, the Vacuum Oil Company of Australia and the newspaper tycoon William Randolph Hearst, he now launched the Wilkins-Hearst Antarctic Expedition, its intention being the establishment of an air base in Palmer Land, from which exploratory flights could be made along the uncharted coasts of the southern reaches of the Antarctic Peninsula. The expedition's aircraft included two Lockheed Vega monoplanes of the type that had proved so successful in the Arctic, and the pilots would be the Americans Carl Ben Eielson, who had been Wilkins' pilot during the trans-Arctic flight, and Joe Crosson.

Departing New York on 22 September 1928, Wilkins and his team travelled south via Montevideo and the Falkland Islands, reaching Deception Island in the South Shetlands on 6 November. Four days later, they unloaded the Vega that Wilkins and Eielson had used earlier in the year. From here, Wilkins explained:

> I planned to use skis, make a flight to reconnoiter [the] Weddell Sea, select a more southerly base, and then when conditions were favorable take the two

planes, alight some five or six hundred miles [805–966km] south of Deception, and with one plane reloaded fly on along the coast to the Ross Sea Barrier.[25]

As John Grierson has remarked, 'The two main needs for the success of this plan were landing areas of sufficient length usable by wheels, skis or floats, one situated at Deception, the other 600 miles south.'[26] Unfortunately, and much to Wilkins's consternation, they found that the ice of Port Foster, the basin-like harbour at the centre of Deception Island, was unexpectedly thin: a mere 61cm. Either the unusual mildness of the season or the warmth from the volcanically influenced beaches surrounding the harbour had melted the ice's edges and left its central portion honeycombed and unstable. 'A violent storm might possibly break it up at any moment,' wrote a dismayed Wilkins. 'Obviously it was unsafe to leave our machine unattended upon its surface.'[27]

Worse was to come. Over the next few days, rain and high temperatures caused much of the remaining snow to melt and puddles of between 15–20cm in depth formed on the bay ice, making a ski take-off absolutely impossible. Unwilling to delay any longer, Wilkins ordered that the aircraft's skis be exchanged for wheels and a runway be prepared on the volcanic tuff and lava of one of the surrounding hills. From this makeshift facility, on 16 November, Eielson and Wilkins made history by becoming the first men to undertake a powered flight in the Antarctic. They spent only twenty minutes in the air, but ten days later both aircraft took off and headed in opposite directions in an attempt to locate a better site from which to operate.

At this point Wilkins, Eielson and Crosson began to appreciate just how enormous were the purely topographical challenges facing aviators in the Antarctic – particularly those who did not enjoy the benefit of working in partnership with land- or ship-based surveyors who could identify safe landing grounds. All but two of the islands they investigated proved to be mountainous and devoid of beaches on which a landing might be attempted. The two low-lying islands, meanwhile – Low Island and Snow Island – lived up to their names, being both low and covered with deep snow, badly crevassed. Wilkins later told his sponsors:

We flew for several hours about the cloud-engirdled mountains; then, as the midnight sun was sinking to its lowest level, we followed the shadowed coast to our base. We had not found a place elsewhere that would serve our purpose.[28]

With no viable alternative available to him, Wilkins and his pilots reluctantly concluded that they must continue to use the Vegas as wheeled land planes, and abandon their skis and floats altogether. However, the kind of flights that they had in mind would require much more fuel than the aircraft had carried up to this point. This, in turn, meant much greater weight and a requirement for a longer airstrip than that previously used. At this critical juncture, therefore, the expedition must undertake a completely unplanned feat of civil engineering. It was, Wilkins acknowledged, a daunting prospect:

> To make a runway half a mile [805m] long … through the mounds of lava that resembled piles of large-sized coke, looked at first like an impossibility. With courage born of necessity we started the job with our hands, wheelbarrows, buckets, rakes, and shovels, cleared many tons of débris and had at last a runway forty feet [12m] wide and about two thousand five hundred feet [762m] long. It had two bends in it of about twenty degrees, and the surface was soft and cindery.[29]

A forced landing at any point during the planned flight would mean almost certain death for both pilot and navigator – not least because there seemed absolutely no likelihood of finding a suitable landing site for a wheeled aircraft – but the most dangerous moment of all would be the attempt to take off, with fuel tanks full to capacity, from this soft-surfaced runway which, despite all their efforts, was still a full 43m shorter than the Vega required.

On 20 December, Wilkins and Eielson decided that they were ready to begin the real work of the expedition. They pumped over 750 litres of aviation fuel into the machine's tanks and bundled their survival packs into the cabin. These contained biscuits, pemmican, chocolate, nuts, raisins and malted milk sufficient for two men to survive for thirty days on a 340g daily ration. 'In case of accident and a forced march home,' Wilkins noted blithely, 'we should each have our own supply if one or the other happened to go through a crevasse.'[30]

In addition, each man carried an alpine rope and a block-and-tackle 'with which he could, if uninjured, haul himself up the rope in a vertical position'. Given the very slim chance of Eielson being able to make a successful forced landing anywhere along the mountainous coast of the Antarctic Peninsula, and the extraordinary obstacles that would face a two-man party trying to walk back along such a route, the thirty days' worth of rations and the thoughtfully provided block-and-tackle probably provided but cold comfort as they climbed aboard.

170

In the event, the first real flight of exploration in the Antarctic went like clockwork. In the course of roughly ten hours, Wilkins and Eielson covered nearly 2,000km up and down the peninsula. Their first major discovery was that previous estimates of the height of the Graham Land Plateau were wildly inaccurate. While Wilkins' charts indicated an altitude of 'from four to six thousand feet' (1,219–1,829m), at the top of this range the Vega was still around 600m below its summit. Eventually, they crossed from the west to the east coast at 2,500m.

Their second observation was that the Antarctic Peninsula was actually an archipelago of large islands, separated by narrow, ice-covered channels:

When we reached a point estimated to be about latitude 71°20'S, longitude 64°15'W, we had used nearly half our supply of gasoline. We had ascertained that we might land with skis almost anywhere in that vicinity and had proved to our satisfaction that Graham Land was not part of the continental area. Storm clouds that we had seen developing behind us threatened to cut us off from our base; and so with the idea of returning safely with the information gathered we swung our airplane to face north and hurried homewards.[31]

Anxiously watching the development of three separate cloud areas, to the west over the southern Pacific, over the Belgica Strait and around Deception Island itself, the two men headed north as fast as their aeroplane would carry them.

The combination of a lighter fuel tank and a tail wind enabled them to maintain a ground speed of 209kph, but low cloud forced them up to an altitude of around 1,520m and for much of their five-hour return flight they navigated by their cockpit instruments alone. Worse still, as they approached the South Shetland island group, they saw that storm clouds completely shrouded Deception Island, making a descent towards its mountainous ring a daunting prospect. Their luck held: at this critical moment, a hole opened up in the clouds 'and Eielson threw the machine into a sharp spiral nose dive and [we] landed within ten hours of the time we started'.[32]

In some respects – perhaps the most important – Wilkins' flight had been enormously successful. He and Eielson had proved that an aeroplane could be flown successfully in Antarctic conditions; they had covered nearly 2,000km in a single flight; they had become the first men to see the plateau that tops the Antarctic Peninsula; and, in the words of one well-informed contemporary commentator, they had 'demonstrated the practical value of

[Wilkins's] methods in a field of peculiar difficulty … [and] obtained such a view of the geography of an area of more than 100,000 square miles as could not have been constructed from all the records of all the explorers that went before.'[33]

In other respects, the flight would prove to have been a failure. In discussing the potential value and pitfalls of aerial observation a year before Wilkins's expedition, Rudmose-Brown had commented that 'The kind of exploration that is now required entails patient observation and accurate measurement. A quick-moving machine cannot help in this, and there is always the probability of mist to hamper the value and imperil the success of aviation in the polar summer.'[34] From the very outset there were doubts regarding some of Wilkins's reported observations and, writing just seven months after Wilkins's return, the Scottish geographer Hugh Robert Mill admitted that 'There still remains in my mind some uncertainty – which, indeed, Sir Hubert Wilkins seems to share – as to whether it is possible to distinguish between actual sea channels blocked with continuous ice and flat-bottomed valleys covered with compacted snow and not depressed below sea level'.[35]

Mill's politely expressed reservations proved to be well-founded because the work of John Rymill's British Graham Land Expedition (BGLE) of 1934–37 would prove conclusively that the supposed straits dividing Graham Land into a number of islands did not exist and that Graham Land was, after all, a peninsula and not an archipelago.

The key difference between the methods adopted by the Wilkins–Hearst Expedition and the BGLE was that the latter deployed both an aeroplane and sledging parties to ensure effective ground control, making their findings truly authoritative. These results would lead James Wordie, who had been one of the first to celebrate Wilkins's discoveries, to remark ruefully that, with the benefit of hindsight, he could see that the aeroplane had been introduced to the Antarctic 'before its uses and limitations in geographical discovery were fully understood'.[36]

★ ★ ★

In discussing the achievements of the Wilkins–Hearst Antarctic Expedition, both real and imagined, Mill openly confessed that his chief fear for Wilkins had always been:

… that his enthusiasm might outrun his discretion and that he might attempt a long flight trusting to luck for a safe landing at the far end. I consider it one of his greatest triumphs that he made sure of his return with the modest gains of a few well conducted flights as a guarantee of greater results later when the fruits of experience have matured.[37]

Given the obvious risks involved, Mill's anxiety appears fully justified – and yet it is also true that, in some respects, one of the most remarkable features of early aviation in Antarctica is that it claimed so few lives.

Wilkins's pioneering achievement was swiftly followed by the even more ambitious exploratory flights of the American aviators Richard E. Byrd and Lincoln Ellsworth, who completed, respectively, the first flight to the Geographic South Pole (28 November 1929) and the first trans-Antarctic flight (23 November–6 December 1935). Although these journeys added relatively little to our understanding of Antarctic geography, especially when compared to the painstaking but less headline-grabbing aerial survey work of Mawson's British, Australian, New Zealand Antarctic Research Expedition (BANZARE) of 1929–31, Hjalmar Riiser-Larsen's *Norvegia* Expedition of 1929–30, and the BGLE (indeed, Ellsworth's observations served to support Wilkins's errors in relation to the Antarctic Peninsula), they were both immensely daring and completed without human loss.

Perhaps more significantly, by touching down no fewer than four times during the course of their 3,200km flight between Snow Hill Island and the Bay of Whales, Ellsworth and his pilot, the British-Canadian Herbert Hollick-Kenyon, proved the accuracy of Ellsworth's conviction that 'it would be possible to find at least as many emergency landing fields as one would expect to find on any trans-continental flight before the development of air-routes'.[38] By disproving the early commentators' belief that it would be impossible to identify suitable landing grounds from the air, Ellsworth had paved the way for an expansion of air operations that would culminate, in 1956, in the establishment from the air of the United States' Amundsen–Scott South Pole Station.

★ ★ ★

While the first flights of exploration in Antarctica were free of fatalities, the same cannot be said of the earliest attempts to derive commercial benefit from aviation. Inevitably, these attempts were connected with that most profitable of Southern Ocean industries: whaling.

From the beginning of the twentieth century, the flensing and dismemberment of all whales harpooned in Antarctic waters were completed either at shore stations, such as that built by Carl Anton Larsen at Grytviken in December 1904, or in the water next to factory ships anchored in sheltered harbours. Although these methods had proved highly successful, creating immense profits for the whaling companies, the need to conduct their operations either on shore or in coastal waters meant that the companies could not avoid the taxes, licences and regulations imposed by the nations that claimed those territories, most notably the United Kingdom. Their solution to this problem, introduced in 1925, was the pelagic whaling vessel: a large floating factory that possessed a built-in ramp, up which whale carcasses could be winched prior to being flensed on deck while the ship was still at sea.

Initially, old freighters and passenger liners were used, the location of their engines amidships making conversion, particularly the construction of onboard slipways, relatively easy. Then, in 1928, the directors of the newly formed Kosmos Whaling Company became the first to commission a purpose-built pelagic whaler, the 18,000-tonne *Kosmos*, which was launched in Belfast at the end of May 1929.[39] Their innovation did not stop there. Fully aware that aircraft had already been used successfully for spotting seals off the coast of Canada and herring in Scottish waters, at the London Olympia Air Show in July the Kosmos directors also announced their intention to pioneer such techniques in the Southern Ocean using a de Havilland Gipsy Moth, equipped with floats and folding wings.

As the pilot, they had recruited the 35-year-old Leif Lier, an experienced Norwegian aviator who had taken part in the search for Umberto Nobile and his airship, *Italia*, the previous year. To further prove his mettle, after the air show, Lier would fly the Moth the 1,570km from the de Havilland factory at Stag Lane in Kingsbury to Oslo (a feat that he completed in just eight hours and fifty-five minutes of flying time).[40]

When the *Kosmos* sailed from Wellington, New Zealand, at the beginning of October, the Gipsy Moth was not the ship's only unusual cargo. Tethered in the shadow of the aeroplane's fuselage were thirty huskies that Captain Hans Andresen had been asked to deliver to Byrd's expedition at Little

America. The dogs were accompanied by the British-Canadian adventurer and ex-Mountie, Alan Innes-Taylor, and as the tugs warped the ship from its berth at the beginning of its long voyage south, he remarked, 'With most of the crew lining the rail, hats went sailing ashore to the hundreds who had come to see us off, sure sign that we'd be back.'[41] It would soon become apparent that such signs could be deceptive.

Six days later, the factory ship and its seven catchers reached the edge of the belt of pack ice lying across the approaches to the Ross Sea, and the hunting began immediately. *Kos 3* chalked up the first kill, a 26m-long blue whale, and soon another eight to ten were being added to the haul every twenty-four hours, mostly blue, fin and humpbacks. The factory ship's two large steam-driven winches hauled the dead whales up onto the offal-strewn meat deck, where more winches helped to tear great, bloody strips of blubber from the carcasses. With scavenging seabirds wheeling above their heads, the flensers then used their long-bladed knives to cut the strips into more manageable chunks before feeding them through hatches into the boiling vats below decks. 'In the cold raw sea air and especially when it is foggy,' Innes-Taylor recalled with disgust:

> ... the sight of 100 men tearing a whale to pieces in the awful stench of corrupt blood and slopping around in it is a carnage beyond description, and sticks in the mind forever ... After a while one gets used to the stench which permeates everything, but one never gets used to the sight of a beautiful streamlined whale being hacked to pieces for oil.[42]

Though some of the whalers might have considered the newfangled floatplane an unnecessary distraction from this more important (and profitable) work, as soon as the seas were sufficiently calm, they used the ship's derrick to swing it overboard. Shortly afterwards, Lier made his first flight – and almost immediately it became apparent that the Kosmos Company's plans for the aerial spotting of whales were deeply flawed. Innes-Taylor put his finger on the chief problem when he asked, 'How did an airplane flying 75 knots/ hour spot whales travelling slowly and then guide a chaser sailing 14 knots to where they were?'[43]

But the pilot also had to overcome the potentially greater dangers of losing his ship at sea and – if he did manage to locate it – finding sea and ice conditions unsuitable for making a landing. According to Hjalmar Riiser-Larsen, a fellow countryman of Lier's who had raced against him in 1919,[44]

and who was now using a Lockheed Vega to undertake aerial surveys and to identify potential new whaling grounds from the ex-whaler *Norvegia*:

> What you look down upon is not a huge white plain: the ice is broken, some cakes drift loosely, some are closely packed; the picture indeed, in black and white and in colours from the diatoms, is the most irregular that could be dreamt of. Moreover, if one is away any length of time ice conditions may have completely altered before one gets back, on which account it is advisable to leave the ship for long flights only when weather conditions indicate that no fog or snow is likely to occur before the return.[45]

To further compound these problems and hazards, Lier's aircraft did not carry a radio, making it impossible for him to report either his sightings without returning to the ship, or his own position in the event of a forced landing.

These dangers did not deter Lier, who not only made spotting flights whenever weather and sea conditions permitted, but also whiled away the evening hours in inventing and debating potential new projects, often with the ship's doctor, Ingvald Schreiner, and Innes-Taylor as fellow schemers. Most of these ideas, including a crossing of Antarctica with dogs, and adventures in the Yukon, were for the future; however, another plan, a flight over the Balleny Islands, seemed capable of more immediate fulfilment.

First sighted in 1839 by British sealing captains John Balleny and Thomas Freeman, the islands form a 257km-long archipelago of three large volcanic islands (Young, Buckle and Sturge) and numerous small islets and stacks, located between 66°15' to 67°10'S and 162°15' to 164°45'E, roughly 240km off the coast of Victoria Land. On 9 February 1839, Freeman had landed on one of the heavily glaciated and rocky islands, making him the first person ever to make a recorded landing anywhere south of the Antarctic Circle. But his visit was one of very few ever made, and the remoteness of the islands, their biological diversity and their status as some of the only truly marine or oceanic islands on this side of Antarctica made them an obvious target for anyone interested in making new discoveries.

Having agreed that Christmas would be the best time to make their attempt, the three conspirators began their preparations by stripping away any unnecessary weight in the Moth in order to make allowance for the extra emergency equipment and rations they would need to carry. This, they hoped, would enable them to maintain the machine's maximum range of 515km. Once they had completed their modifications, Lier made a successful

trial flight on 20 December and, according to Innes-Taylor, the trio 'now felt confident that when we had a perfect day, with calm and unlimited visibility, we would go'.[46]

That day dawned on 26 December. Originally, it had been agreed that Lier would be accompanied by Innes-Taylor, who had served with the Royal Canadian Flying Corps towards the end of the war, but, as he dressed, the Canadian was interrupted by Schreiner:

> The doctor came to my cabin and asked me if he could go in my place. There was no sickness aboard at the moment, he said, and it was a chance for him to get away from the ship for a few hours. I didn't have the heart to refuse him, but I said he should be sure to get the captain's permission to go. He went off and returned shortly, happy that the captain, after a lot of persuading, had said yes, he could go. It was disappointing, but then I thought there would be another time.[47]

It would prove a fateful decision for both men – and, for Schreiner, a fatal one.

Shortly afterwards, the Gipsy Moth, with its serial number N42 emblazoned on its fuselage, was swung out from the *Kosmos* and refuelled. Lier and Schreiner clambered aboard and, with a final cheerful wave, began their run. To Innes-Taylor, watching from the ship, it seemed to take the heavily laden aircraft an inordinately long time to lift off, but the floats rose into the air at last, streams of water pouring from their sides, and in no time at all the little aeroplane had dwindled to a speck in the western sky. Then it disappeared.

Later that day, one of the catchers' captains reported that Lier and Schreiner had landed close to his vessel, perhaps to report a whale sighting, but that they had flown away after only a very brief pause, keeping to their westerly course. Neither man, nor their aircraft, was ever seen again.

★ ★ ★

In his account of the tragedy, first published a year after his death, Innes-Taylor asserted that by 4 p.m. on 26 December he had joined Captain Andresen on the bridge of the *Kosmos* to look out for the Gipsy Moth, which, by his estimation, had sufficient fuel for just one more hour of flying. Perhaps it was at this point that he told the captain that Lier and Schreiner

had not intended simply to complete another search for whales and that, instead, they had intended to fly over the Balleny Islands, over 240km to the west – a flight that would take the small aircraft close to the limit of its range.

Whatever Andresen's personal feelings regarding this clear breach of discipline, his professional response was to order all the catchers to post special lookouts and to return to the factory ship for re-bunkering at the earliest opportunity so that they could then begin a systematic search. By 7 p.m. all seven catchers were steaming westwards in an agreed pattern and Andresen had used his radio to alert the captains of all the other whaling ships of the emergency. By 8 a.m. 27 December, no fewer than sixteen catchers had joined the rescue attempt. But to no avail: none found so much as a scrap of wreckage.

Inevitably, opinions regarding the accident varied. Listening to the details of the unfolding tragedy over 1,000km to the south at Little America, Byrd believed that engine failure must have been the primary cause:

> ... for visibility, according to Captain Andresen, remained clear and the pilot was skilful. It is unlikely that he became lost. A number of the men here, including Owen and Petersen, knew the pilot, and so the tragedy strikes personally. For I believe it is a tragedy. Even assuming the landing was made safely, the plane could not long exist in the heavy seas which ran on the following day. I can imagine no worse predicament than to be forced down in the vicinity of the pack ... The fliers carried emergency rations for only two days. I am sure they are lost.[48]

Riiser-Larsen, too, appears to have believed that Lier had been forced to make an unplanned water landing, and he stated his conviction that it would have been completely impossible for the two men to have reached the Balleny Islands.[49] Innes-Taylor disagreed. More than half a century later, he remained certain that his friends had reached their destination, and that 'somewhere high on the islands' mountaintops, my two friends lie amidst the wreckage of their plane, enveloped by that peace to be found where no man has ever trod or ever will'.[50]

Whether they landed on the sea, or crashed into a mountainside, there can be little doubt that Lier's attempt to reach the Balleny Islands crossed the narrow line that separates daring from foolhardiness. Russell Owen, an American journalist with Byrd at Little America, had met Lier the previous year and thought him 'always careful, knowing the dangers of getting out of touch with the ships',[51] but in making this flight, the Norwegian had chosen to operate at the Gipsy Moth's maximum range, leaving him with absolutely no contingency in the event of an accident or miscalculation. Moreover, as Grierson has stated, 'if they did lose their bearings the chances of rescue without radio were almost a million to one against'.[52] Most importantly, the flight was not connected with the work for which Lier had been employed; it was not authorised by the ship's captain; and, given the short amount of time that would have been available to the two men once they reached the island group, it was highly unlikely to produce any meaningful results in terms of survey or other observations. In the parlance later adopted by many BAS personnel, it was a 'jolly': an excursion designed almost exclusively for pleasure. In this respect, then, the loss of N42 and its crew can be compared with the series of accidents that claimed so many British lives in the Antarctic during the decades following the end of the Second World War.

★ ★ ★

Lier and Schreiner became the first airmen to die in the Antarctic – but they would not be the last. Indeed, statistically, accidents during air operations have accounted for more deaths than any other single cause in that hostile region – and more than many other causes combined. Even when the 257 fatalities sustained in the Air New Zealand disaster of 28 November 1979 are discounted, in the seven decades between 1929 and 1999 in excess of ninety individuals died in more than twenty-five separate air accidents.[53]

Until the end of the Second World War, air operations remained on a small scale, consonant with the expeditions of which they formed a part. Up to 1946, even the most ambitious explorers seldom included more than twenty or thirty men in their shore parties, supported by perhaps one or two ships and, if they were lucky (and well financed), an equal number of aircraft. This pattern began to change with the United States Antarctic Service Expedition (Byrd's third) of 1939–41, during which fifty-nine men overwintered at three separate bases, but the most radical departure came with the post-war Operation Highjump.

This expedition, launched by the United States Navy, would involve some 4,700 men, thirteen ships, including icebreakers, destroyers, tankers, a submarine and an aircraft carrier, and over thirty aircraft (including, for the first time, helicopters) – but it would remain in the Antarctic for just one austral summer, that of 1946–47. Its purposes would be fivefold: to test personnel and equipment in extreme cold; to consolidate and expand US sovereignty over as large an area of the continent as possible; to assess the practicality of establishing permanent manned bases; to test the feasibility of developing air facilities on the ice; and, lastly, to undertake a scientific programme including hydrography, meteorology, geology (including aerial prospecting for uranium), magnetism and survey. In the words of Lisle A. Rose, the expedition's leading historian, 'For the first time in its history the US Navy was to make Antarctic operations a major component of its mission. The partial militarization of South Polar research and exploration was about to begin.'[54]

So far as aerial operations were concerned, these would be designed to achieve a systematic expansion of the air exploration of Antarctica, particularly its coastal rim, using a combination of ship- and land-based aircraft, all of which would be equipped with the very latest technology, including the trimetrogon system for hitherto unimaginably accurate aerial photography, radar, magnetometers and JATO (Jet Assisted Take-Off) boosters. If all went according to plan, by the end of the summer, the pilots and navigators of the US Navy would have done more to extend the aerial survey of Antarctica than any previous expedition.

The aircraft to be used for the majority of this ambitious long-range operation included six Douglas R4D Skytrain (or Dakota) transports, which would fly fan-shaped missions southwards from the crystallised snow runway of the expedition's planned Little America IV base on the Ross Ice Shelf, and a total of six twin-engine Martin PBM Mariner flying boats, which would conduct wide-ranging coastal surveys from the seaplane tenders USS *Pine Island* and USS *Currituck*.

After weeks of hectic preparation, the 14,225-tonne *Pine Island*, which formed the centre of the expedition's Eastern Task Group, sailed from the vast naval station in Norfolk, Virginia, on the afternoon of 2 December 1946. Accompanied by her escorts, the destroyer *Brownson* and the fleet oiler *Canisteo*, she completed her 16,000km voyage south without a hitch, and on Christmas Day reached the northern edge of the pack ice.

Up to this point conditions had proved unexpectedly benign, with even the 'Roaring Forties' failing to live up to their fearsome reputation, but now, just as the task force prepared to begin its real work, the weather suddenly deteriorated. Between Christmas Day and 29 December, a combination of fog, snow and ocean swells made it impossible to launch any of *Pine Island*'s Mariners, *George I*, *George II* and *George III*, and an attempt to do so resulted in minor damage to one of *George I*'s wing floats.

After four days of frustrating inactivity, shortly after midday on the 29th, the weather began to clear and the swell to subside. With *Pine Island* listing a full three degrees as her giant deck crane strained under the weight of the 15,000kg aircraft, *George I* was lowered gingerly over the side and refuelled, two rearming boats holding her steady as the aviation fuel poured down a hose strung out from the ship. Once her fuel gauges indicated 'full', the boats manoeuvred her away from *Pine Island* and then cast off the towropes. Shortly afterwards, with her twin Wright R–2600 radial engines roaring, she took to the air, the first of the Eastern Task Group's fixed–wing aircraft to do so. Having received favourable weather and visibility reports from the crew of *George I*, *George II* followed in her wake at 6.30 p.m.

After a successful flight lasting around ten hours, *George I* returned to the ship at 11.05 that night. Anxious to make the most of the continued good weather and the twenty-four hours of daylight, *Pine Island*'s commander, Captain Henry Caldwell, ordered that the aircraft should be refuelled immediately. Her tired aircrew, however, would be relieved and allowed to get some rest, their places being taken by Ralph 'Frenchy' LeBlanc (pilot), Bill Kearns (co-pilot), Owen McCarty (photographer), Max Lopez (navigator), Wendell K. Hendersin (radioman), Jim 'Robbie' Robbins (radar operator), Bill Warr (crew chief) and Fred Williams (flight engineer). 'We had flown together on only a few short checkout flights prior to storing our plane on board the USS *Pine Island* in Norfolk,' Robbins recalled, '... plus one test flight in Panama on the way south. However, all of us were volunteers and had many hours in PBMs.'[55] Robbins even enjoyed the advantage of having previously flown in northern Greenland and Arctic Canada, making him unusually well qualified for the task in hand.

But the weather was turning. As the crew gathered their gear on *Pine Island*'s flight deck ready to transfer to *George I*, LeBlanc, 'a lanky Cajun from Louisiana',[56] and one of the navy's most experienced PBM pilots, shared with them the latest meteorological reports. These indicated that a potentially severe storm appeared to be moving directly into their planned flight path. According to Robbins:

[LeBlanc] stipulated he was not about to make this flight, in adverse weather conditions, without first discussing it with his crew. In my opinion, he obviously felt such a flight under these conditions (especially in a seaplane) was above and beyond the call of normal duty assignments.[57]

The mission, he told them, would be undertaken only with a crew made up of volunteers. 'We all agreed,' wrote Robbins, 'we were ready and raring to go.' Finally, and perhaps to demonstrate that he would not ask anything of his men that he would not do himself, Captain Caldwell told the crew that he, too, would join them, as a supernumerary, or 'volunteer observer'.

With its new crew of nine, *George I* took to the air on its second Antarctic flight at a little before 3 a.m. 30 December. Already heavily laden with personnel and fuel, and with water cascading through damaged hatches, the seaplane bounced across 3km of ocean before heaving itself into the air with the aid of its four JATO bottles. It was, observed Robbins, 'by far, the longest take-off run I have ever been in, or heard of'.[58] Almost immediately they were enveloped in a snowstorm, with zero visibility at 240m above sea level, but with reports of improved conditions over the coast some 380km to the south, they continued on over the pack. The radar, too, seemed to be functioning well, and the size and density of the scattered icebergs below meant that they showed up well on Robbins's flickering screen.

After three uneventful hours, *George I* was closing rapidly on the coast in the vicinity of Thurston Island, Antarctica's third largest island, lying at 72°06'S, 99°00'W off the north-west end of Ellsworth Land. LeBlanc accordingly increased altitude to a little over 300m. 'I kept a constant vigil on the radar scope,' wrote Robbins, 'informing the pilot of any significant changes. The last reading was "mountain range twenty miles [32km] ahead and scattered icebergs". This was in total agreement with our charts.'[59]

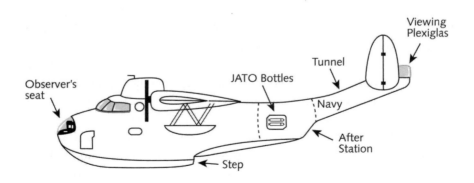

Martin PBM Mariner 'George I'

For a while it looked as though conditions might improve, and Kearns took over the controls to let LeBlanc rest. But moments later, *George I* ran into 'ice blink', and with a shallow overcast above, and a fine driving snow obscuring the land below, the light filtering through the clouds bounced off the snow 'in a million directions, as if each fragment were a tiny mirror'.[60] To complete the pilots' bafflement, at this point the altimeters, which measure the height of an aircraft from the ground, began to give confusing and rapidly changing readings. 'A friend of mine,' announced Kearns, 'once rammed into the top of a glacier in Greenland in this kind of weather. Let's get the hell out of here!'[61]

LeBlanc nodded agreement, and Kearns banked the aircraft to begin a 180-degree turn. But ice now encrusted each of the Mariner's 18m wings and it responded sluggishly to his demands. Seconds later, and mid-turn, 'a crunching shock ran through the plane and reverberated all along the hull'.[62] The pilots reacted instinctively, Kearns slamming home the throttles and LeBlanc giving full low pitch to the propellers to maximise their pulling power. At the same time, they strained back on the yokes as hard as they could without causing the engines to stall catastrophically. Kearns remembered that he breathed a sigh of relief as the Mariner began to climb – but it was premature, as 'At almost the identical moment, a tremendous explosion literally blew the plane apart'.[63]

In an instant, the helpless crew of *George I* were caught in a violent, whirling maelstrom, with men, kit and aircraft parts flying in all directions. 'Something grabbed me squarely by the seat of the pants,' Kearns recalled, 'and threw me upward against the cockpit glass. In that split second, I knew I was headed straight for the starboard propeller. How I missed that meat cleaver, I'll never know.'[64] But he did miss it, and woke some time later, in one piece but 'full of pain, and nearly frozen'.

Owen McCarty, who had been dozing in a rear compartment, hurtled nearly the whole length of the fuselage, striking his head as he passed through one of the internal hatches. He also regained consciousness lying in the snow – though all he could do was sit 'for hours, holding my head in my hands, before I could gather my wits enough to take steps to keep from freezing to death'.[65] His confusion is hardly surprising as his injuries included, as well as a dislocated thumb, cracked ribs and a broken leg, a 7in cut to his head. 'With my fingers I can feel my skull,' he noted in his diary later that day,[66] and Robbins believed that the photographer would probably have bled to death had the cold not caused rapid coagulation.

Caldwell, who had been seated at the very front of the plane, was hurled straight through the Plexiglas nose of the Mariner, but sustained only relatively minor injuries, including damaged and loosened teeth, a broken nose and a smashed ankle. Miraculously, Warr and Robbins, both of whom had been riding just aft of the aircraft's control room, escaped practically unscathed, suffering nothing worse than minor cuts and bruises.

In the minutes immediately following the explosion, these five survivors – with the exception of McCarty who, by his own admission, felt 'too dazed to know exactly what was happening'[67] – extracted themselves from the snowdrifts and staggered about the crash site, each initially fearing that he alone had survived, and each experiencing a rush of relief as he discovered his companions. Around them, the blizzard continued to rage, the curtains of driven snow lit eerily by the fires burning in the wreckage. 'Then,' Kearns recalled with a shudder, 'an agonizing scream cut through the wail of the wind. It was Frenchy's voice.'[68]

Those who could ran towards the remains of the flight deck, which lay on its side enveloped in fire. When the explosion tore the aircraft apart, LeBlanc had been the only member of the crew wearing his safety harness, and now they found him still strapped into his seat, with the flames leaping around him as he screamed. Kearns reached him first, but a broken right shoulder made it impossible for him to release the buckle until Robbins and Warr arrived. The three men dragged the pilot from the twisted wreckage and beat out the flames with their gloved hands. 'Frenchy's face, arms and legs were burned black and were already starting to swell,' Kearns later reported. 'He was only half-conscious, writhing in pain and muttering unintelligibly.'[69] While Kearns treated LeBlanc with antibiotic sulfadiazine tablets – the only medical supplies that they could locate – Robbins and Warr went to search for the three missing crewmen.

They found Ensign Max Lopez kneeling in the snow, with the back of his head missing; the upper half of radio operator Wendell Hendersin's body lay nearby, its upright position giving the impression that he was buried to his waist. Presumably both men had hit the propellers that Kearns had been lucky enough to miss as he flew through the cockpit's Plexiglas canopy. Williams was sprawled on the snow close to the edge of a huge fire pit created by the thousands of litres of aviation fuel shed by the Mariner's ruptured tanks. 'Upon kneeling next to him,' Robbins wrote thirty-five years later:

… it was obvious his condition was extremely critical. The internal injuries he sustained were apparently extensive, since he could not move at all and was hemorrhaging from the mouth and nose. His back appeared to be broken and we agreed that moving him would only compound the problems.[70]

Having covered the injured man with a blanket and a piece of canvas engine cover, Warr and Robbins erected a windbreak made from a piece of decking and then went to assist the others. 'I told him we would be in earshot for anything he needed, and that we had to keep moving as other crew members needed help, too. He seemed to understand.'[71] Williams died two hours later. Lopez, Hendersin and Williams became the third, fourth and fifth airmen to die in the Antarctic and, surprisingly perhaps given the scale and daring of US operations over recent decades, the first Americans.

With all the crew accounted for, the primary concern now must be survival. The 23.5m fuselage had broken into three parts: the wings and centre section formed one, the burning flight deck another, and the waist and tail section the third. This last portion was by far the largest and the only one into which all six men could squeeze. Writing in the third person nine years later, Kearns observed:

Some sort of luck was with them, for in the drifting snow they found sleeping bags, still neatly rolled in their khaki containers. Robbins and Warr rigged one for Frenchy and carried him into the severed waist. Then the rest crowded in.[72]

The same two men rigged a parachute across the gaping hole at the end of their refuge to prevent the snow blowing in and, before taking shelter themselves, searched the wreck site for vital food and equipment. 'The initiative and energy of these two saved our lives,' McCarty recorded gratefully.[73]

The survivors could count themselves lucky in that the aeroplane wreckage was concentrated in a small area, with the three main pieces lying within a few metres of each other. This meant that the PBM's stores and equipment were also tightly grouped, some within the smashed fuselage, and some strewn about the snowfield on which it rested. Had the pilots managed to gain more altitude before the explosion, the picture might have been very different – and, of course, the crew might all be dead. Over the next few days, searches resulted in the recovery of a sleeping bag for each man, blankets, a stove, two tents which eased the cramped conditions in

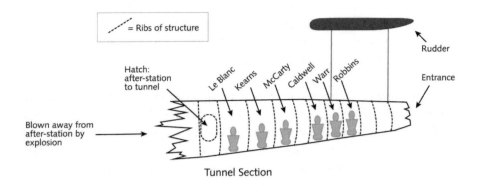

= Ribs of structure

Hatch:
after-station
to tunnel

Le Blanc
Kearns
McCarty
Caldwell
Warr
Robbins

Rudder

Entrance

Blown away from
after-station by
explosion

Tunnel Section

Wreckage of 'George I'

the fuselage, ample food and fuel – sufficient, indeed, to last for weeks if necessary – and a 'Gibson Girl' hand-cranked transmitter, which they used to send a pre-programmed emergency message, though they had no way of knowing whether anyone heard it. To everyone's astonishment, McCarty even succeeded in finding his wedding ring, which had become dislodged in the crash. Most had also been fortunate to sustain only relatively minor injuries; the worst being fractures to Kearns's upper arm and shoulder and breaks to Caldwell's and McCarty's lower limbs.

The exception, of course, was LeBlanc, who had suffered major burns to his face, left arm and hand, and to his thighs and back. 'His face was covered with a hard, black crust and swollen to inhuman shape,' Kearns reported. 'His hands were bloated like fat sausages.'[74] Initially, it appeared that his eyes might also have been scorched and that he would be permanently blinded. On that first afternoon, McCarty noted that the pilot 'started to get delirious and tried to get up. He said he was going to the sick bay to see Doctor Williamson. I had to curse at him to make him stay still and rest.'[75] Over the coming days, LeBlanc lurched between delirium, sleep and spells of surprisingly cheerful lucidity – though Robbins observed, 'His mouth was burned to the point that he had to break his lips open with the fingers of his one good hand.'[76] All knew that his life hung by the merest thread and that, to have any chance of survival, he must be rescued soon.

But in those first few days, rescue seemed only a remote possibility. *George I* had crashed in a largely unexplored and poorly mapped area and

already the screaming blizzard had begun to bury the wreckage. Caldwell feared that the storm might have blown them off course and, when they had flown away from *Pine Island, George II* was the only other airworthy aircraft within 4,500km, as *George III* had been stripped of a wingtip float in order to replace the one damaged during the aborted launch of *George I* on 26 December. 'The situation of the survivors was anything but hopeful,' opined Kearns. 'They might almost have been stranded on the far side of the moon.'[77]

On 2 January 1947, the third day after the crash, a period of clear, bright weather began – but the men's pleasure soon changed to disgust when they saw a group of skuas circling overhead 'like evil omens'[78] and dipping occasionally to investigate the shallow graves of their dead comrades. They managed to frighten the birds by discharging a broken shotgun at them and, on the 5th they moved the bodies and buried them properly, close to the PBM's starboard wingtip, with their heads to the south. 'It's just one week tonight since we left the ship,' McCarty noted glumly in his diary that evening. 'God knows it seems longer. Spirits are low. We can't understand why there has been no plane yet.'[79]

The explanation was a combination of poor weather and misfortune. *George I* had been expected to return to *Pine Island* by 12.45 p.m. on 30 December. Though worrying, her radio silence could be explained by adverse meteorological conditions, or by mechanical failure, but when she failed to reappear at the allotted time, Commander Isador Schwartz, Caldwell's executive officer, ordered that lost aircraft procedures be initiated. The ship's radio officers transmitted hourly messages to the missing crew, advising them to remain with their machine and to man their radio on the hour, every hour, while *George II* was made ready for a rescue flight. But, of course, whatever the PBM's state of readiness, she could not take to the air in zero visibility – and for nearly two days a combination of dense fog and snow squalls rendered *Pine Island*'s crew helpless.

At last, on the morning of New Year's Day, the fog cleared sufficiently for *George II* to be swung overboard and for refuelling to begin – but when the fog closed in once more, Schwartz had no choice but to order that the preparations be halted. Given that the fog might just as easily clear again, at least for the relatively short amount of time necessary to get the PBM airborne, he instructed that she be secured to the ship's stern by a 90m line, rather than being brought back on board. In order to protect the fragile seaplane, refuelling boats stationed themselves either side, like grooms holding the bridle of a wayward stallion, but this precaution proved inadequate in the face of the unpredictable ocean swell and, at a critical moment, the PBM was driven forward uncontrollably until, with a resounding crash, she struck the towering side of the ship. On inspecting the damage, the disconsolate aircraftsmen quickly realised that they would be better employed making *George III* airworthy than in attempting to straighten *George II*'s buckled port wingtip and aileron – and yet more precious time had been lost.

George III finally took to the skies on 5 January but completed only a brief search over *George I*'s last reported position before being forced back by more bad weather. Another flight on the 6th met with exactly the same result and when fog and snow squalls closed in, air operations again ground to a halt. In an attempt to make his own luck, four days later Captain George Dufek, commander of the Eastern Task Group, ordered that his ships steam 160km west in the hope of finding better conditions. Previously, he had been reluctant to move in case the missing PBM limped back only to find the flotilla missing; now that seemed unlikely.

When the sun began to burn away the fog in the early hours of 11 January, it appeared that his gamble had paid off. Ships' crews, engineers and airmen leapt to work and by 4.30 a.m. the newly repaired *George II* rested on the water in the lee of *Pine Island*, the great fuel line linking ship to seaplane pulsing with the steady flow of thousands of litres of pumped gasoline. By 7 a.m. the PBM was airborne and winging her way towards Thurston Island.

At the crash site, meanwhile, conditions had slowly but surely deteriorated. LeBlanc's periods of lucidity had decreased in length and frequency and, while Kearns believed that he 'clung to life with amazing tenacity',[80] the pilot's chances of survival appeared to be dwindling rapidly. 'The poor guy is so badly burned that at times he can't remember what happened or where he is,' McCarty noted in his diary:

> Kearns says he kept asking him to call Doctor Williamson. He can never seem to get enough water, and is constantly eating snow through a hole in the wreckage, which only makes him more thirsty … I hope he can hold out until rescue comes, but he looks bad![81]

Burns, it soon turned out, were not the only problem. The intense cold made their lungs hurt when they breathed deeply, and one night LeBlanc told Kearns that his feet had begun to trouble him and that he couldn't wriggle his toes. The co-pilot pulled off his friend's boots and socks, and later admitted, 'what he saw made his stomach turn over'.[82] LeBlanc's feet had turned a sickly grey-white colour and felt cold to the touch. They also emitted a pungent odour, indicating the presence of gangrene. Kearns was grateful when his patient lapsed back into delirium before learning the truth.

Though LeBlanc's condition remained by far the worst, McCarty also observed that his own left thigh had taken on the appearance of 'a balloon filled with water', his head wound had begun to leak pus into his flying helmet, and he continued to suffer severe headaches and dizzy spells. With their fractures untreated, and with no painkillers to ease their discomfort, Caldwell and Kearns were also suffering. The group still possessed ample food and fuel, but their limited equipment meant that it seemed to take an eternity to melt cups of snow. With his dehydration accelerated by his burns, all agreed that LeBlanc must have first call on the water they managed to generate, but all felt a raging and insatiable thirst.

Inevitably, the weather added to their woes, with snow and fog making the launch of a search-and-rescue mission seem only a remote possibility. And even if *George II* and *George III* took off successfully, would they look in the right place? Kearns and Caldwell disagreed regarding their location – Kearns insisted that they had crashed on Thurston Island, while Caldwell believed (wrongly) that they had strayed over the Fletcher Islands – and their debates must have caused additional concern that the hoped-for rescue missions from *Pine Island* might be misdirected. Nonetheless, every day the walking wounded staggered about the wreckage, sweeping the accumulated snow from the dark blue wings and fuselage of the PBM, so that they would be more obvious from the air. And day after day, they cranked the handle of the Gibson Girl in the vain hope that their signal would be heard hundreds of kilometres away.

The skies over Thurston Island cleared on the twelfth day. During the morning, patches of blue appeared among the clouds, and by noon the crew of *George I* had begun to feel uncomfortably warm in their flying suits. For the first time, they could obtain a better impression of their immediate surroundings. 'Under other conditions,' Kearns observed, 'this would have been a beautiful spot':

> They were high on a mountain ridge, and at their backs rose other higher mountains, merging in the far distance into an unending whiteness almost without horizon. Beneath them, the ever-moving sea ice was broken

189

occasionally by open leads that showed dark water, and interspersed with great 'growler' bergs that crashed and groaned as they shifted with the currents. Except for the reverberating noises of the bergs, and the whisper of shifting snow, silence pressed around them like a blanket.[83]

The depression that had prevailed for the previous few days gave way to renewed optimism, with all convinced that, if the improved conditions were not merely a local phenomenon, the *Pine Island* must surely be able to launch one, or both, of its remaining PBMs.

The accuracy of this prediction was proved on the morning of Saturday, 11 January when, as he sat in the fuselage changing his socks, Kearns heard a new sound, 'like the beat of props that comes before you catch the full engine sound'.[84] McCarty spotted *George II* first, but only in time to see the huge seaplane fly directly over their position, apparently blind to their frantic signals. 'How it could fly so close and fail to see us, we could not understand,' he wrote, shortly afterwards. 'One of the mainstays of our morale has been the thought that our blue-black wreckage stood out like a sore thumb.'[85]

Desperate to ensure that they could not be missed a second time, they now pulled out their rubber dinghy and filled it with everything both non-essential and inflammable, including pieces of cardboard, wood, paper, cloth and manila line. They then doused the pile of rubbish with gasoline and waited, praying that the PBM crew would fly in a standard grid pattern, known as a 'ladder search'. If they were right, the PBM should appear again at a distance no greater than 15km.

At 10.20 a.m., Caldwell, who had been standing on the broken wings scanning the horizon shouted, 'Airplane!' Robbins immediately stepped forward and tossed a match into the dinghy. 'BOOOOOMMMM!! Everything seemed to explode in my face – no chance to turn away! … I was very lucky to get off with only my eyebrows and eyelashes singed off.'[86] In the perfectly calm conditions a column of thick black smoke rose 90m into the air – surely this must be visible to the crew of *George II*? Incredibly, for a moment – 'the longest moment of their lives,' thought Kearns[87] – it seemed that they hadn't seen it, as the great blue aeroplane flew on without changing course. Then, suddenly, the pilot dipped his wings and began a long fast dive towards the men on the ground. 'From that moment,' wrote McCarty, 'our worries were gone. We all shouted and jumped around. Each thanked God in his own way. There's no way to express our happiness, but all of us felt mighty good.'[88]

But their ordeal was not quite over. Having thrown down emergency supplies, including extra clothing, food and bedding, Lieutenant Jim Ball, the pilot of *George II*, also dropped a note stating that the closest point at which a PBM could safely land lay some 16km to the north of the crash site. On returning to *Pine Island*, Ball would pass this vital information on to the crew of *George III*, so that they could land and await the arrival of Caldwell and his men. This, of course, meant that the survivors, three of them with broken limbs, must now not only drag themselves that distance across completely unknown country, but also man-haul the dead weight of the crippled and badly burned LeBlanc. Given that many of them would almost certainly die if forced to spend a night in the open, they must also complete the journey against the clock. Their only alternative was to wait in the hope that *Pine Island* might eventually be able to push close enough to Thurston Island to enable one of her short-range helicopters to effect a rescue. 'We held a conference,' McCarty recorded, 'and decided to try it.'[89]

The 16km journey took over ten hours to complete. Having loaded their emergency sledge with sleeping bags, a water breaker, chocolate and cigarettes dropped by *George II*, and the compass from the wrecked aeroplane's instrument panel, the crew lifted LeBlanc into place and lashed him securely into a sitting position, as warm and as comfortable as they could make him. Fully loaded, the sledge weighed in excess of 90kg. All knew that the trek ahead would be arduous and profoundly uncomfortable; for the pilot it would be agony. Practically everyone who has endured it has at some point attested to the 'pure soul-destroying labour'[90] of man-hauled sledging, but their catalogue of injuries must surely result in the experience of Caldwell's crew being ranked as one of the most extreme in the annals of Antarctic exploration.

Sometimes they travelled over a well-crusted surface and made good progress; at others, they found themselves floundering up to their waists in soft snow, or negotiating a field of crevasses of unknown width and depth. But the variable quality of the surface and the need to keep moving as quickly as possible were not their only worries. Would the ice close to their planned take-off site be strong enough to bear their weight and that of the heavy sledge? Would it be possible to transfer LeBlanc to that most unstable of watercraft, a rubber dinghy? Would they even be able to find the waiting PBM in the fog that now began to roll in from the sea? And, if they did so, would there be sufficient visibility for it to take off?

To add to their woes, hours into their trek they discovered that their compass had become dislodged by the constant bumping and that it had disappeared into the snow.

Their anxiety over becoming completely lost was somewhat alleviated by their first sight of the rescue plane, far to the north, riding easily and idling its engines in open water. But the fog remained a concern and, calling on their last reserves of energy, they attempted to move more quickly. 'Distance was very deceiving,' McCarty recalled, 'and in spite of our increased speed and frantic efforts to beat the fog, we seemed never to grow closer.'[91] They also found themselves crossing a thin crust and time and again the photographer fell through, pulling Kearns or Warr down with him. And yet it was only McCarty who broke through, Robbins attributing his repeated misfortune to 'his weight combined with his comparatively small feet'.[92] On one occasion he fell up to his waist, and when he looked down he realised that his legs were swinging over a blue hole at least 2m deep.

And then, suddenly, unexpectedly, they were no longer alone. Out of the fog loomed two men, Lieutenant Commander John 'Dixie' Howell and Chief Photographer's Mate Dick Conger, from *George III*. 'There was no laughing or cheery greetings,' recalled Conger:

> The survivors were past that stage. First in line was Lieutenant Kearns, who looked as if he couldn't believe it. Second was Chief McCarty, a fellow photographer and a good friend. I slipped an arm around his shoulder and said a few words. He just let out a joyful sob and said, 'I never was so glad to see a photographer in my life'.
>
> I am a photographer by trade, and I had a camera with me while ashore, but when these struggling men came into sight, I forgot my calling, I forgot I had a camera, and didn't even think of getting exclusive pictures. The survivors were important and everything else was incidental. I saw quite a bit during the war, but I can say that I never have seen such real heroism as I did that night on the ice. How those men ever traveled over ten miles of ice, snow and crevices will always be a mystery to me.[93]

★ ★ ★

More than thirty years after his joyous return flight to *Pine Island* aboard *George III*, 'Robbie' Robbins reconsidered the events that had resulted in the loss of his aircraft, the deaths of Hendersin, Williams and Lopez,

and the near-miraculous survival of the remaining members of *George I*'s aircrew. In retrospect, he felt convinced that the first impact, the 'crunching shock' that Kearns reported, had ruptured the PBM's hull fuel tank. Too preoccupied with keeping their aeroplane airborne to notice the dropping needles of their fuel gauges, the pilots initially thought they had enjoyed a miraculous escape, whereas, in fact, high octane aviation fuel had begun to stream from the shattered tank. When this came into contact with the hot engine exhausts, a catastrophic explosion became inevitable. Though their low altitude had been the cause of the accident, ironically it also helped to save the lives of most of the crew because, instead of being hurled into the air hundreds of metres above the earth, they fell relatively short distances into the surrounding snow drifts. In two out of three cases, the men who died might also have survived relatively unscathed, had they not had the misfortune to strike the PBM's propellers as they were thrown from the disintegrating aircraft.

But why did *George I* hit the ground in the first place? The answer is that, as with so many air accidents, in the moments before impact LeBlanc and his crew encountered the 'perfect storm': a devastating combination of meteorological, navigational, topographical, technical and human factors that served to seal their fate.

When describing his own experience of flying in 'ice blink' nearly two decades earlier, Byrd had remarked that it would be easy 'for a careless or intimidated pilot to fly his plane straight down into the snow. There was no point on which to pin the nose of the plane for steady, level flight. Only a milky, trembling nothingness.'[94] While there is no real evidence of carelessness on the part of LeBlanc and Kearns – though LeBlanc's decision to fly at an altitude of just 300m in poor visibility and over largely unknown territory seems questionable – the conditions they encountered on their approach towards Thurston Island clearly left both pilots disorientated. In his semi-official account of both the expedition and the accident, Byrd blamed the crew's lack of familiarity with the prevailing conditions, emphasising, 'In all their years of flying they had come across nothing even remotely like it.'[95] He also admitted that, in his view at least:

> Responsibility for the tragedy was mine. I had briefed and alerted the expedition on that strange phenomenon of multiple light reflection visibility … but that it did not get down through the chain of command to the pilot of that plane was my fault.[96]

Blind and bewildered, LeBlanc and Kearns became totally reliant on Lopez's navigation and on the radar readings provided by Robbins. But, in 1946, mapping of the area was at best incomplete, and at worst utterly inaccurate – as is evidenced by the fact that, for twenty years following its discovery by Byrd in 1940, the island was thought to be a peninsula. The very purpose of Operation Highjump's aerial survey was to correct such flaws.

Work undertaken by BAS and other research bodies over subsequent decades has also shown that Thurston Island is an area of particularly high deposition, resulting in the creation of large snow mounds, as difficult to map and as changeable as the sand dunes of the Sahara Desert. Crucially, these mounds – and, indeed, the underlying coastline of Thurston Island itself – have very gentle gradients, rendering them all but invisible to the relatively early radar carried by *George I*. For his part, Robbins became convinced that the unusual topographical characteristics of Thurston Island had caused the accident, later stating his belief that:

> This 'no returns' phenomenon was the first ever 'stealth radar' happening. The uncharted area from the coast to 800 feet [244m] in altitude where we hit was such a gradual incline that there was nothing for the radar to see.[97]

In the few minutes before the impact, he felt absolutely certain that his equipment was functioning well and that its readings corresponded with the charts. His misplaced confidence – which seemed to be justified both by the radar's ability to pick up accurately the icebergs below, and by his own 'vast polar experience'[98] – almost certainly contributed to the pilots' slow response to the fluctuating altimeter readings, readings that would soon prove to be devastatingly accurate.

Finally, should *George I* have been airborne in the first place? The meteorological conditions during the last few days of December 1946 had proved extremely treacherous, with short spells of fine weather quickly giving way to much longer periods of fog, interspersed with snow squalls. The rational response to the prevailing conditions would have been to wait before launching long-range surveys. But the expedition would be limited to just one austral summer and its window of opportunity to achieve the desired results was necessarily limited. This knowledge almost certainly added to Caldwell's impatience after days of enforced inactivity and encouraged him to order flights that he knew to be extremely dangerous.

Recording his own experiences spotting whales in the Antarctic during the same period, John Grierson acknowledged:

> There is nothing more trying to a flier than days, maybe weeks, between flights in the isolation of a ship ... I must confess that I infinitely prefer to take risks myself in the cockpit than to stay in the security of a ship.[99]

He also recognised:

> When such vast sums of money as are represented by a ship costing one and a half million and by an expedition whose running expenses amount to half a million, are at stake, those responsible for the success of the expedition would need to be superhuman not to have some misgivings occasionally.[100]

How much greater must those misgivings be when the costs involved are as vast as those required for Operation Highjump, and when the outcome of the expedition would affect not only personal but national prestige?

Described by George Dufek as 'a good leader, a horse of a man ... capable, determined, and aggressive',[101] perhaps on this occasion Caldwell's determination to succeed – and, equally perhaps, his fear of failure – overwhelmed his discretion. If this was indeed the case, he would not be the first polar explorer to give way to such pressure, nor the last.

6

'Cold, Very Cold'

Deaths by Hypothermia

When, on 29 March 1912, Captain Scott wrote his last exhortation, 'For God's sake look after our people',[1] two members of his Polar Party, 'Titus' Oates and 'Taff' Evans, were already dead, and Scott, 'Uncle Bill' Wilson and 'Birdie' Bowers had just a few hours left to live. The surviving trio had used the last of their fuel to make two cups of tea apiece on the 20th, and they had consumed their remaining food, which they ate cold, sometime between then and the date of Scott's final journal entry. All were suffering from frostbite of varying degrees of severity – on the 19th Scott had written of his right foot, 'Amputation is the least I can hope for now'[2] – and their lack of fuel meant that they could no longer even melt snow to drink, let alone cook food or keep warm. 'Every day,' Scott noted:

> … we have been ready to start for our depot 11 miles [17.7km] away, but outside the door of the tent it remains a scene of whirling drift. I do not think we can hope for any better things now. We shall stick it out to the end, but we are getting weaker, of course, and the end cannot be far. It seems a pity but I do not think I can write more.[3]

In the century since Scott pencilled his final words, debate has raged over what caused, or most contributed to, the tragedy that overwhelmed his party. In turn, the spacing of the depots, the quantity and quality of the food, the decision to commence the journey so late in the season, the selection of five men instead of four, the distractions of an extensive scientific programme, the timing of Oates's suicide, Scott's leadership and

planning, and his choice of ponies and man-hauling as his main means of locomotion have all been analysed and argued over ad nauseam.

In reality, of course, while some or even all of these factors may have played a part in the disaster, ultimately none of them single-handedly determined the fate of the Polar Party. But, as Susan Solomon has cogently argued in her book, *The Coldest March*, one factor did make all the difference between life and death. According to Solomon, a comparison of the detailed meteorological data collated by George Simpson, meteorologist on the *Terra Nova* Expedition, with information gathered over the last decades of the twentieth century from an array of automated weather stations in Antarctica, 'points not to errors made by men but toward the capriciousness of nature as the stunningly decisive blow to the survival of Scott, Bowers, Wilson, and Oates'.[4]

Based upon their own observations and those of previous expeditions, including Scott's *Discovery* Expedition and Shackleton's *Nimrod* Expedition, the Polar Party anticipated that, when they descended the Beardmore Glacier to reach the Great Barrier on their return journey, they would experience a welcome rise in temperature. This comparative warmth – or lesser cold – would play a vital role in enabling them to maintain the daily mileages that they knew to be essential if they were to reach their winter quarters at Cape Evans before the end of the sledging season. Initially, reality matched their expectations, and analysis first published by Solomon in 1999 'reveals that the minimum daily temperatures experienced by Scott and his men from about February 10 through 25, 1912, while on the southern end of the Ross Ice Shelf were comparable to the climatological average.'[5]

Of course, this does not mean that the journey up to this point was trouble free. On 11 February, for instance, Scott recorded that his party had endured the 'worst day we have had during the trip', though he also admitted that this was 'greatly owing to our own fault', as they had steered too far to the east of their proper path.[6] The following day, another navigational error resulted in their arriving 'in a horrid maze of crevasses and fissures', leaving them in a 'very critical situation'.[7] Then, on 17 February, 'Taff' Evans, whose physical and mental condition had been giving increasing cause for concern, collapsed. 'I was the first to reach the poor man,' recorded Scott, 'and [was] shocked at his appearance; he was on his knees with clothing disarranged, hands uncovered and frostbitten, and a wild look in his eyes ... He died quietly at 12.30 a.m.'[8] In the absence of a post-mortem, the exact cause of Evans' decline and death could not be determined, but Wilson believed it to be brain damage sustained in an earlier fall. 'It is a terrible thing to lose a companion in this way,' wrote Scott. But then, with exceptional candour, he admitted, 'Calm reflection shows that there could not have been a better ending to the terrible anxieties of the past week.'[9]

Although the rest of the party were now relieved of the burden of a dying man, their progress continued to be disappointing, largely due to the poor quality of the surface on which they were travelling. 'I am anxious about the Barrier surfaces,' Scott admitted on the 18th. 'The surface was every bit as bad as I expected,' he recorded the following day; 'Same terrible surface' on the 20th; and 'really terrible surface,' four days later. Then, at last, the surface began to improve and with it the daily averages: 'Day yields 11.4 miles [18.3km],' he noted with evident relief on 25 February, 'the first double figure of steady dragging for a long time', and, on the 26th, 'Nine hours' solid marching has given us 11½ miles [18.5km]'. However, in the same entry he made the ominous observation that the day had been 'cold, very cold. Nothing dries and we get our feet cold too often.'[10]

Between 10 and 24 February, the temperatures recorded by the Polar Party had ranged between −11°C and −27°C, which is normal for the season. But during the night of 26–27 February, the temperature dropped precipitously, to an extraordinary −38°C. The following night, the mercury fell to below −40°C and it was still −36°C when the day's march began. 'There is no doubt,' wrote Scott with remarkable understatement, 'the middle of the Barrier is a pretty awful locality.'[11] Matters did not improve over the coming days and, according to Solomon:

> From the end of February until the last temperatures were recorded on March 19, Scott and his men struggled through three weeks when almost every daily minimum temperature was a bitter and debilitating 10–20°F colder than what can now be shown to be typical based on many years of observations in this region … Minimum temperatures day after gruelling day were forty to fifty degrees colder than those that Lieutenant [Teddy] Evans had encountered on the Barrier just a month before.[12]

To all intents and purposes, from the night of 26–27 February, the fate of Scott and his companions was sealed.

The immediate effects of this catastrophic drop in temperature were twofold. First, it became ever more difficult for the remaining four men to

propel their sledge. On 3 March, having covered a mere 7km in four and a half exhausting hours, Scott observed:

> One cannot consider this a fault of our own – certainly we were pulling hard this morning …
>
> It was more than three parts surface which held us back – the wind at strongest, powerless to move the sledge. When the light is good it is easy to see the reason. The surface, lately a very good hard one, is coated with a thin layer of woolly crystals, formed by radiation, no doubt. These are too firmly fixed to be removed by the wind and cause impossible friction on the runners. God help us, we can't keep up this pulling, that is certain.[13]

Scott was right: though their growing debility would inevitably reduce their pulling power, the fault did not lie with his men. Instead, the plunging temperature prevented the formation of lubricating meltwater between the sledge runners and the snow surface. The production of meltwater is influenced by factors including the temperature at the snow surface, the weights being carried on the sledge and the speed of movement, but, in essence, the lower the ambient temperature, the greater the friction, and the more difficult the pull.[14] These, then, were the conditions that produced what Scott described as the 'sandy frost-rime'[15] that so retarded their progress.

The second effect of the cold was a substantial increase in the dual risks of frostbite and hypothermia. One recent clinical account of the identification and treatment of cold injuries states:

> The amount of muscle and fat a person has may be more important than his or her age in defending against hypothermia. Less body fat decreases tissue insulation. Malnutrition and exertion decrease the fuel available for heat generation.[16]

We now know that the calorific intake of Scott's Polar Party fell woefully short of what they required to fuel the colossal exertion of man-hauling – potentially 2,500 calories per day less than they needed during their trek across the Polar Plateau[17] – with the result that, by the time they descended to the Great Barrier, they had burned off a considerable amount of body fat and even muscle. On their slim rations, the more they struggled across a worsening surface, the more weight they lost and the more exhausted they became, leaving them ever more susceptible to the increasing cold.

The devastating impacts of cold and malnutrition soon became apparent. On 2 March, Oates revealed the condition of his feet to his companions, 'the toes showing very bad indeed, evidently bitten by the late temperatures'.[18] Three days later, his feet were 'in a wretched condition':

> One swelled up tremendously last night and he is very lame this morning. We started march on tea and pemmican as last night … Marched for 5 hours this morning over a slightly better surface covered with high moundy sastrugi. Sledge capsized twice … Our fuel dreadfully low and the poor Soldier nearly done. It is pathetic enough because we can do nothing for him; more hot food might do a little, but only a little, I fear. We none of us expected these terribly low temperatures, and of the rest of us Wilson is feeling them most; mainly, I fear, from his self-sacrificing devotion in doctoring Oates's feet. We cannot help each other, each has enough to do to take care of himself.[19]

By 6 March, Oates could pull only occasionally and his morale was failing fast, 'his spirits only come up in spurts now, and he grows more silent in the tent'. Like Evans before him, he had become 'a terrible hindrance', delaying the party's departure after each camp as he struggled to don his footgear and then reducing their progress as they waited for the shambling wreck to catch up. 'He asked Wilson if he had a chance this morning,' Scott noted on 10 March, 'and of course Bill had to say he didn't know. In point of fact he has none.'[20]

By 12 March, Oates' hands, too, were 'pretty well useless'. Worse still, Wilson's debility had also increased and on the 14th Scott observed that the doctor experienced great difficulty in removing his skis. The crisis for Oates came on the morning of either 15 or 16 March (Scott had lost track of dates):

> He slept through the night before last, hoping not to wake; but he woke in the morning – yesterday. It was blowing a blizzard. He said, 'I am just going outside and may be some time'. He went out into the blizzard and we have not seen him since.[21]

Although Scott opined that Oates's suicide was 'the act of a brave man and an English gentleman', by this point he knew that it would make no material difference to the chances of the remaining trio:

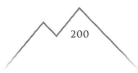

Assuredly the end is not far. I can only write at lunch and then only occasionally. The cold is intense, −40° [C] at midday … we are all on the verge of serious frostbites, and though we constantly talk of fetching through I don't think any one of us believes it in his heart.[22]

On the 18th, Scott recorded, 'My right foot has gone, nearly all the toes', and the next day he and his companions pitched their tent for the last time, with further movement prevented by the onset of a blizzard from the nor'-nor'-west. This day, 19 March, would also be the last upon which Scott recorded the temperature: it was −40°C.

As a scientist, George Simpson felt convinced that 'the weather played a predominating part in the disaster',[23] and Solomon's comparison of Simpson's data with that gathered from the automated weather stations set up in the 1980s proves beyond any reasonable doubt that Scott and his men experienced a lengthy period of abnormal cold that they could not have predicted. Scott himself was absolutely certain that the weather had brought about his downfall, and in his 'Message to the Public', which he wrote around the time of his last journal entry, he insisted:

> … that our arrangements for returning were quite adequate, and that no one in the world would have expected the temperatures and surfaces which we encountered at this time of the year. On the summit in lat. 85° 86° we had –20°, -30° [−29°C to −34°C]. On the Barrier in lat. 82°, 10,000 feet lower, we had −30° [−34°C] in the day, −47° [−44°C] at night pretty regularly, with continuous head wind during our day marches. It is clear that these circumstances come on very suddenly, and our wreck is certainly due to this sudden advent of severe weather, which does not seem to have any satisfactory cause.[24]

Cold, then, created the conditions that brought about Scott's death and those of his four companions. The actual cause of death, however – the cause that, in other circumstances, would have been entered on a death certificate by an attending physician – was almost certainly hypothermia, complicated by frostbite, vitamin deficiencies, malnutrition and dehydration.

In the words of Dr Henry Guly, a retired member of the British Antarctic Survey's Medical Unit (BASMU) and the author of numerous papers on medicine and illness during the Heroic Age:

Three types of accidental hypothermia are recognised. Acute hypothermia (often called immersion hypothermia) is caused by sudden exposure to cold such as immersion in cold water or a person caught in a snow avalanche. Exhaustion hypothermia is caused by exposure to cold in association with lack of food and exhaustion such that heat can no longer be generated. Chronic hypothermia comes on over days or weeks and mainly affects the elderly.[25]

Evans' head trauma – which none of his companions described in detail – would have made him particularly susceptible to hypothermia, and his reported cognitive dysfunction, delirium and ultimate coma all appear to be absolutely typical of the condition. In their turn, Scott, Bowers and Wilson were almost certainly victims of exhaustion hypothermia, caused by excessive and protracted cold. Only Oates' death varied from this pattern. Though he, too, exhibited all the symptoms of exhaustion hypothermia, his final decision to leave the tent meant that, ultimately, he died of acute (or immersion) hypothermia amidst the whirling snows of the blizzard that raged outside.

A party led by Dr Edward Atkinson discovered the bodies of Scott, Wilson and Bowers seven and a half months later. 'We have found them,' Apsley Cherry-Garrard wrote in his diary on 12 November. 'To say it has been a ghastly day cannot express it – it is too bad for words.'[26] Later, he described the scene inside the tent:

> Bowers and Wilson were sleeping in their bags. Scott had thrown back the flaps of his bag at the end. His left hand was stretched over Wilson, his lifelong friend ... I feel sure that he [Scott] had died last.[27]

Almost immediately, this description of the two friends, bound in death, entered the already potent mythology of the *Terra Nova* Expedition: Scott's last, intensely human urge to rest his hand upon the body of his dead friend providing the final act in a tragedy that he had already described so compellingly in his diary and in the elegiac prose of his 'Message to the Public'.

There is, though, another, and rather more clinical, interpretation of Scott's last act. When, on 17 February, he, Wilson, Bowers and Oates had retraced their steps to find Evans, they discovered him on his hands and knees in the snow, his 'clothing disarranged' and his 'hands uncovered'.

As Henry Guly has confirmed, we now 'know that "paradoxical undressing" (i.e. the patient undressing despite being cold, either because of confusion or because they believe they are too warm) can be a feature of hypothermia'.[28] This was the behaviour of Evans in his last moments of consciousness. Though the interpretation sits ill with the more romanticised notions of Scott's death – notions to which Cherry-Garrard undoubtedly subscribed – perhaps Scott's open sleeping bag and his hand thrown across Wilson were also indications not of a final act of friendship, but of the pathology of the hypothermia that ultimately killed him.

★ ★ ★

In later years, the deaths of Scott's Polar Party would come to epitomise both the heroism and the ills of Antarctic exploration during the Heroic Age – and yet, in almost every respect, the circumstances of their deaths were unique and wholly unrepresentative of this or any other epoch. Scott, Wilson and Bowers expired at a point approximately 79.6°S 170°E; they had been on the trail for nearly five months; they had already trudged more than 2,500km; and they were still about 270km from their hut at Cape Evans. Scott admitted that 'we took risks',[29] but, ultimately, the last members of his five-man team, malnourished and exhausted, fell victim to a highly unusual and sustained period of intense cold that drastically reduced their progress and massively increased their exposure to the twin spectres of frostbite and hypothermia.

In contrast, practically every other cold-related death in the Antarctic has occurred during a local excursion, usually on well-trodden paths and often just a matter of metres from the warmth and security of a base hut. Those who have died in this fashion have been fit and well fed and they have fallen victim to predictable local conditions. In many cases, their deaths have been entirely avoidable, in a way that the deaths of Scott and his men – at least according to the persuasive analysis of Solomon and Simpson – were not.

The routine of any Antarctic base is punctuated by the need to undertake a range of outdoor tasks. With the evolution of polar bases and the development of our attitudes to ecology, many of these chores have changed, or been eradicated altogether, but traditionally they included some that were necessary for the welfare of the expedition members, such as the fetching of fuel, food and snow, hunting for penguins and seals, and the clearing of windows, doors and chimneys. Others – including visits to the Stevenson

Screen, the magnetic hut, and the edge of the sea ice – formed part of a base's scientific programme. Finally, dogs, when present, must be fed and watered and have their chains dug out to prevent strangulation. And, of course, the ease with which these duties were completed was entirely dependent upon the weather.

Overall, the meteorologists were perhaps the most to be pitied, as their work necessitated visits to the monitoring equipment every few hours, day and night, regardless of darkness, gales, drift and freezing temperatures. One of the best descriptions of these regular forays was provided by Vivian Fuchs, during the Commonwealth Trans-Antarctic Expedition's winter on the Filchner Ice Shelf in 1957:

> As [the] hour approaches [the] observer dresses appropriately for outside conditions and attempts to glide stealthily from [the] living room to avoid waking irate light sleepers ... Once outside, [his] route leads over hard snow crust surface above [the] sounding-board roof which vibrates to every crunching footstep. Happily unconscious of this and, striving to find a way through driving drifts, [he] falls down [a] six-foot drift slope, finally arriving at the screen which is certainly full of snow. Clears it sufficiently to read instruments – crunches [his] way back over roof, trips over aerial mast stay, falls up [the] six-foot slope and regains tunnel entrances. Now frozen and covered in snow, [he] compromises with seven doors by leaving most of them open. In Met office [he] records and codes observations then back to recline on bunk till repeat performance 3 a.m.[30]

Meteorology, explained Hannes La Grange, the expedition's South African meteorologist, is 'like a religion, either you believe in it, or you don't',[31] and throughout the expedition he conducted his routine observations with unwavering dedication. Equally impressive, though, was the commitment displayed by the amateurs that most expeditions included in their staff: men who, in normal circumstances, would not be expected to pursue with such rigour the arcane mysteries of a science in which they had received no formal training, but who, in the punishing Antarctic environment, often demonstrated the passionate conviction of converts.

Given the nature of their duties, the frequency with which their observations must be taken and the conditions in which they worked, it is not surprising that a number of meteorologists have fallen victim to the very phenomena that they have sought to study – and, all too often, experience has provided little or no immunity. One such victim was André Prud'homme, senior meteorologist with the Expéditions Polaires Françaises, and the first Frenchman to die on the Antarctic continent.

Funded through a combination of private finance and a grant from the National Assembly, the first French expedition to the Antarctic since Charcot's Heroic Age voyages of 1903–05 and 1908–10 landed on the Adélie Coast, in the French Antarctic sector, early in 1950. A twelve-man team under the command of André-Franck Liotard reached Cape Margerie on 18 January and work began immediately on the construction of the expedition's main base, which they named Port Martin Station after the expedition's second in command, J.A. Martin, who had died en route to the Antarctic. The site of the base lay close to the winter quarters of Mawson's AAE (67°0'S 142°40'E) and, as Paul-Émile Victor, the veteran director of the Expéditions Polaires Françaises, would later declare, the conditions proved just as hostile as those faced by the Australian expedition nearly four decades earlier:

> In Adélie Coast, the winds come directly from the Pole without meeting any obstacle in between, and they reach speeds of 100mph [161kph], and even 150mph [241kph] or more at certain points. There are blizzards on an average of eight days out of ten in this land near the South Pole which Mawson had christened the 'home of the blizzard'. Human efficiency was drastically reduced in these conditions. The efficiency of scientific equipment was also endangered; anemometers toppled over, radio antennas were twisted out of shape, recording instruments were filled with powdery snow; the variations in the magnetic field were so great that they exceeded the instruments' capacity to compensate; radio contact was often blacked out.[32]

Despite these challenges, over the next six months Liotard's party made twelve journeys inland, using both dog teams and Studebaker Weasels. One of these expeditions covered 604km on the glacial highlands, while another located a large emperor penguin rookery on the Pointe Géologie Peninsula, only the fifth such rookery to be discovered up to that date.

Liotard's party was relieved on 9 January 1951 by a team under the leadership of Michel Barré, and the extensive scientific programme continued uninterrupted. In April, further journeys commenced and, on

10 June, an eight-man party reached the rookery at Pointe Géologie where, for only the second time in history, they observed the remarkable incubation rituals of the emperor penguin.[33]

The extraordinarily harsh winter of 1951 was André Prud'homme's first experience of the Antarctic, and it fascinated him. On his return to France in 1952, he wrote up his meteorological observations, including an exposition of his novel theories on wind phenomena, which were then published in 1957.[34] This publication established the 37-year-old Prud'homme as France's leading specialist in Antarctic meteorology and guaranteed him a place on the scientific staff of the French contingent of the IGY, which based itself at the new Dumont D'Urville Station on Petrel Island, one of the islands of the Pointe Géologie archipelago, roughly 62km to the west of Cape Margerie.

Mario Marret, who spent a winter on Petrel Island studying the newly discovered emperor penguin colony, described the whole of Pointe Géologie as:

> A large zoo without bars, in an unspoiled natural reserve where petrels, penguins, Cape doves, skuas and seals disported themselves, fished, built their nests, coupled, were born, fluttered around learning to fly, chattered and squawked, and increased and multiplied without let or hindrance – almost.[35]

Fascinating though its fecundity might make it to biologists, Petrel Island also has its attractions for meteorologists. Of particular interest is the relative benignity of the local climate, which compares very favourably even with Port Martin, just a few kilometres down the coast. The mean temperature is considerably higher, and the surrounding islands provide protection from the worst of the blizzards that batter the neighbouring shores.

These, then, were the phenomena that Prud'homme studied throughout the IGY. The work of the expedition was, in Victor's opinion, slow and unglamorous,[36] but Prud'homme's research flourished throughout 1958, and he planned to share his findings with the Melbourne meteorological conference scheduled for February 1959.[37]

On 7 January, just twenty hours before the expected arrival of the veteran relief ship *Norsel*, Prud'homme left the living quarters of Dumont D'Urville Station to complete what would have been one of his last rounds of meteorological observations prior to his departure from the Antarctic. He was never seen again, and the mystery has never been satisfactorily resolved.

Prud'homme was both highly experienced in Antarctic conditions and very familiar with the layout of the base and the surrounding terrain. When he left the hut at 3.30 p.m., a blizzard was blowing, but these were relatively commonplace, despite the shelter afforded by the islands of the archipelago. The anemometer registered a wind speed of around 97kph, but visibility was not unusually poor and the meteorological shelters lay only 90m from the hut's door. However, Petrel Island is so rocky and uneven that it had been necessary to erect a scaffold to provide suitable foundations for the huts, and recent snowfalls had made the surface particularly treacherous; perhaps, then, Prud'homme slipped and sustained a head injury. Or, he might have become disorientated in the blizzard conditions and fallen victim to acute hypothermia. Whatever the cause of his confusion, the most probable explanation for his disappearance is that he quite simply walked straight into the sea and drowned. When he failed to return, his colleagues sounded the alarm, and by 6 p.m. every man on the base had joined the search. The arrival of the *Norsel* enabled the searchers to extend their operations using whaleboats and helicopters, but to no avail. Prud'homme had vanished.

In contrast, there can be no doubt regarding the circumstances of Shin Fukushima's death, and they further evidence the bewildering effects of blizzard conditions. Fukushima, a 28-year-old geophysicist specialising in cosmic rays and aurora, served with the fourth Japanese Antarctic Research Expedition, based at Syowa Station on East Ongul Island in Queen Maud Land. On the afternoon of 10 October 1960, he and Yoshio Yoshida, a geomorphologist and dog handler, left their base to feed the expedition's dog teams and to inspect sledges that had been prepared for a planned traverse of the fast ice in Ongul Strait. On leaving the hut, the two scientists encountered a blizzard far more severe than the one that had claimed Prud'homme's life the previous year and, with a wind velocity of 33m per second, visibility was reduced to just 1m.

They quickly located the dogs and fed them with the table scraps that Yoshida carried, but then they agreed that it would be foolish to try to find the sledges in the whirling maelstrom. Instead, they would return to the safety of their living quarters. 'Before long,' recalled Yoshida, 'Shin's back disappeared from my poor visual field – my eyes are very short-sighted and at that time I did not use my eyeglasses due to the heavy blizzard.'[38] In these conditions, shouting to attract attention would be futile, but Yoshida was lucky: quite by accident he stumbled across a pressure ridge that he recognised, and this enabled him to work out his position in relation to the hut entrance. Shortly afterwards, at around 3 p.m., he burst through the door, mildly frostbitten and with his clothes full of drift snow.

Fukushima was not so fortunate. When Yoshida returned alone, Dr Tetsuya Torii, the base leader, immediately initiated a search, with the Japanese personnel aided by a party of visiting Belgians from the Roi Boudouin Base. But conditions were so bad that two of the search parties became so disorientated themselves that they were unable to retrace their steps to the hut and spent over twenty-four hours outside. None found any trace of the missing geophysicist.

The mystery surrounding Fukushima's disappearance was finally resolved on 10 February 1968, when a geological survey party stumbled across his frozen corpse on the western edge of West Ongul Island. A combination of exceptionally light snowfall in recent years and warm weather had combined to reveal his body which, according to one report, 'had almost the appearance of life'.[39] Even more extraordinary than the reappearance of Fukushima's lifelike body after nearly eight years, was its location. We now know that, after becoming separated from Yoshida, he had walked some 6km from Syowa Station (the total distance he travelled potentially being even greater, if divergences from a direct course are taken into account). Perhaps he had mistakenly tried to locate Yoshida, whom he knew to be short-sighted, or he had simply become completely disorientated.

All the time, as he trudged forward through the blizzard, the effects of acute hypothermia would have been taking their toll on his mind and body. As his core temperature dropped below the 36–38°C norm, he would have become increasingly tired; his dexterity and reaction times would have slowed and his judgement would have become more impaired, rendering him incapable of remedying his initial mistake. With a core temperature below 35°C, he would have been shivering violently, while deteriorating motor skills and muscle co-ordination would have slowed his walking pace, until it became a stumble, and his mental faculties would have become ever more clouded. Once his core temperature dropped below 32°C, acute energy loss would have prevented further shivering, and his temperature loss would have accelerated. By this point, Fukushima would have been only semi-conscious, and no longer aware of his surroundings. It may have been at this stage that he collapsed, or deliberately sat or lay down in the snow, too exhausted and confused to continue. By the time his core temperature reached 30°C he would have lost consciousness, his pulse would have become almost

unmeasurable, his breathing shallow and erratic, and his pupils dilated and unresponsive to light. Death would have followed soon afterwards.

The terrifying ease with which the onset of a blizzard could disguise landmarks and make even well-known surroundings completely unfamiliar was described by Hal Lister, base leader at South Ice, the forward glaciological research station of the Commonwealth Trans-Antarctic Expedition. During the winter of 1957, Lister, like so many scientists before and since, willingly left the safety of the expedition hut to undertake routine observations – in his case, the measurement of snow accumulation. Just a few metres from the trapdoor he found himself completely disorientated by a combination of thick, sizzling drift and a freakish change in wind direction. For two hours he stumbled among the sastrugi, blinded and directionless:

> The distance from South Ice could surely be no more than 300 yards [274m] yet I could see nothing but snow lines and hummocks. By this time I was not sure of distance or of direction … I had to wait and hope that the weather would ease a little or my colleagues would fire a flare to give me a glimpse of direction. To keep warm I walked the square … I lay down for five minutes, walked ten yards and back and lay down again, sheltering behind a higher sastrugi, then repeated the process hoping someone would realise that I was outside longer than usual.[40]

Eventually, frostbitten and exhausted, Lister saw a light twinkling through the sheets of drift: a Tilley lamp suspended from the top of the Dexion mast by one of his companions, anxious at his absence. Wondering whether he was hallucinating, Lister staggered towards the beacon, his thick beard a mass of snow, ice and frozen mucus, and his hands thrust into his armpits to protect them from severe damage. Eventually, the light led him to the mast and on to the trapdoor and safety.

Given that detailed and frequent scientific observations have been integral to the work of most expeditions, and that the greatest value can be obtained from these observations if they are maintained uninterruptedly no matter what the conditions, to most observers it will appear extraordinary that the well-being of scientists, and those undertaking more mundane but essential tasks, has not been routinely safeguarded by the rigging of lifelines running between a station's buildings and other key installations. After all, it requires nothing more complicated than the driving in of stakes at set intervals and the uncoiling of rope or wire. Additional security would be achieved

through the insistence that, in blizzard conditions, anyone venturing outdoors should link themselves to the lines using a combination of belts and carabiner clips. And yet, all too often, lifelines have not been rigged, either because they were thought to be a nuisance or, as one FIDS veteran recently admitted, 'because we could always find something more interesting to do'.[41] In the absence of these, surely the simplest of expedients, Lister's luck held. Prud'homme's and Fukushima's did not.

★ ★ ★

If a blizzard can so effectively confound the recognition of well-known landmarks around a base, its ability to bewilder in less familiar surroundings must increase tenfold. This reality was most tragically evidenced at Stonington Island during the austral winter of 1966.

Sir Ranulph Fiennes has written that any expedition to Antarctica 'is almost wholly dependent, both for its success and for its ultimate survival, upon teamwork ... the man who fuels the stove or minds the storeroom becomes as essential as even the most fêted explorer'.[42] It was in recognition of this truth, and in order to maintain morale, that BAS developed the practice of allowing men usually employed on its bases to undertake short recreational sledging journeys. Although such excursions facilitated the development of field craft and helped to keep dog teams in good condition, their primary objective was fun, and, as Vivian Fuchs recognised, 'these "jollies" were greatly prized by the static staff'.[43]

Throughout the sledging season of 1965–66, John Noel, a radio operator and mechanic, and Tom Allan, a carpenter and general assistant, had remained at Base E on Stonington Island, undertaking unglamorous but essential routine observations and maintenance duties while their companions took part in sledging expeditions. Poor weather had made completion of the field work difficult and time-consuming,[44] but by the middle of May all of the sledge parties had returned safely and, on the 19th, Terry Tallis, the base leader, contacted Port Stanley to request permission for the two men to undertake their own small-scale excursion towards the Northeast and McClary glaciers. Travelling no further than 50km from the base, they would take two dog teams, each of nine dogs, and rations and fuel for thirty days – though they expected to be absent for no more than ten. As Tallis later confirmed, it was considered 'customary for base members, who are not field workers, to have a short holiday',[45] and, as he anticipated, no objections were raised.

Delighted to have received a 'green light' for their jaunt, on 21 May Noel and Allan undertook a preliminary day trip to lay a small food depot at the foot of the 826m Walton Peak, which they also climbed. At lunchtime two days later, they set off in earnest, Noel driving the 'Trogs', and Allan the 'Moomins'. During the routine radio schedule at 5 p.m. the following evening, Noel transmitted the somewhat cryptic message, 'Position East Butson and on the move, "Manking" in'.[46] Later discoveries proved that they had camped that night on Butson Ridge at an altitude of 610m, and that the next day they had pushed on towards Square Bay via a mountain route.

From this point forward, Tallis received no further updates by radio, but he felt no immediate concern as the silence was almost certainly due to interference caused by the worsening weather. After logging receipt of the field party's message, he noted in his diary that the weather at Base E had become overcast, with a wind which, in the absence of an anemometer, he estimated at 25–30 knots. 'Wind increasing and ice breaking up, which was about 3–4 inches [7–10cm] thick,' he observed the next day. 'Late afternoon and evening the wind was gusting 80–100 knots, the whole base hut was shaking, items falling off shelves and two very large crates with coal bags on top of them were blown away and not seen again.'[47] Experience had shown that wind speeds might be 10–20 knots higher in Noel and Allan's locality, so the break in communications came as no surprise.[48] According to surveyor Neil Marsden:

> Radio communication was never brilliant in those days and especially up the top of the North-East [Glacier], so we didn't hear from them after three days but we didn't particularly worry about it, the wind blew up and there was a lot of drift around … but it was nothing unusual to be out of contact.[49]

The base receiver remained silent even after a calm settled on Stonington Island on 28 May – but this, too, could be explained. After all, while the pair's No. 68 field radio set had been used by the earlier field parties and had functioned well at that time, equipment breakdowns remained fairly commonplace. Even when they failed to return at the expiry of their allotted ten days on 2 June, their delay could have been caused by any number of minor accidents; besides, the men were known to be competent, well equipped and accompanied by two strong dog teams. More than four decades later, Tallis admitted, 'We were, of course, very worried about them,'[50] but it wasn't until 7 June, with Noel and Allan now

overdue by five days, that he advised Stanley of his decision to dispatch a search party made up of Neil Marsden and geologist Keith Holmes.

The two men left the base at first light (11 a.m.) on the 7th, Holmes driving the 'Giants', and Marsden the 'Komats'. Like Noel and Allan before them, that afternoon they camped on Butson Ridge, roughly 18.5km from the base, and undertook a search for the pair's first campsite. The next morning, they sledged to the head of the McClary Glacier and while Holmes walked up a rocky spur overlooking the lower portion of the glacier, Marsden sledged downhill to search for tracks. 'Continued northwards,' they reported on their return, 'and were beginning to descend the glacier to Square Bay when Holmes, who was following, spotted what we were looking for about 100 yards [91m] to the west on a steepish slope below a rocky bluff.'[51]

According to Marsden:

> We saw these black specks in the snow and we found Tom and John and they were both dead, all the dogs were dead … the big black speck … was the top half of John Noel; he was buried from [the] waist downwards. He was sort of looking out towards a rocky slope about a hundred yards away … and at the bottom of this rocky slope was Tom Allan lying on his back.[52]

Having first confirmed that the men and dogs were all dead, Holmes and Marsden immediately turned back to base, so that they could report their findings without trusting them to a radio signal, which they knew could be intercepted by amateur shortwave radio buffs in the Falklands.[53] They covered all 43km in the half-light of the afternoon, arriving at Base E with their grim tidings at 7 p.m. that evening.

Unfortunately, this understandable decision to return without having completed any further investigations gave rise to some inaccurate speculation regarding the deaths of Noel and Allan. In particular, on 9 June, Vivian Fuchs wrote to the families of the dead men, telling them that both had 'lost their lives on a sledging journey when their camp was destroyed by high winds'.[54] The following day, a BAS press release repeated the conjecture, stating:

> The camp appeared to have been destroyed by exceptionally high winds … which had strewn the snow with areas of rock fragments torn from the nearby cliffs. It is thought that some of these fragments could have cut up the tent which then blew away … There was no sign of the sledge, nor of the boxes

and gear which it carried. It is presumed that these were also blown away, or that they have been buried beneath the snow.[55]

Only when a second, four-man party returned to the scene on 12 June could a clearer picture be obtained of Noel and Allan's last movements and the circumstances of their deaths.

A detailed excavation of the site resulted in the discovery of the men's map and of Allan's camera. Together, the map and the film in the camera revealed that the pair had camped on East Butson on the night of 24 May and that a wind had been blowing at the time. Subsequent photographs, probably taken the following day, showed that the gale had continued, and probably increased in force – just as it had at the base. Crucially, the dig also resulted in the discovery of a sledge; the main pyramid tent – unstrapped, but still with the sledge; the small, emergency 'pup' tent; and the frozen corpses of the missing dogs, still in their traces. Finally, when the diggers broke into a snow cave, with a 2.5m diameter, and equipped with water, food, bedding, Primus stove, and fuel, they conclusively dispelled the original theory that the men had succumbed to the cold when a powerful gust of wind whipped their tent away. One mystery had been resolved – but another took its place: if Noel and Allan had been able to create a warm and well-stocked emergency shelter, why had they died?

A closer examination of Allan's body revealed that, while he was fully dressed for outdoor work, he had not tied or tucked in his windproof trousers. He was also wearing two left-foot mukluks. This appears to indicate either that he donned his clothes in an emergency or, perhaps more probably, that he dressed fairly carelessly, expecting to return to the snow cave after only a short absence. A small shovel lay by his side. In contrast, when the recovery team began to dig out Noel's body, they found that he was actually standing in the entrance to the snow cave. Moreover, his clothing indicated that he had never intended to leave it, as he had donned only his upper outdoor garments, including his anorak, snow goggles and gloves, but with only his combat trousers and felt slippers below the waste. After he died, the windblown drift had filled any gaps around his torso so that, when discovered, he was still standing, with his arms resting on the surrounding snow surface.

In a later press release, dated 21 July, Fuchs attempted to make sense of the tragedy, and his reconstruction remains compelling. In his opinion, the pair must have been quite relaxed when they broke camp on 25 May, because they clearly intended to follow their original plan of heading for Square Bay. However, either the weather proved more severe than they had at first appreciated, or it quickly worsened, because they had not travelled far when they made their decision to stop again. At this point the plateau rises sharply to a little over 1,500m in the east, but then falls away sharply to the north and west via two wide glaciers. This topography causes much turbulence as the katabatic wind pours down from the plateau, before being channelled across the twin glaciers. In the lee of the neighbouring bluff the wind regularly deposits a considerable portion of the loose snow that it sweeps off the plateau.

Faced with these conditions, Noel and Allan clearly decided to stop and make camp. But, by the time they had unfastened the sledge ropes, conditions must have deteriorated to such a degree that they realised it would be impossible to erect the tent, so, instead, they grabbed their shovels and started to dig. In the circumstances, this decision had been absolutely the right one. They also erected a windbreak using dog-food boxes, probably in an attempt to prevent the drifting snow from immediately filling the hole that they were excavating. Having hollowed out a cave large enough to accommodate them, they then dragged in all their essential equipment, including sleeping bags, food, fuel and Primus – but not their radio – before blocking the entrance with a bag of personal gear. Clearly the conditions had been too poor for them to tend to the dogs, so they simply left them in their traces. As Tallis noted in his accident report, 'Some of the dogs in both teams were notable "Chewers" … Conditions must have been severe if the dogs were not interested in getting loose and returning to base.'[56]

Why did Allan leave the safety of the snow cave? Interviewed forty-five years later, Neil Marsden stated that, in his opinion, and in that of the other members of the recovery party, 'they must have run out of oxygen'.[57] He also speculated on whether, fearful of asphyxiation, Allan might have set out 'to look for a crevasse for them to get into' as an alternative, better ventilated shelter. Although this scenario is possible – the annals of Antarctic exploration are, after all, full of incidents of near suffocation in tents, ship's cabins, snow caves and motor vehicles – the pair's state of dress makes Fuchs's alternative reconstruction more believable.

The dogs, Fuchs pointed out, would have needed to be dug out and brought to the rapidly rising surface level every few hours. This would have been standard practice, and the two men would almost certainly have taken it in turns to perform an unpleasant but essential task. The fact that the searchers located one team on the surface while the other had become buried also indicates that the work was still under way when the men died. In Fuchs' opinion:

> Since Allan was found fully dressed with a shovel beside him, it seems probable that he was freeing the dogs. Because he was found 100 yards [91m] from the campsite it is likely that in going to dig up the second team he missed his way in the dark and the driving snow. He would then have wandered searching for the entrance to the cave. Meanwhile Noel, alarmed at the failure of Allan to return, must have gone to the entrance and stood shouting in an effort to guide him back … (It would have been entirely wrong for Noel to start searching, for then the entrance would have disappeared beneath the snow and both men would have been left wandering in the blizzard).[58]

Clearly Allan could not hear Noel's calls, and he did not find his way back. As for Noel, though he could have retreated into the cave at any time, instead he remained at the entrance trying desperately to save his friend. Eventually both men, just a few metres apart, succumbed to acute hypothermia. 'It was,' Fuchs opined in his later history of BAS, 'a tremendous example of courage that he remained to the last, and most assuredly he gave his life for his friend.'[59]

In retrospect, it is difficult to disagree with Fuchs' summation. In the years after the death of Scott's Polar Party, much was made of Oates' decision to walk into the blizzard in what many saw as an heroic effort to save his companions. And yet, by the time he acted, Oates' move could make no material difference to the fate of the remaining trio: his suicide was the act of an exhausted man who, after weeks of intense suffering, had reached the limit of his endurance. Noel's act was very different: at any point during the blizzard he could have re-entered the cave and plugged the entrance. He had ample food and fuel and his survival would have been almost guaranteed. In the last minutes of his life, the effects of hypothermia would almost certainly have reduced his ability to think clearly, but his decision to remain exposed for so long was, by any standard, a profoundly selfless act.

★ ★ ★

Over the course of the last seventy or so years, our understanding of how the human body responds to extreme cold has grown rapidly. We now know, for instance, that temperature regulation is controlled by the hypothalamus; the mechanisms we unconsciously employ to prevent heat loss and to maintain core body temperature include the narrowing of blood vessels (vasoconstriction) and the excretion of stress hormones such as adrenalin, noradrenalin and cortisol; and heat loss is initially countered by an increased metabolic rate.[60] As we have seen in this chapter, we are also much more familiar with the pathology of hypothermia, and with the progression of its observable symptoms. However, while we are able to make some generalisations regarding physiological characteristics that might inhibit the onset of hypothermia, with physically fit individuals tending to demonstrate improved cold tolerance, it is still impossible to accurately predict who in a group of apparently similar individuals will survive sustained subjection to extreme cold, and who will not. For this reason, some stories of survival raise as many questions as stories of death: a fact powerfully demonstrated by events on Heard Island in May 1952.

First sighted by British sealers in 1833, Heard Island is located at 53°S 73°30'E. Though it lies roughly 1,000km north of the western sector of the Australian Antarctic Territory, its position on the southern side of the Antarctic Convergence, where the cold Antarctic waters of the Southern Ocean mingle with warmer sub-Antarctic waters, results in its classification as an Antarctic island. At its greatest extent, it is about 40km long and 20km wide, with the central portion rising steeply towards the volcanic craters of Big Ben (2,745m) and its neighbour, Mawson Peak (2,896m). The island remains volcanically active, with smoke and steam issuing from both mountains, and fresh lava flowing on its south-western flanks.

'From the sea Heard Island presents a forbidding and desolate appearance,' wrote Phillip Law, director of ANARE, in 1953:

> Sheer black rock-faces alternate with the terminal ice-cliffs of the glaciers, against which the surf breaks unceasingly. The higher slopes of the island are usually covered in clouds and are seldom visible. As the principle axis of the island lies in the direction of the prevailing north-westerly winds, and as there are no deep indentations in the coastline, no all-weather anchorages exist; Atlas Cove and Corinthian Bay are the best.[61]

During the winter, the entire island is blanketed with snow, but in the summer the lower slopes of the Laurens Peninsula, which juts out from its north-western edge, Atlas Cove, the Rogers Head Peninsula and the Spit, which forms the island's south-eastern tip, are ice-free. Steep terrain and heavily crevassed glaciers make overland journeys extraordinarily difficult, but the heavy surf and boisterous weather of the 'Furious Fifties' render the use of small boats around the coast even more perilous; they also tend to make landing operations, in the words of one ANARE ship's officer, 'a race against the elements'.[62]

Altogether, then, Heard Island presents a grim and forbidding face to the world. 'It accorded with my preconceived ideas,' recalled Arthur Scholes, an English radio operator who accompanied the first ANARE expedition to the island in 1947, 'and looked as though it would have knocked the heart out of any adventurer.'[63] And yet the features that made the island so repugnant to all but the most hardened explorer also made it an ideal training ground for Australia's nascent post-war Antarctic programme, which intended to build upon the earlier work of Mawson's AAE, and his BANZARE of 1929–31. Given that the island's earliest visitors had confined

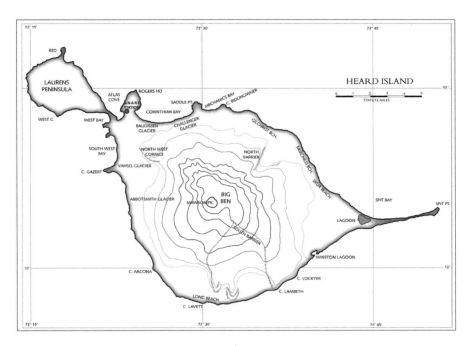

themselves to slaughtering almost the entire population of elephant seals, much work remained to be undertaken in the fields of geology, zoology, geomagnetism, seismology and, most importantly since Australian weather is profoundly influenced by climatic conditions in the Antarctic and the Southern Ocean, meteorology.

The base established by the first ANARE expedition in December 1947 had been built at Atlas Cove, a fjord-like feature that must once have formed the bed of a long-extinct glacier, its shore a barren plain of black volcanic sand, known as the 'Nullabor', which stretches towards the Baudissen Glacier on the main island's north-western shoulder. Over the next four years, that first spartan base had gradually evolved to become, in the words of Peter Lancaster Brown, the stores officer with the 1952 contingent, 'a town planner's nightmare'.[64] Each of the succeeding expeditions had contributed to the 'ribbon development', and by 1952 the two dormitories, kitchen, mess hut, bathhouse, engine room, laboratories and recreation hut were joined together by a warren of interconnecting corridors. 'One need never brave the outdoors before breakfast,' noted a slightly disapproving Brown, 'save for the need to comply with Nature's demands, the place for which lay directly outside the door of the sleeping huts.'[65] Law, too, confirmed that great pains had been taken to ensure the comfort and maintain the morale of each year's fourteen-man overwintering party, with the station's amenities including 'a library, a radiogram, a piano, table tennis, regular film screenings and free issues of cigarettes and liquor'.[66]

And yet, despite these luxuries and the expeditionaries' own efforts to maximise the comfort of their year-round base, it was to be expected that the type of men who volunteered for service with ANARE would embrace every opportunity to escape the hut in order to explore the island. To men of their stamp, the inherent difficulty and danger of such excursions formed a major part of their appeal.

Brown, who was described as a 'tall, rangy Englishman' by one of his companions,[67] had served with British Army Intelligence and as an RAF observer during the war. He was also an experienced mountaineer, and throughout his year with ANARE he made a number of treks, some on foot and some with his party's dog teams. His enthusiasm for field work was clearly infectious because, in late May, Alistair 'Jock' Forbes, the expedition's Scottish dog handler decided that he, too, would lead a short expedition. He would be accompanied by two of the Australian personnel, Dick Hoseason, the radio operator, and Lawrie Atkinson, a weather observer, and they chose as their objective Saddle Point, a stubby spur of land separated from the base hut by the Baudissen and Challenger glaciers. 'It was of no use telling him not to go,' Brown later wrote, 'and during the following two days I helped the trio to prepare their field equipment. Also I promised to lead them through the maze of pressure ridges on the Baudissen Glacier … I would return to Base after having seen the other party safely on its way.'[8]

The weather on the morning of 26 May was far from ideal for a trip designed exclusively for pleasure, with the air temperature of −1°C made to feel much cooler by a wind of 16kph. 'After breakfast it took a long time and a great deal of patience to adjust the pack frames of the Saddle Point party,' observed Brown. 'As they were all short men, the bulky fifty-pound [23kg] loads dwarfed all three of them – they looked like overloaded porters on a Himalayan march.'[69]

Having traversed the black sand of the Nullabor, the party donned crampons, roped up and began their ascent of the glacier. It proved to be hard work, with the unseasoned Atkinson and Hoseason clearly struggling with their heavy loads. Given that their journey had only just begun, Brown admitted to some anxiety about the trio's abilities, and especially about Atkinson, who seemed to be the weakest member of the party. 'But,' he reasoned, 'to ask them to turn back … would be an insult to their manhood – Forbes would certainly have refused.'[70] Instead, they continued at a snail's pace.

At an altitude of 300m above sea level, the wind increased and began to lift the loose powdery snow so that visibility rapidly dwindled. The timing could not have been worse because the party had now entered an area of bad crevassing, where a deviation from the correct path would lead them into impossible ice falls. As by far the most competent member of the group, Brown pushed on ahead, so that he could establish the safest course and leave a trail of footprints that the less experienced could easily follow without undue risk. 'Imagine my horror,' he spluttered:

… when, during a lull in the wind, I glanced back to look for Forbes and his team, and saw them 200 yards [183m] too far over to the right. I had purposely taken a long detour round what I knew to be a heavily crevassed area. Our footprints were unmistakeable – signposts to the correct route to follow – yet in spite of these, Forbes, in his supreme over-confidence, had cut off the corner.[71]

Furious at what he saw as their wilful stupidity, Brown subjected the trio to a 'torrent of abuse' when they caught up, and from that point onwards they followed his instructions unquestioningly; nonetheless, such behaviour hardly boded well for the future, especially since the novices would soon be deprived of Brown's expertise.

Soon afterwards, with order restored and with the worst of the crevasses behind them, Brown decided that it was now safe to allow Forbes, Atkinson and Hoseason to continue unchaperoned towards Saddle Point. According to his own account, his last injunction to them before they parted ways was to avoid, at all costs, the beach below the ice cliffs. Though such a route would obviously be crevasse free, it could also leave them trapped between the unscalable cliffs on the one hand, and the bitterly cold and turbulent waters of Corinthian Bay on the other.

Having said their farewells, Brown watched the three men as they trudged away, shouting while they were still within earshot, 'Bring me back some Saddle Point rock!' In reply, Forbes 'turned and grinned at me and waved goodbye'.[72]

That evening, as agreed with the field team, Brown and Jim Carr skied from the base to the north-western limit of the Corinthian Bay beach in order to exchange signals by Aldis lamp and hand torch. The air temperature had fallen to −4.5°C, and with a fresh breeze of 32kph producing a significant wind chill, the two men felt cold, despite their fur-lined Labrador anoraks and windproofs. Darkness had long since fallen and the beam from the Aldis lamp should have been clearly visible to the men encamped at the other side of the bay. At 7.55 p.m. precisely, Carr began to flash the signal, 'Hello, Saddle Point. Hello, Saddle Point', repeating it over and over again for the next fifty or so minutes. There was no reply.

★ ★ ★

The inhabitants of the base hut felt very little anxiety about the field party that night, with most subscribing to the view that, after their unaccustomed exercise, Forbes, Hoseason and Atkinson had simply forgotten to keep the agreed 'sked' and were already comfortably settled in their sleeping bags. In fact, by the time Carr finally switched off the Aldis lamp at 8.45, Hoseason was dead, Forbes was either dead or dying, and Atkinson was drifting in and out of consciousness in the throes of hypothermia.

After separating from Brown early that afternoon, the three men had descended onto the moraine that separates the Baudissen and Challenger glaciers. At Little Beach, the sand strip beneath the moraine, they had taken a short rest and embarked on a hunt for seals. During their search, Forbes had noticed a long but narrow stretch of sand running along the foot of the ice cliffs that form the seaward face of the Challenger Glacier. Despite Brown's earlier warnings, all three agreed that the beach appeared quite safe and that the completion of their journey to Saddle Point via this level and comparatively sheltered path seemed infinitely preferable to once again donning their crampons for the climb up and across the next glacier. Heaving their heavy packs back onto their shoulders, the three men set off at once, delighted that they had found so easy a route.

Halfway along the beach, they realised the full magnitude of their mistake. All previous expeditions to Heard Island had remarked on the violence of the surf, and numerous ships and small boats had been wrecked after being driven in under the 15–30m ice cliffs. Now, without any warning, a great surf suddenly bubbled and tumbled across the narrow beach, catching the heavily laden trio completely unawares. It 'caught us napping – knocking us completely over,' Atkinson told his friends the following day.[73] He provided more detail at an official hearing the following year:

> Suddenly Hoseason gave a shout and went out on a wave. As he was dragged out he tried to get out of his pack. Another wave brought him in. I grabbed him while Forbes removed his pack. The next wave dragged us both out. I dumped my pack and rode the next breaker in pulling Hoseason with me, but in the scramble against the ice cliff I lost hold of Hoseason and Hoseason washed out again. I dug my ice axe into the cliff and held on with assistance from Forbes. When Forbes and I looked around there was no sign of Hoseason and he did not reappear.[74]

Hoseason's last plaintive cry as the sea pulled him away from the cliffs was 'Save me, lads, save me!'[75] But Forbes and Atkinson could do nothing as they fought for their own lives. As the sea retreated to gather strength for its next onrush, the two drenched men half-ran, half-staggered back to the moraine. They had lost everything but the clothes on their backs: packs, ice axes, emergency rations – all were now being tossed about in Corinthian Bay, along with the body of their drowned friend.[76]

Their first instinct was to push on towards Saddle Point, though in the absence of fuel, dry clothing, a tent or any means by which to communicate with the base, this aim appears somewhat nonsensical. In the event, within a few hundred metres they realised that they would never make it, as Atkinson, as well as being wet and bitterly cold, was clearly in a state of shock and would be unable to proceed much further. Recognising that their only chance now lay in one of them reaching the base to summon aid, Forbes told his companion to find what shelter he could while he re-crossed the Baudissen Glacier, following the footprints they had made that morning. With no viable alternative suggestion to offer, Atkinson agreed. Forbes then set off at what Atkinson thought was 'an incredible speed', striding up the sloping gradient of the moraine and up onto the ice of the glacier. 'I felt sure he would get through all right.'[77]

In comparison with the confident and purposeful Forbes, Atkinson knew that he was in a parlous condition:

> The next hour or so was a complete blank. When I came to, it was dark and I could see the lights of the Base across the bay … I wandered about a bit to try and warm up, then I sheltered behind a couple of boulders – that kept the wind away. At any moment I expected help to arrive. The night dragged by – how long it seemed. Sometimes I dozed in a kind of stupor, not sleep but not consciousness either, I seemed suspended between the two. I must be in hell, I thought.[78]

At first light, he knew that something must be wrong, that Forbes must have been delayed. He realised, too, that he could wait no longer. But, with his hands and feet already frostbitten, attempting to cross the Baudissen Glacier would be little short of suicide. That left only one, equally suicidal, alternative: the beach below the ice cliffs.

The beach between the Baudissen Glacier ice front and the waters of the bay is even narrower than that below the Challenger Glacier, but this time luck was on Atkinson's side. With the tide at its lowest, he made his way across the black sands as quickly as his frostbitten feet would carry him; the sea to his right frothed and rippled menacingly but, thankfully, it showed no signs of repeating the sudden onslaught that had overwhelmed his party the previous day. Later Atkinson admitted that, by this time, he had become completely desensitised to both pain and fear:

Neither the sea nor the ice cliffs held any terror for me any longer. A week ago I would rather have suffered the loss of a limb than walk beneath those cliffs, but like my body, my nerves were frozen numb and lifeless – an anaesthetic against any fear.[79]

At times the path disappeared altogether and, with the water too deep to wade through, he plunged in bodily, and swam:

When I reached 'The Nullabor', I felt no relief; I had nothing left to feel with. A seal pup lay across my path, and I kicked at it. Funny, I thought, I can see my boot pushing into its skin yet I can't feel it. How I found the Base I don't know …[80]

The final stages of Atkinson's approach were witnessed by the men at Atlas Cove. At noon on 27 May, meteorologist Ken Hall was on his way to manufacture hydrogen for that afternoon's radiosonde balloon flight when he noticed that the interest of the husky puppies had been piqued by something on the Nullabor. He glanced in the same direction and was, in the words of Jim Carr's later account, 'astonished to see a man staggering drunkenly across the flat plain towards camp'.[81]

Hall and the others half-dragged, half-carried the bewildered man to the hut and quickly learned what had happened. Clearly, there could be no doubt that Hoseason was dead – but the faintest glimmer of hope remained that Forbes might still be alive somewhere on the Baudissen Glacier. Quickly, and with hardly a word spoken, they packed a tent, equipment and emergency rations and, within an hour of Atkinson's appearance, Brown, Carr, Hall and three of the husky pups set out towards the ice slopes.

'How had Atkinson managed to reach the Base before Forbes?' asked Brown as they trudged uphill:

… and where was Forbes? Could it be possible he was still alive, that he was lost, blindly wandering about the upper snowfields of the glacier? In the past I had admired his great tenacity; he may have dug a hole and taken shelter from the wind.[82]

Carr, on the other hand, entertained 'no illusions that our comrade would be found alive'.[83] And Carr would be proved right.

For two hours, the three men followed the tracks made by the outgoing party the previous day. The high cloud base made for good visibility and the tracks proved fairly easy to trace, except in those areas where the wind had swept away the snow to leave only bare, blue ice. The relatively clear skies also intensified the cold and, as they climbed higher onto the dazzling white slopes of the glacier, their condensing breath froze on their beards and in their hoods.

By 3 p.m., they had reached the narrow path through the crevasse field, where Brown had berated a penitent Forbes for his foolhardiness; just beyond, Brown could see the point at which they had separated, Brown to return to the base, and Forbes and his companions to continue on towards Saddle Point. Here, with just half an hour of daylight remaining, they found what they had been looking for. 'We topped a small rise,' wrote Carr, 'and saw that our search was ended; the body lay half buried in snow, with the dogs standing around, looking in puzzled manner at the still form.'[84] Typically, Brown's account of the discovery was more brutal, 'Forbes was almost buried beneath the drift – quite lifeless – a frozen lump of flesh', though he also noted that the dead man's face 'had all the expression of a gentle sleep, like some effigy of a saint'.[85]

Both men agreed that Forbes' body lay very close to the outward tracks, proving that he had been on the right path when he died. However, Brown's description both of Forbes and of the surrounding area provides important additional detail that enables us to reconstruct his last minutes. According to his account:

> There was no sign of his gloves, his ice axe or his precious pack; his windproof open – his shirt undone; his hands so frozen that he had been unable to prevent his clothing working loose … In the bare glimmer of daylight that remained, we could see tracks leading up and down the mountain. Uncertain footprints not knowing the right direction to take; he'd dropped exhausted by his efforts and died peacefully on his bed of snow.[86]

In fact, Forbes' open clothing and the missing gloves that he almost certainly discarded, rather than lost accidentally, are absolutely typical of the 'paradoxical undressing' so common in cases of acute hypothermia. His 'uncertain footprints', too, are consistent with the behaviour of a victim of hypothermia whose faculties are becoming increasingly clouded as his core body temperature plummets. Even 'the expression of a gentle

sleep' can be described as being fairly typical of death by hypothermia, which, by its terminal stages, is largely free of distress.

★ ★ ★

In many respects, the most remarkable feature of the Heard Island tragedy is not that Forbes and Hoseason died, but that Lawrie Atkinson lived.

Having seen the bodies of Scott, Wilson and Bowers in November 1912, Apsley Cherry-Garrard expressed his conviction that Scott had been the last of the three to die. He also commented, 'Once I had thought that he would not go so far as some of the others. We never realised how strong that man was, mentally and physically, until now.'[87] Similarly, Atkinson, supposedly the weakest of the Heard Island trio, had been the only survivor. Hoseason, of course, had drowned – but what factors had enabled Atkinson to live while Forbes, by all accounts a determined and physically strong individual, had perished?

In the case of Scott's Polar Party, the experiences of the last four were broadly similar: they endured the same temperatures and the same surface conditions, and they shared the same food in the same quantities. The disparity in their survival times can therefore be attributed, in large part, to their physiological differences, including size, amount of subcutaneous fat, quantity of muscle, physical fitness, circulating levels of hormones and underlying medical conditions, with all of these factors interacting.

Though such physiological factors would also influence the eventual fates of Forbes and Atkinson, their experiences were not only very different from those of Scott's party four decades earlier, but also from each other's. In Brown's estimation, both men were of short stature, and on the afternoon of 26 May both were soaked to the skin – but there the similarities ended. While Atkinson remained at sea level, Forbes embarked on a trek across a glacier, at a significantly higher altitude. Although the temperatures cited by Brown, both before the accident and during the subsequent search, fall within the seasonal range recorded by ANARE observers between 1948 and 1950,[88] at sea level they are likely to have been marginally higher. Atkinson would also have benefited from the minimal amount of shelter afforded by the large boulders, whereas Forbes would have been almost completely exposed to the westerly wind sweeping across the Baudissen Glacier. Once on the glacier, Forbes' wet clothes would have made him particularly vulnerable. Finally, the very fact that Forbes was on the move

may have counted against him, as physical exertion reduces the amount of fuel the body has available for heat generation, making the hiker more susceptible to hypothermia than the sitter.[89]

When Atkinson finally staggered into the base at Atlas Cove on 27 May he was, in Carr's opinion, in a 'dreadful condition, suffering from exposure, exhaustion and frostbite'.[90] Brown agreed, noticing that he was 'almost unconscious; his hands puffed and white – utterly lifeless. His eyes were bloodshot, and his bare, dishevelled head dripping wet like the rest of his body.'[91] These descriptions and the testimony of Atkinson himself give us, perhaps, the best available insight into the experience of the less fortunate Forbes.

★ ★ ★

Although, in its immediate aftermath, the *Melbourne Argus* proclaimed that the Heard Island accident equalled 'in tragic heroism the death of Oates and of other great men who went before them',[92] in reality, the deaths of Forbes and Hoseason were the product of their own errors. Certainly, their ANARE colleagues were in no doubt about the matter, with the typically outspoken Brown pointing to the 'gross errors in his [Forbes'] judgement' as the primary cause of the accident.[93]

Of course, human error and misjudgement have played a significant role in many Antarctic fatalities attributable to hypothermia. Sometimes death has resulted from an act of omission, such as the failure to rig lifelines at Petrel Island in 1959 and at Syowa in 1960; on other occasions, acts of commission have been responsible, with Forbes' recommendation that his party should follow the beach path, and Hoseason and Atkinson's acceptance of that advice, surely ranking as one of the more extreme examples of a wilful disregard of obvious safety precautions. But, in most cases, the deaths have resulted from simple miscalculation: in particular, a decision to travel, or to leave a secure shelter, in bad weather.

In attempting to undertake a necessary and routine duty during the blizzard near Square Bay, Tom Allan made just such a miscalculation. As Mario Marret remarked after experiencing the blizzard conditions of Adélie Land:

There are times when you have to stay put and do nothing ... You can do nothing against the forces of nature when they are really loose. All you can do is to wait until they have blown themselves out.[94]

When summing up the circumstances surrounding the deaths of Forbes and Hoseason, Jim Carr observed that they should serve 'as a perpetual reminder to those who face the hazards of Antarctica that there is room for only one mistake, and [that] the last'.[95] The same maxim could be applied with equal relevance to the deaths of Prud'homme, Fukushima, Allan – and many more.

'THEY ARE OF THE TYPE ...'

RISK AND RISK-TAKING IN THE ANTARCTIC

In the Antarctic, men have died for many reasons. Some have been ill-prepared, in terms of either equipment, experience or training; some – but very few – have died because of equipment failure; some have died because of somebody else's blunder; and some, perhaps all, have been unlucky. Most, though, have died because they made a mistake, or a series of mistakes, in one of the most unforgiving environments on the face of the planet. With the immense benefit of hindsight, the majority of those mistakes appear well-intentioned, understandable and eminently forgivable; only a tiny minority seem to have resulted from a wilful disregard for personal safety.

Where fatal errors of judgement have occurred, it is natural that we should want to understand the circumstances and behaviours that gave rise to them. And yet, while a significant number of studies have sought to identify the kind of personalities that are best suited to living and working in the Antarctic, remarkably little has been done to explore attitudes to risk. In his influential review of safety provisions in BAS, Sir Donald Logan wrote of the young men who applied for service with the Survey: 'They are of the type that for recreation at home might certainly ride large motorcycles, go skiing or mountaineering, and perhaps take up the even more hazardous sports such as hang-gliding.'[1] However, more recent research conducted in non-polar environments has drawn important distinctions between the motivations and psychology of those who undertake the different forms of 'extreme sport' to which Logan alluded, and this research makes his characterisation of Antarctic explorers as 'thrill-seekers' seem somewhat misguided.

In particular, while there is clear evidence that some sports such as skydiving are attractive to those seeking what is commonly described as 'an adrenalin rush', activities like expeditionary mountaineering – which has much closer parallels with Antarctic exploration – have a very different appeal.[2] After all, though expeditionary work often includes moments of intense, even spiritual, exhilaration – such moments are attested to in many polar expedition diaries from all periods – these brief flashes are usually attained only at the expense of weeks or months of unremitting, and often repetitive and tedious, manual labour. The experiences of those participating in Antarctic expeditions are, then, very far removed from those enjoyed by individuals who hurl themselves from an aeroplane at 4,000m or race a motorcycle down country lanes for pleasure.

Of course, a voluntary decision to embark on a venture that will, by its very nature, place the individual in an environment more extreme than most of us will ever encounter must indicate an enhanced willingness to tolerate risk. Indeed, for a certain category of men, the very existence of those risks – and the opportunity to overcome them – constitute some of the Antarctic's chief attractions. In his investigation into the deaths of Dai Wild, Jeremy Bailey and John Wilson in 1965, Willoughby Thompson remarked, 'An extraordinary fact of life in the British Antarctic Territory … is the youth of the persons serving there … There is, and must be, a fair amount of devil-may-care in their attitude to life.'[3] Thompson therefore conflated youth with risk-taking.

However, while it is true that the huge majority of casualties featured in this book were younger than 35, with most still in their twenties, in reality this was merely a reflection of the broader demographic of the overwintering population – a demographic that was itself, in large part, a product of the recruitment process, where older recruiting officers gave preference to youth, fitness and the absence of dependants. Once these influencing factors are taken into account, there is very little evidence that, in the Antarctic context, youth can be equated with risky behaviour.

Generally speaking, it will be accepted that, in any high-risk situation, experience will be of more consequence than age. But experience, too, can influence behaviour in potentially unexpected ways. In a paper entitled 'Perceptions of Danger, Risk Taking, and Outcomes in a Remote

Community',[4] Robin Burns and Peter Sullivan have shown that, in their relatively small sample group of Australian Antarctic Division personnel, those with previous Antarctic experience judged the environment to be less risky than did the 'first-timers'.[5]

On the one hand, it may be that their first-hand knowledge of the various hazards enabled these individuals to manage those hazards effectively, thereby removing much of the risk. In the words of Burns and Sullivan, such people 'are aware of the risks to which they are likely to be exposed but either believe that they know how to reduce them or accept them as part of the situation'.[6] On the other hand, it is equally possible that familiarity has bred contempt. According to Pete Salino, who was stationed at Faraday at the time of the 1982 disaster in which three men died:

> With sustained exposure to risk you develop a better understanding of the risks but also become habitualised to and accepting of them. I think this is manifest in the way you become less likely to take what you perceive as a high risk but more likely to routinely take what you think of as low risks. Of course, the outcome in either case could be fatal.[7]

Interviewed in 2009, veteran expeditionary Ken Blaiklock demonstrated just such an acceptance when discussing the once common practice of dog sledging in two-man teams:

> I should think ninety per cent of sledging is done with two people. I mean you know the risks, you know that if somebody falls down a crevasse it's very difficult for one person to get him up – it has been done, but it's jolly difficult – but you weigh that with the advantages. Two people and two dog [teams] is a very strong team so far as logistics go: you're carrying the minimum amount of food, tents and sledging gear; you only need one ice axe, and one ice spear and one tent, one stove and you've got two sledges with all the rest ... so you've got tremendous range ... my view was the risks were minimal.[8]

With the benefit of several years' worth of accumulated knowledge of Antarctic fieldwork, Blaiklock considered the risk worth taking. Pointedly, in the same interview, he also laughed at what he perceived to be the unnecessary anxiety of a much less experienced team member when asked to undertake a journey of this type. 'I think he was very concerned that there were only two of us, and if one had an accident it virtually meant the death of the other one.' This was just the kind of stoicism exhibited by Scott as he lay dying in his tent on the Great Barrier in March 1912. 'We took risks, we knew we took them; things have come out against us, and therefore we have no cause for complaint, but bow to the will of Providence, determined still to do our best to the last.'[9] Essentially, in both cases, the risks were calculated and guarded against – but the possibility of their materialising despite the safeguards was always understood and accepted.

Outside the specific Antarctic context, much work has been done to define the personality traits that are typical of risk-takers; these include impulsivity, extraversion, sensation seeking and low self-control.[10] Overall, there could hardly be a greater contrast with the 'ideal' characteristics for an overwinterer, as identified by every Antarctic leader from Shackleton to Fuchs, and from Fuchs to present-day behavioural researchers like Lawrence A. Palinkas – but which were perhaps best summarised by ANARE director, Phillip Law, as 'character, "guts" and "stickability"'.[11] Inevitably, the acceptance of such analysis and categorisation then begs the question, did any of the individuals who died in the Antarctic exhibit the traits of the typical risk-taker and, if so, were they habitual or merely momentary aberrations, the product of unusual situations and particular stresses?

Only in a very small number of cases has it been suggested, by contemporaries, that the victims of an accident not only took a risk, but that, more generally, they exhibited the kind of 'devil-may-care' attitude alluded to by Willoughby Thompson. In his account of the 1952 Heard Island disaster, for instance, Peter Lancaster Brown certainly characterised 'Jock' Forbes as foolhardy – but, as the most experienced glacier traveller in the party, it might also be that Brown felt at least partially responsible for the deaths of Hoseason and Forbes and that, in his account of the tragedy, he sought to deflect blame.

Another example is Bernie Gunn's appraisal of Lieutenant Tom Couzens, who died when his Sno-Cat plunged into a crevasse near Cape Selborne in November 1959. Though Gunn's criticism is implied, rather than overt, his account of the accident clearly indicates that he felt that Couzens verged on being reckless – and it is interesting to note that Gunn's assessment is supported by the ex-tank commander's military service papers, in which he is described by one senior officer as demonstrating 'a slightly irresponsible tendency'.[12]

In both these cases, then, there is reason to believe that the decisions and behaviours that produced fatal consequences were fairly typical of the men involved. In other examples, Leif Lier's decision to embark upon a highly dangerous flight to the Balleny Islands on 26 December 1929, without the knowledge or sanction of the ship's captain, and Bertil Ekström's fast driving in poor visibility on the night of 23 February 1951, both appear to have been the results of irresponsible behaviour rather than of particular situational stresses or strains.

In some circumstances, a degree of irresponsibility might be looked upon with a kindly or forgiving eye, particularly where it is seen to be a product of youthful high spirits and inexperience – but such indulgence seldom extends to high-risk environments. And in this regard, it *is* possible to draw parallels between expeditionary activity and extreme sports. In their 2016 study into the twin aspects of enjoyment and risk in skydiving and mountaineering, James Hardie-Bick and Penny Bonner pointed out:

> Skydivers carry out safety checks on their kit before jumping, climbers think carefully about the weather conditions, white water rafters know all about the currents they have to negotiate and divers ensure they have checked their oxygen … this suggests a group of people who take responsibility for their actions within a highly specific terrain.[13]

A key aspect of such activity, it seems, is the effective management of the inherent risks. Where individuals were perceived to be deliberately increasing risk, and reducing control, these individuals 'gained a negative reputation for themselves … those who engaged in chronic, excessive risk-taking were frequently the subject of gossip and gained reputations as "unsafe" or "accidents waiting to happen"'.[14]

Such, according to Dick Richards and Ernest Joyce, was the reputation of Aeneas Mackintosh, who died when making an unnecessarily early crossing of the sea ice between Hut Point and Cape Evans in May 1916, and when their arguments failed to dissuade him from his chosen course of action they refused to accompany him. In this scenario, the aberrant behaviour – when judged against the Antarctic 'norm' – was Mackintosh's impetuosity. The caution displayed by Richards and Joyce, on the other hand, appears entirely consistent with what one much more recent expeditionary has described as a deeply felt reluctance to travel with risk-takers.[15]

In contrast with the actions of Mackintosh, Forbes and Couzens, those of Ambrose Morgan, John Coll and Kevin Ockleton in 1982 – which also appear to have been the result, primarily, of a willingness to take an unnecessary risk – were altogether less typical of the men involved. In his accident report, their base leader, Len Airey, described the men variously as 'keen and able', 'very sensible', and 'capable and keen', though he also acknowledged that they differed in terms of experience.[16] Thirty-five years later, this assessment was supported by fellow Faraday Base veterans Graham Hurst and Pete Salino, indicating that the trio's decision to cross young sea ice in unstable weather conditions was a product of a set of distinct circumstances and motivations – in particular, their boredom and frustration after weeks of isolation on Petermann Island – rather than a display of ingrained recklessness. It seems highly improbable that these men were in any way ignorant of the risk that they took. Instead, their decision was an example of the kind of 'optimism bias' alluded to by Dr Des Lugg, for many years head of polar medicine with the Australian Antarctic Division: 'During fifty-five years' close association with the Antarctic, one has observed an attitude in Antarctic circles that "it can never happen to me" ... when some are forced to make crucial decisions, many throw caution to the winds.'[17]

Given the unavoidable – and often extremely unpredictable – variations in how individuals will react to different situations and pressures, the onus must be on their employer to ensure that, so far as is practicable, training and procedures instil consistency in behaviour and reaction. Throughout the history of FIDS and BAS, the linchpin in the British response to this requirement has been the fostering of continuity. From its very inception, the organisation has sought to guarantee the effective transfer of knowledge through the retention of experienced personnel at each of its bases, a process that began as early as 1946, when Alan Reece, Victor Russell and Frank White – all of whom had overwintered during 1945 – remained at the bases established by Operation Tabarin in order to ensure that they could share their acquired expertise with the incoming FIDS novices. This policy – which many veterans have argued constitutes one of the great strengths of the BAS model – has remained the norm, and today BAS not only contracts most of its field staff for two summers and one winter, but also maintains an Antarctic Employment Pool to ensure that it can call upon experienced personnel who might wish to return to the Antarctic after a break of six months or more.[18]

This continuity also shaped attitudes to risk because, as Pete Salino has confirmed, 'Culture on a base really relied on the previous winterers who indoctrinated the next generation … In the end it [safety] came down to the atmosphere and attitudes on the base itself.'[19] Naturally, the individuals most influential in setting the culture were the base leaders – though it was also accepted that, at its most successful, theirs would be a 'consensual control', with the leader being a 'first among equals'.

Inevitably, the relationship with BAS headquarters in Cambridge must be very different. Ideally, this relationship would acknowledge the truth of polar historian Hugh Robert Mill's 1905 assertion that:

> The worst risk which the commander of a government expedition of exploration runs is to be hampered by the minuteness of his instructions which he dares not disobey even when unforeseen circumstances turn them into a prohibition of all progress.[20]

In other words, the organisation would set the framework of what survey and scientific work should be conducted, but it would leave the day-to-day pursuit of that work to the men on the ground and carefully avoid unnecessary, and potentially counterproductive, interference. This 'light touch' would become ever more important throughout the 1960s, '70s and '80s as wider societal changes, in particular the erosion of traditional attitudes to authority and discipline, came to be felt even in the remotest outposts of empire. As Salino has observed:

> There was a lot of difference between Cambridge and the men in the field … They were a bunch of old guys who went to the Antarctic in the Heroic Age. We wouldn't have taken any notice anyway! Whilst respecting their experience, we didn't look up to them as authority figures![21]

Logan, too, recognised both the need for freedom of action and the fact that adventurous young men would reject the imposition of restrictions from on high. They would be, he opined, 'self-reliant, confident types' who would find opportunities to explore, no matter what obstacles were placed in their way.[22] Moreover, these were precisely the kind of men that BAS wished to employ and, in terms of recruitment, it would be counterproductive to introduce too many restrictions on their autonomy.

Despite the high incidence of deaths among BAS personnel in the years immediately preceding its issue (between February 1980 and August 1982, the organisation sustained no fewer than six deaths in three separate incidents), Logan's report on the Survey's safety provisions was very far from being critical in its tone. Instead – and no doubt to the immense relief of the management of both BAS and its parent body the Natural Environment Research Council (NERC) – he concluded, 'the level of health and safety at present provided by BAS is about right'.[23] He recognised not only that the challenges of living and working in the Antarctic are unique and, in assessing the appropriateness of training and safety protocols, 'experience gained over a period must play a large part', but also that BAS's policy of recruiting young men for two-year tours was 'a strength'.[24] He made no recommendations regarding the culture of BAS and supported the continuation of recreational journeys, despite the fact that the majority of recent casualties had occurred during such non-essential excursions. Logan's one caveat was that BAS, as well as ensuring 'that candidates have the hazards of Antarctica fairly explained to them before they accept the engagement', should also provide documentation containing 'a clear and fair indication of the challenge which the Antarctic presents to those living there, the hazards to life and the need for safety procedures and vigilance'.[25] In his opinion, responsibility for personal safety must continue to rest, in large part, with the individual.

At an organisational level, this view is still firmly held in BAS: those venturing to the Antarctic must take responsibility for their own well-being. What *has* changed is the level of training that such individuals are given prior to embarkation. Considerable emphasis has always been placed on the sharing of veterans' experience, but in the decades following Logan's review, the mechanisms by which this process occurs have been formalised, systemised and tracked. As in the worlds of skydiving, white-water rafting and climbing, culturally, the greatest respect is accorded not to those with experience, but to those who balance their experience with preparation. John Hall, BAS Head of Operations Delivery and one of the key figures in the development of the Survey's attitudes to health and safety, has recounted how he sought to shock new recruits into a realisation of the challenges ahead:

One of my presentations was titled 'Active Learning' and 'Learning from Accidents'. The first page was a quote from William Edwards Deming, 'Learning is not compulsory ... neither is survival'. I wanted to shock people into thinking hard about the reality of where they were going – so started by asking for a show of hands who had considered that they may not return. I only wish I had kept statistics on the show of hands over the years to see how the number had changed because it certainly has. This presentation gave a short, rather sombre summary of FIDS/BAS fatalities since 1948 ... More important however [there] followed a walk through and discussion of some real case studies of near misses that under marginally different circumstances could have led to a fatality – this was the 'learning from accidents'.[26]

According to Hall, a gradual shift in cultural attitudes began to take effect from the early 1970s onwards, with greater oversight of field activities from BAS headquarters in Cambridge, the continuity of managers, both at the Antarctic stations and on the royal research ships, and the 1974 Health and Safety at Work Act all playing their part. As a result, 'Health & Safety is not something that sits on the side of our activity it really has become embedded in our culture'.[27]

The impact of these changes is best evidenced by BAS's fatality statistics. In the thirty-four years between 1948 and 1982, twenty-six FIDS or BAS personnel died in the Antarctic, twenty-four of them as a result of accidents. In the three and a half decades between 1982 and the time of writing, BAS has suffered just one fatality. As it seems reasonable to assume that the personnel recruited by BAS since 1982 are not markedly different from those employed in the immediate post-war decades – being, for the most part, adventurous, scientifically trained and subject to exactly the same kind of selection procedures – it must also be assumed that the significant reduction in casualties is due to the cultural shift alluded to by Hall.

This supposition is further underpinned by the fact that the increased focus on health and safety has at no point resulted in the curbing of recreational journeys. Crucially, instead of being dismissed as 'jollies', these excursions are now recognised – and encouraged – as essential training exercises, serving to familiarise novices with the terrain, weather, surface conditions and equipment. The critical difference is that, now, no distinction is made between recreational and work activities.

The death toll of Antarctic expeditionaries during the twenty-first century proves beyond any doubt the truth of Sir Donald Logan's concluding remark, 'Health and safety precautions are not perfect – people do still fall ill and accidents regrettably do still happen',[28] but the relatively low number of fatalities, particularly when considered as a proportion of the number of personnel as a whole, also serves to prove that the hazards inseparable from the prosecution of Antarctic survey and science are now much better understood then they once were – and the risks are better managed. It is also true that each and every tragedy described in this book has served as a stepping stone to that improved understanding and better management.

NOTES

Introduction

1   Cherry-Garrard, *The Worst Journey in the World*, p.587.

2   *Ibid*.

3   Hillary, *No Latitude for Error*, p.13.

4   Bruce Davis has applied the term to an even longer period from 1890 to 1945, but this is not the accepted norm. See Bruce Davis, 'The Australian Antarctic Research Program in Focus' in Aant Elzinga (ed.), *Changing Trends in Antarctic Research* (Dordrecht: Kluwer Academic Publishers, 1993), p.118.

5   These expeditions included one Belgian, two German, seven British, one Japanese, one Swedish, two French, one Norwegian and one Australian.

6   The author is indebted to Joan N. Boothe, author of *The Storied Ice*, for sharing her detailed analysis of the numbers involved in the Heroic Age expeditions. Boothe to the author, 10 August 2014.

7   Hayes, *The Conquest of the South Pole*, p.29.

8   The eight included the five men of Scott's polar party (British); Belgrave Ninnis of the AAE (British); Robert Brissenden, also of the *Terra Nova* expedition (British); and Richard Vahsel of Filchner's Second German Antarctic Expedition (German). Of these, six were included in shore parties and two were onboard ship.

9   See British Antarctic Monument Trust, www.antarctic-monument.org 'Those Who Died'.

10   IGY population statistics drawn from Walter Sullivan, *Assault on the Unknown* (New York: McGraw-Hill, 1961), p.306.

11 *Ibid.*, p.298.

12 The term 'wind chill factor' was coined by the American scientist Paul Siple to describe the accelerating effect of the wind on the process of heat loss (a result of the removal of the surface layer of warm air and its replacement with cold air). See Ashcroft, *Life at the Extremes*, p.152.

13 BBC, 2LO–5XX–S.B, Bickerton, 'Australian [*sic*] Antarctic Expedition', 17 March 1927.

14 F.H. Bickerton, *A Log of the Western Journey*, 31 December 1912. SPRI MS1509.

15 Quoted in Sullivan, *Assault on the Unknown*, p.299.

16 The copy was manufactured by Larcum Kendall.

17 Quoted by David Pratt, 'Performance of Vehicles Under Trans-Antarctic Conditions', Institution of Mechanical Engineers, *Proceedings of the Automobile Division* (1958–59), No. 6, p.196.

18 Author's interview with Ken Blaiklock, 1 June 2009.

19 Hampshire Record Office, George Marston to Hazel Marston, May 1914.

20 Author's interview with Ken Blaiklock, 1 June 2009.

21 This same equipment was subsequently purchased by Aeneas Mackintosh for use by the Ross Sea Party during the *Endurance* Expedition.

22 Mitchell Library, MSS382/2, A.L. McLean Diary, 28 February 1913.

23 Goldsmith Diary, 1 November 1956.

24 Author's interview with Ken Blaiklock, 1 June 2009.

25 Eric Back, 'Cold Weather Hazards', in *The Medical Press*, 9 November 1955.

26 During the infamous, if inaccurately named 'Race to the South Pole', Edmund Hillary adopted precisely the same tactics in order to conceal his vehicle movements from the expedition committees in London and New Zealand – and from Fuchs.

27 Coroner's report, 'In the matter of an inquest into the death of Rodney David Marks who died at South Pole Station, Antarctica', 16 September 2016. I am indebted to retired coroner Richard McElrea, for generously facilitating access to his formal inquiry report, held by the New Zealand Coroner's Office.

28 *Ibid.*

29   *Ibid.*

30   *The Telegraph*, 14 December 2006.

31   Hayes, *The Conquest of the South Pole*, pp.30–31.

32   See, in particular, Stephanie Barczewski's *Antarctic Destinies: Scott, Shackleton and the Changing Face of Heroism* (London: Hambledon Continuum, 2007) and Max Jones' *The Last Great Quest: Captain Scott's Antarctic Sacrifice* (Oxford: Oxford University Press, 2003).

33   Expeditions' scientific reports, which were often voluminous and usually published over a number of years, are excluded from this analysis. As an example, the scientific reports of Douglas Mawson's Australasian Antarctic Expedition (AAE, 1911–14) were published over thirty-one years (1916–47), filling twenty-two volumes with over 4,000 pages of text, plates, charts and maps.

34   See Haddelsey with Carroll, *Operation Tabarin: Britain's Secret Wartime Expedition to Antarctica* and Haddelsey, *Shackleton's Dream: Fuchs, Hillary & the Crossing of Antarctica*.

35   George Lowe, 'The Commonwealth Trans-Antarctic Expedition 1955–58', in *The Mountain World 1960–61* (Malcolm Barnes, ed.), p.243.

36   Author's interview with Rainer Goldsmith, 3 May 2009.

Chapter 1

1   See, for instance: Palinkas, Gunderson, Holland, Miller and Johnson, 'Predictors of Behavior and Performance in Extreme Environments: The Antarctic Space Analogue Program', in *Aviation, Space, and Environmental Medicine*, Vol. 71, No. 6 (June 2000), and Lugg & Shepanek, 'Space Analogue Studies in Antarctica', *Acta Astronautica*, Vol. 44, Nos 7–12, (1999), pp.693–99.

2   Friedman, 'Fire Safety in Spacecraft', in *Fire & Materials: An International Journal*, Vol. 20 (1996), pp. 235–43.

3   During a short field trip to Wiencke Island in November 1944, Ivan Mackenzie Lamb, botanist on Operation Tabarin, undertook a novel experiment to determine whether the Antarctic lichen *Neuropogon* could be used as fuel. He and his two companions succeeded in collecting and burning sufficient lichen to make tea and to fill two

thermos flasks. While it would be impossible to collect enough for routine cooking and heating, the experiment did prove that the material could be harvested and stored for use in an emergency. See BAS AD6/1A/1944/B, I.M. Lamb, Operation Tabarin (Base A) Official Diary, 18 November 1944.

4   http://antarcticfire.org/index.html.

5   Though financed by the British newspaper magnate, Sir George Newnes, only two of the ten members of the shore party, William Colbeck and Hugh Blackwell Evans, were British; the remainder were Norwegian (six) and Australian (one). Borchgrevink himself was of mixed parentage, his father being Norwegian and his mother English.

6   Bernacchi, *To the South Polar Regions: Expedition of 1898–1900*, p.134.

7   Borchgrevink, *First on the Antarctic Continent: Being an Account of the British Antarctic Expedition, 1898–1900*, p.150.

8   *Ibid.*

9   Bernacchi, *To the South Polar Regions: Expedition of 1898–1900*, pp.139–40.

10   *Ibid.*, p.140.

11   BBC Archives, BBC 2LO-5XX-S.B, F.H. Bickerton, 'Australian Antarctic Expedition', p.3.

12   BAS, AD6/1/ADM 4.2, Marr to A.C. Cardinall, 13 February 1944.

13   William Ellery Anderson, *Expedition South*, p.45.

14   James, *That Frozen Land*, p.78.

15   In fact, this 'jetty' and the approaches to Hut Cove proved to be the only real disadvantages of the location. In his interim report on the establishment of the base, William Flett noted, 'Unfortunately, the ship could not lie off this site, as the sea, in its immediate neighbourhood, is dotted with sea-stacks, reefs, and submarine pressure ridges due possibly to the movement of the sea ice.' (See BAS AD6/1D/1945/C, Flett, 'Interim Report on the Establishment of Base D'.) These obstacles meant that heavily laden boats could only reach the jetty at high tide, so deliveries had to be timed very carefully.

16   Taylor, *Two Years Below the Horn: A Personal Memoir of Operation Tabarin*, p.193.

17   *Ibid.*

18   *Ibid.*

19   In a similar accident, FIDS Base B, Deception Island, was gutted by
     fire in September 1946, possibly as a result of clothes being left to
     dry too close to the stove; there were no casualties.

20   Taylor, *Two Years Below the Horn: A Personal Memoir of Operation
     Tabarin*, pp.277–78.

21   AD6/24/1/10, BAS Oral History Recording, Frank Elliott
     interviewed by Margaret Martin, 7 October 1997.

22   *Ibid.*

23   *Ibid.*

24   AD6/2D/1948/H, Sladen, 'Hope Bay Base Journal', November 1948.

25   *Ibid.*

26   *Ibid.*

27   *Ibid.*

28   In his report on the fire, Sladen recommended that all such doors should
     be made to open inwards in order to make access and egress easier.

29   AD6/2D/1948/H, Sladen, 'Hope Bay Base Journal',
     November 1948.

30   *Ibid.*

31   *Ibid.*

32   *Ibid.*

33   *Ibid.*

34   *Ibid.*

35   *Ibid.*

36   AD6/2D/1948/H, Sladen to Frank Elliott, 10 November 1948.

37   AD6/2D/1948/H, Sladen, 'Hope Bay Base Journal', November 1948.

38   *Ibid.*

39   *Ibid.*

40   *London Gazette*, 21 June 1949.

41   AD6/2D/1948/H, Sladen, 'Hope Bay Base Journal',
     November 1948.

42   AD6/24/1/10, BAS Oral History Recording, Frank Elliott
     interviewed by Margaret Martin, 7 October 1997.

43   AD7/D/1/1948, 'Hope Bay Base Journal', entry by John O'Hare,
     24 November 1948.

44   O'Hare, quoted in the *Daily Mail*, 9 March 1949.

45   AD7/D/1/1948, 'Hope Bay Base Journal', entry by John O'Hare,
     29 November 1948.

46   *Ibid.*, 1 December 1948.

47   *Ibid.*, 30 November 1948.

48   BAS G62/1/3, Frank Elliott, memoirs written in preparation for interviews with Geoffrey Hattersley-Smith, March 2012.

49   Ken Blaiklock in conversation with the author, 10 February 2017.

50   Mrs Jocelyn Sladen to the author, 8 February 2017.

51   Ken Blaiklock in conversation with the author, 10 February 2017.

52   Taylor, *Two Years Below the Horn: A Personal Memoir of Operation Tabarin*, p.192.

53   AD6/24/1/10, BAS Oral History Recording, Frank Elliott interviewed by Margaret Martin, 7 October 1997.

54   Bernard Stonehouse, 'Fire Precautions at Antarctic Stations', *Polar Record*, Vol. 6, Issue 46 (July 1953), pp.743–45.

55   *Ibid.*

56   *Ibid.*

57   Béchervaise, *Blizzard and Fire: A Year at Mawson, Antarctica*, pp.11–13.

58   Dewart, *Antarctic Comrades: An American with the Russians in Antarctica*, p.139.

59   *Ibid.*

60   Dewart, *Antarctic Comrades: An American with the Russians in Antarctica*, p.140.

61   '8 Scientists Die at Soviet Base', *The Times*, 20 August 1960.

62   Béchervaise, *Blizzard and Fire: A Year at Mawson, Antarctica*, pp.14–15.

63   Ignatov, *Where It's Coldest*, p.80.

64   *Ibid.*, p.23.

65   The author's account of the fire at Vostok is largely based upon the following report: Theodore Shabad, 'Russians Reveal Tale of Survival in the Long Polar Winter', *The New York Times*, 26 April 1983. This article itself was based substantially upon official Soviet press releases.

66   Ignatov, *Where It's Coldest*, p.55.

67   Tatiana Yakovleva, '45th birthday of Russia's Antarctic station Vostok', *Pravda*, 16 December 2002.

68   Just one month after the survivors of the Vostok fire were relieved, another (non-fatal) fire destroyed the mobile shelter that housed the station's drilling equipment. Ice core drilling did not resume at Vostok until 1984.

69   Thomson, *The Coldest Place on Earth*, p.155.

70   *Ibid.*, p.192.

71   *The New York Times*, 26 April 1983.

72   Referring to a visit he made to the Brazilian station during the 1990s, Ken Blaiklock has commented, 'I'm not at all surprised there was a fire there … The base hut was partly covered in a snow-drift and the main and only easy entrance was down a ladder into a small room where all the outer clothing was hung. Some of the anoraks were hanging over the electric fire with red hot open elements, and we were horrified. We stayed inside the main base rooms as little as possible.' Blaiklock to the author (undated letter, received 20 February 2017). Given this experience, it is tempting to speculate on whether poor fire safety contributed to the Brazilian tragedy.

73   *The Times*, 6 February 1961.

74   'Fire Guts British Antarctic Lab', sciencemag.org, 5 October 2001.

75   'Brazil to open $52 million research base in Antarctica', SciDev.net, 13 September 2013.

76   'UK Climate research destroyed by Antarctic fire', AAP Newsfeed, 18 December 2001.

77   Bernard Stonehouse, 'Fire Precautions at Antarctic Stations', *Polar Record*, Vol. 6, Issue 46 (July 1953), pp.743–45.

Chapter 2

1   Source: Thomas & Dieckmann, 'Antarctic Sea Ice – a Habitat for Extremophiles', *Science*, Vol. 295, Issue 5555 (25 January 2002), pp.641–44.

2   T.W. Edgeworth David, 'Antarctica and Some of its Problems', *The Geographical Journal*, No. 6, Vol. XLIII (June 1914), pp.605–27. David estimated that Mawson's AAE (1911–14), the results of which had not yet been published, would probably increase the area of charted coastline by some 2,000km.

3   *Ibid.*

4   R.N. Rudmose-Brown, 'Some Problems of Polar Geography', *Scottish Geographical Magazine*, 43:5 (1927), pp.257–81.

5   *Ibid.*

6   Frank Debenham, 'The Future of Polar Exploration',
     The Geographical Journal, Vol. 57, No. 3 (March 1921), pp.182–200.

7   Andrew Taylor, *Two Years Below the Horn: A Personal Memoir of
     Operation Tabarin*, p.124.

8   *Ibid.*

9   *Ibid.*, p.265.

10   See Fuchs, *Of Ice and Men: The Story of the British Antarctic Survey,
     1943–73*, pp.66–67.

11   Shackleton, *South: A Memoir of the Endurance Voyage*, p.304.

12   Joyce, Ernest, *The South Polar Trail: The Log of the Imperial Trans-
     Antarctic Expedition*, p.186.

13   *Ibid.*

14   *Ibid.*, pp.186–87.

15   *Ibid.*, p.187.

16   Quoted by R.W. Richards, *The Ross Sea Shore Party, 1914–17*,
     p.38.

17   *Ibid.*

18   *Ibid.*

19   *Ibid.*

20   *Ibid.*

21   Joyce, *The South Polar Trail: The Log of the Imperial Trans-Antarctic
     Expedition*, p.187.

22   Shackleton, *South: A Memoir of the Endurance Voyage*, p.304.

23   R.W. Richards, *The Ross Sea Shore Party, 1914–17*, p.38.

24   Shackleton, *South: A Memoir of the Endurance Voyage*, pp.304–05.

25   Letters Patent of 21 July 1908. Quoted in Christie, *The Antarctic
     Problem*, p.301.

26   TNA, PREM 3/141, 'Most Secret Cipher Telegram from Air
     Ministry to Mideast', 2 February 1943.

27   *The Times*, 6 January 1947.

28   *Ibid.*, 5 March 1948.

29   BAS, AD6/1/ADM (Item 22), 'Operation Tabarin Political
     Instructions', November 1943.

30   TNA CO 537/4010, 'Political Instructions to the Leader of FIDS',
     4 November 1948. Quoted in Dodds, *Pink Ice: Britain and the South
     Atlantic Empire*, p.19.

31   Fuchs, *A Time to Speak: An Autobiography*, p.175.

32   Dodds, *Pink Ice*, p.20.

33   AD6/2Y/1958/H, John Paisley, 'Report on the Loss of the Base Y Dion Island Depot-Laying Party in May 1958'.

34   FIG Archives, 'Coroner's Inquest into the Deaths of Black, Statham and Stride', 30 April 1959. Deposition of David McDowell, Senior Meteorologist, Base Y.

35   John Paisley Journal. Quoted in Fuchs, *Of Ice and Men: The Story of the British Antarctic Survey, 1943–73*, p.192.

36   FIG Archives, 'Coroner's Inquest into the Deaths of Black, Statham and Stride', 30 April 1959. Deposition of Ray McGowan, wireless operator, Base Y.

37   *Ibid.*

38   John Paisley Journal, 30 May 1958. Quoted in Fuchs, *Of Ice and Men: The Story of the British Antarctic Survey, 1943–73*, p.192.

39   AD6/2Y/1958/H, John Paisley, 'Report on the Loss of the Base Y Dion Island Depot-Laying Party in May 1958'.

40   BAS Sound Archive, David McDowell interviewed by Chris Eldon Lee, 6 July 2012.

41   *Ibid.*

42   FIG Archives, 'Coroner's Inquest into the Deaths of Black, Statham and Stride', 30 April 1959. Deposition of David McDowell, senior meteorologist, Base Y.

43   Peter Gibbs in an email to the author, 20 January 2017.

44   AD6/2Y/1958/H, John Paisley, 'Report on the Loss of the Base Y Dion Island Depot-Laying Party in May 1958'.

45   FIG Archives, 'Coroner's Inquest into the Deaths of Black, Statham and Stride', 30 April 1959. Deposition of David McDowell, senior meteorologist, Base Y.

46   *Ibid.* Deposition of John Paisley, base leader, Base Y.

47   'David McDowell Remembers', February 2009. Courtesy of the British Antarctic Monument Trust.

48   FIG Archives, 'Coroner's Inquest into the Death of Neville Mann', 11 March 1964. Maurice Sumner, 'Report on the Loss of Neville Mann', Surveyor, 30 August 1963.

49   BAS AD6/2F/1982/H, Draft of a letter from Richard Laws to John Prescott MP, 18 October 1982.

50   BAS AD6/2F/1982/H, Len Airey, 'Report of the Journey to Petermann Island by John Coll, Kevin Ockleton and Ambrose

Morgan, 11 July–15 October 1982'. Note left by Coll, Ockleton and Morgan, July 1982.

51 *Ibid.*

52 Graham Hurst, interviewed by the author, 23 January 2017.

53 BAS AD6/2F/1982/H, Len Airey, 'Report of the Journey to Petermann Island by John Coll, Kevin Ockleton and Ambrose Morgan, 11 July to 15 October 1982'. Note left by Coll, Ockleton and Morgan, July 1982.

54 *Ibid.*

55 *Ibid.*

56 *Ibid.*

57 *Ibid.*

58 Airey, *On Antarctica*, p.174.

59 BAS AD6/2F/1982/H, Len Airey, 'Report of the Journey to Petermann Island by John Coll, Kevin Ockleton and Ambrose Morgan, 11 July to 15 October 1982'. G.L. Hurst, 'Note on Medical Conditions', 4 November 1982.

60 Pete Salino interviewed by the author, 6 February 2017.

61 BAS AD6/2F/1982/H, Len Airey, 'Report of the Journey to Petermann Island by John Coll, Kevin Ockleton and Ambrose Morgan, 11 July to 15 October 1982'.

62 Pete Salino to the author, 19 February 2017.

63 BAS AD6/2F/1982/H, Len Airey, 'Report of the Journey to Petermann Island by John Coll, Kevin Ockleton and Ambrose Morgan, 11 July to 15 October 1982'. 'Diary of Events'.

64 BAS AD6/2F/1982/H, Len Airey, 'Report of the Journey to Petermann Island by John Coll, Kevin Ockleton and Ambrose Morgan, 11 July to 15 October 1982'. 'Diary of Events'.

65 Airey, *On Antarctica*, p.177.

66 BAS AD6/2F/1982/H, Len Airey, 'Report of the Journey to Petermann Island by John Coll, Kevin Ockleton and Ambrose Morgan, 11 July to 15 October 1982'. Telegram from Airey to R.M. Laws, director, BAS, 17 August 1982.

67 BAS AD3/2/121/70/11 'Administration NERC 1982 Review of Safety Provisions in BAS' by Sir Donald Logan. BAS Board of Inquiry into the loss of Morgan, Coll and Ockleton.

68 BAS AD3/2/121/70/11, BAS press release.

69   BAS AD6/2F/1982/H, Len Airey, 'Report of the Journey to Petermann Island by John Coll, Kevin Ockleton and Ambrose Morgan, 11 July to 15 October 1982'.

70   *Ibid*. Peter Salino, 'Report of Petermann Search Party'.

71   *Ibid*.

72   FIG Archives, 'Coroner's Inquest into the Deaths of Morgan, Coll and Ockleton'. Rex Hunt to the Coroner, British Antarctic Territory, 18 March 1983.

73   FIG Archives, 'Coroner's Inquest into the Deaths of Morgan, Coll and Ockleton'. Professor J. Nelson Norman to the BAT Coroner, 7 February 1983.

74   *Ibid*.

75   John Dudeney to the author, 16 December 2016.

76   BAS AD6/2F/1982/H, Len Airey, 'Report of the Journey to Petermann Island by John Coll, Kevin Ockleton and Ambrose Morgan, 11 July to 15 October 1982'. 'Diary of Events'.

77   Pete Salino to the author, 19 February 2017.

78   BAS AD6/2F/1982/H, Len Airey, 'Report of the Journey to Petermann Island by John Coll, Kevin Ockleton and Ambrose Morgan, 11 July to 15 October 1982'.

79   John Dudeney to the author, 16 December 2016.

80   I am most grateful to Matthew Hall, Professor of Law & Criminal Justice at the University of Lincoln for his help in differentiating between the available inquest verdicts.

81   BAS AD3/2/121/70/11 'BAS Board of Inquiry into the Loss of Morgan, Coll and Ockleton'.

82   *Ibid*.

83   *Ibid*. Interviewed on 23 January 2017, Graham Hurst thought the idea that BAS could have stiffened the morale of the party a 'load of rubbish; [it] wouldn't have made any difference. They would have just pooh-poohed it.' Pete Salino was even more forthright, dismissing the idea as 'cobblers' (author interview, 6 February 2017).

84   BAS AD3/2/121/70/11 'BAS Board of Inquiry into the Loss of Morgan, Coll and Ockleton'.

85   John Dudeney to the author, 20 October 2016.

86   Sir Donald Logan, 'A Review of Safety Provisions for Staff and Property in the British Antarctic Survey, with Particular Reference to Operations in Antarctica', June 1982.

87   *Lords Hansard*, Columns 473–74, 4 July 2008, Lord Grocott, 'Health & Safety (Offences) Bill'.

88   NERC to Sir Donald Logan, 21 January 1982. Quoted by Logan, 'A Review of Safety Provisions for Staff and Property in the British Antarctic Survey, with Particular Reference to Operations in Antarctica', June 1982.

Chapter 3

1   Giaever, *The White Desert: The Official Account of the Norwegian–British–Swedish Antarctic Expedition*, p.176.

2   Charles Swithinbank, *Foothold on Antarctica: The First International Expedition Through the Eyes of its Youngest Member*, p.180.

3   D.L. Pratt, 'Performance of Vehicles under Trans-Antarctic Conditions', *The Institution of Mechanical Engineers: Proceedings of the Automobile Division*, 1958–59, No. 6, pp.193–225.

4   Shackleton, *The Heart of the Antarctic: Being the Story of the British Antarctic Expedition, 1907–1909*, Popular Edition (London, Heinemann, 1914), p.14.

5   *Ibid.*

6   *Ibid.*, p.89.

7   *Ibid.*, pp.89–90.

8   *Ibid.*, p.166.

9   *Ibid.*, p.14.

10   See, for example, Franz Pfeifer, 'Convertible motor car and self-propelled sledge', US Patent 863633, application filed 15 December 1905.

11   Charcot, *The Voyage of the Pourquoi-Pas: Journal of the Second French South Polar Expedition, 1908–10*. Quoted in Aubert, Skelton, Frenot & Bignon, 'Scott and Charcot at the Col du Lautaret: 1908 Trials of the first motor-driven sledges designed for transport in the Antarctic', *Les Cahiers illustrés du Lautaret* (2014), No. 5, p.35.

12   Reginald Skelton Diary, 3 February 1902. Quoted in Aubert, Skelton, Frenot & Bignon, 'Scott and Charcot at the Col du Lautaret: 1908 Trials of the first motor-driven sledges designed for transport in the Antarctic', *Les Cahiers illustrés du Lautaret* (2014), No. 5, p.10.

13   Scott Diary, 24 October 1911.

14   Griffith Taylor, *With Scott: The Silver Lining*, pp.91–92.

15   Evans, *South with Scott*, p.55.

16   Griffith Taylor, *With Scott: The Silver Lining*, p.92.

17   Scott Diary, 5 January 1911.

18   *Ibid.*

19   *Ibid.*, 6 January 1911.

20   Griffith Taylor, *With Scott: The Silver Lining*, p.87.

21   Cherry-Garrard Diary, 8 January 1911. Quoted in Cherry-Garrard, *The Worst Journey in the World*, pp.93–94.

22   Evans, *South with Scott*, p.56.

23   Scott Diary, 8 January 1911.

24   Evans, *South with Scott*, pp.166–67.

25   Scott Diary, 24 October 1911.

26   Evans, *South with Scott*, p.167.

27   Scott Diary, 27 October 1911.

28   *Ibid.*

29   Edgar Evans, quoted by Scott in his diary, 27 October 1911.

30   Lashly Diary, 28 October 1911. Quoted in Cherry-Garrard, *The Worst Journey in the World*, p.322.

31   Lashly Diary, 1 November. Quoted in Cherry-Garrard, *The Worst Journey in the World*, p. 323.

32   *Ibid.*, pp.323–24.

33   Interview with Bernard Day, *The New York Times*, 16 February 1913.

34   *Ibid.*

35   Ponting, *The Great White South*, p.77.

36   Evans, *South with Scott*, p.173.

37   J. Stephen Dibbern, 'The First Attempts at Motor Transport in Antarctica, 1907–1911', *Polar Record*, Vol. 18, No. 114 (1976), pp.259–67.

38   Scott Diary, 17 October 1911.

39   D.L. Pratt, 'Performance of Vehicles under Trans-Antarctic Conditions', *The Institution of Mechanical Engineers: Proceedings of the Automobile Division* (1958–59), No. 6, pp.193–225.

40   SPRI MS1509, Bickerton, 'Western Sledging Journey', p.1.

41   BBC 2LO-5XX-S.B., Bickerton, 'Australian Antarctic Expedition', p.4.

42   SPRI MS1509, Bickerton, 'Western Sledging Journey', p.7.

43   *Ibid.*, p.8.

44   *Ibid.*, p.9.

45   *Ibid.*, p.3.

46   Mawson, *The Home of the Blizzard*, Vol. 2, (1915), p.6.

47   SPRI MS1509, Bickerton, 'Western Sledging Journey', p.9.

48   D.L. Pratt, 'Performance of Vehicles under Trans-Antarctic Conditions', *The Institution of Mechanical Engineers: Proceedings of the Automobile Division* (1958–59), No. 6, pp.193–225.

49   SPRI MS1456/38, 'Report of the Conference of a Committee of the RGS with Sir Ernest Shackleton', 4 March 1914.

50   *The Motor*, 1914. Quoted in David L. Harrowfield, 'Intentions – Hopeful: The Ross Sea Party Girling Motor-Sledge in Canterbury Museum. Shackleton's Imperial Trans-Antarctic Expedition, 1914–1916', *Records of the Canterbury Museum*, Vol. 27, (2013), pp.97–111.

51   For a comprehensive description of the Girling motor-crawler and its history, see David L. Harrowfield, 'Intentions – Hopeful: The Ross Sea Party Girling Motor-Sledge in Canterbury Museum. Shackleton's Imperial Trans-Antarctic Expedition, 1914–1916', *Records of the Canterbury Museum*, Vol. 27, (2013), pp.97–111.

52   SPRI MS1456/38, 'Report of a Conference of a Committee of the RGS with Sir Ernest Shackleton', 4 March 1914.

53   *The Times*, 28 May 1914.

54   Edvard Welle-Strand in the *Bergens Aftenblad*, 20 May 1914. Translation courtesy of Finn R. Jørstad.

55   Mitchell Library, State Library of NSW, MSS 2198/2, Frank Wild Memoirs, p.120.

56   Hampshire Record Office, George Marston to Hazel Marston, May 1914.

57   SPRI MS GB015 – MS1537, A.L.A. Mackintosh Diary. Quoted in Harrowfield, 'Intentions – Hopeful: The Ross Sea Party Girling Motor-Sledge in Canterbury Museum. Shackleton's Imperial Trans-Antarctic Expedition, 1914–1916', *Records of the Canterbury Museum*, Vol. 27, (2013), pp.97–111.

58   Hocken Library, Dunedin, MS 0231;1424, James Paton Diary. Quoted in Harrowfield, 'Intentions – Hopeful: The Ross Sea Party Girling Motor-Sledge in Canterbury Museum. Shackleton's Imperial Trans-Antarctic Expedition, 1914–1916', *Records of the Canterbury Museum*, Vol. 27, (2013), pp.97–111.

59 RGS MS RGS/CB7/Livingston, David. A.H. Ninnis, 'Diaries of the Ross Sea Party'. Quoted in Harrowfield, 'Intentions – Hopeful: The Ross Sea Party Girling Motor-Sledge in Canterbury Museum. Shackleton's Imperial Trans-Antarctic Expedition, 1914–1916', *Records of the Canterbury Museum*, Vol. 27, (2013), pp.97–111.

60 SPRI MS 1456/33, Leslie Thomson Diary. Quoted in Harrowfield, 'Intentions – Hopeful: The Ross Sea Party Girling Motor-Sledge in Canterbury Museum. Shackleton's Imperial Trans-Antarctic Expedition, 1914–1916', *Records of the Canterbury Museum*, Vol. 27, (2013), pp.97–111.

61 RGS MS RGS/CB7/Livingston, David. A.H. Ninnis, 'Diaries of the Ross Sea Party'. Quoted in Harrowfield, 'Intentions – Hopeful: The Ross Sea Party Girling Motor-Sledge in Canterbury Museum. Shackleton's Imperial Trans-Antarctic Expedition, 1914–1916', *Records of the Canterbury Museum*, Vol. 27, (2013), pp.97–111.

62 Frank Debenham, 'The Future of Polar Exploration', *The Geographical Journal*, Vol. 57, No. 3 (March 1921), pp.182–200.

63 R.N. Rudmose-Brown, 'Some Problems of Polar Geography', *Scottish Geographical Magazine*, 43:5, (1927), p.268.

64 Byrd, *Discovery: The Story of the Second Byrd Antarctic Expedition*, p.17.

65 E.J. Demas, 'Tractor Operations on the Second Byrd Antarctic Expedition', *Polar Record*, Vol. 2, Issue 12 (July 1936), pp.175–84.

66 Byrd, *Discovery: The Story of the Second Byrd Antarctic Expedition*, p.17.

67 E.J. Demas, 'Tractor Operations on the Second Byrd Antarctic Expedition', *Polar Record*, Vol. 2, Issue 12 (July 1936), pp.175–84.

68 Byrd, *Discovery: The Story of the Second Byrd Antarctic Expedition*, p.17.

69 E.J. Demas, 'Tractor Operations on the Second Byrd Antarctic Expedition', *Polar Record*, Vol. 2, Issue 12 (July 1936), pp.175–84.

70 *Ibid.*

71 *Chicago Daily Tribune*, 25 October 1939. Quoted in Freitag and Dibbern, 'Dr Poulter's Antarctic Snow Cruiser', *Polar Record*, 23 (143), pp.129–41 (1986).

72 Freitag and Dibbern, 'Dr Poulter's Antarctic Snow Cruiser', *Polar Record*, 23 (143), (1986), pp.129–41.

73 Poulter, unpublished manuscript. Quoted in Freitag and Dibbern, 'Dr Poulter's Antarctic Snow Cruiser', *Polar Record*, 23 (143), (1986), pp.129–41.

74   US Navy official accident report. Quoted in 'Operation Highjump, 1946–47', Chapter 6, www.south-pole.com.

75   John Williams, recorded interview: https://sites.google.com/site/wilkesstationhistory/home/years/1959/hartley-robinson-1959.

76   'Development of Weasel, 1 July 1942', US National Archives and Records Administration, Records of the OSRD, NC-138, Entry 1, Office of the Chairman, NDRC, and the Office of the Director, OSRD: General Records, 1940–47, Box 55. Quoted by Henry Hemming in *Churchill's Iceman: The True Story of Geoffrey Pyke: Genius, Fugitive, Spy*, p.301.

77   For full details of the development of the Weasel, and of Geoffrey Pyke's remarkable career, the reader is directed to Henry Hemming, *Churchill's Iceman: The True Story of Geoffrey Pyke: Genius, Fugitive, Spy*.

78   John Giaever, *The White Desert: The Official Account of the Norwegian–British–Swedish Antarctic Expedition*, p.158.

79   Swithinbank, 'Mechanical Transport of the Norwegian–British–Swedish Antarctic Expedition, 1949–52', *Polar Record*, Vol. 6, Issue 46 (July 1953), pp.765–74.

80   *Ibid.*

81   Sullivan, *Assault on the Unknown: The International Geophysical Year*, p.299.

82   Quoted in George J. Dufek, *Operation Deepfreeze* (New York: Harcourt, Brace & Company, 1957), p.134.

83   John C. Cook, 'An Electrical Crevasse Detector', US Patent 2885633 A, application filed 8 April 1957.

84   John C. Cook, 'An Electrical Crevasse Detector', *Geophysics*, Vol. 21, No. 4 (October 1956), pp.1055–70.

85   *Ibid.*

86   Sullivan, *Assault on the Unknown: The International Geophysical Year*, p.299.

87   http://geokem.com/Antarctic/, Gunn, *Land of the Long Day*, Chapter 23, unpaginated.

88   *Ibid.*

89   *Ibid.*

90   *Ibid.*

91   *Ibid.*

92   BAS H/1965/Z, 'Crevasse Accident, 12 October 1965', Statement by John Ross, 22 January 1966.

93   *Ibid.*

94   *Ibid.*

95   *Ibid.*

96   In the circumstances, it seems probable that Bailey was referring to the morphine-based painkiller, Omnopon. According to Ken Blaiklock, 'When sledging in the days of FIDS, we each used to carry a small packet of morphine with us', Blaiklock to the author, 16 October 2016.

97   BAS H/1965/Z, 'Crevasse Accident, 12 October 1965', Statement by John Ross, 22 January 1966.

98   P.G. Law, 'Personality Problems in Antarctica', in *The Medical Journal of Australia*, Vol. 1, No. 8 (20 February 1960), p.277.

99   Fuchs and Hillary, *The Crossing of Antarctica: The Commonwealth Trans-Antarctic Expedition, 1955–58*, p.310.

100 BAS Archives, edited transcript of a recording of Dr Gordon Bowra interviewed by Chris Eldon Lee, 21 September 2010. Transcribed by Andy Smith, 25 March 2011.

101 BAS Archives, edited transcript of a recording of Bill Bellchambers interviewed by Chris Eldon Lee, 12 December 2011. Transcribed by Andy Smith, 3 September 2012.

102 Roderick Rhys Jones to the author, 7 June 2017.

103 BAS Archives, Inquest No. BAT 1/66, 'Inquiry into the Deaths of David Wild, Jeremy Bailey and John Wilson, Inquiry of 16 February 1966'.

104 *Ibid.*

105 BAS Archives, E37/G1/10, 'Board of Inquiry into the Deaths of John Anderson and Robert Atkinson'.

106 Swithinbank, 'Motor Sledges in the Antarctic', *Polar Record*, Vol. 11, Issue 72 (September 1962), pp.265–69. In an email to the author dated 7 March 2017, David Pratt remarked, 'I would take issue with Charles if he were with us. The breakdowns per mile of Sno–Cats versus Skidoos in my view depends on (1) preparation (2) vehicle loading (3) the driver (4) the time pressures of the operation (5) finance. Certainly [the] Skidoo is easier to drive.'

107 Boyles, Schmutzler & Rowley, 'Snowmobiles in Antarctica', *Arctic*, Vol. 32, No. 3 (September 1979), pp.189–200.

108 *Ibid.*

109 BAS Archives, E37/G1/10, 'Board of Inquiry into the Deaths of John Anderson and Robert Atkinson'.

110 *Ibid.*, evidence of D. Fletcher, BAS HQ.

111 BAS H/1965/Z, 'Crevasse Accident, 12 October 1965', Board of Inquiry's Findings, 16 February 1966.

112 *Ibid.*

113 BAS Archives, Sir Donald Logan, 'A review of safety provisions for staff and property in the British Antarctic Survey with particular reference to operations in Antarctica', October 1982 (issued January 1983).

114 BAS Archives, E37/G1/10, 'Board of Inquiry into the Deaths of John Anderson and Robert Atkinson'. Evidence of Stephen Tait.

Chapter 4

1 R.E. Priestley, 'The Psychology of Exploration', in *Psyche*, Vol. 2 (1921), p.20.

2 Editor's introductory note to R.E. Priestley, 'The Psychology of Exploration', in *Psyche*, Vol. 2 (1921), p.18.

3 Frederick A. Cook, *Through the First Antarctic Night*, pp.303 and 365.

4 Henryk Arçtowski, 'The Antarctic Voyage of the *Belgica* during the years 1897, 1898 and 1899', in *The Geographical Journal*, Vol. 18, No. 4 (October 1901), p.381.

5 Erik Ekelöf, 'Medical Aspects of the Swedish Antarctic Expedition, October 1901–January 1904', in *The Journal of Hygiene* (1904), p.531.

6 E.A. Wilson, 'The Medical Aspect of the *Discovery*'s Voyage to the Antarctic', in *The British Medical Journal* (8 July 1905), p.79.

7 E.A. Wilson Diary, 13 August 1902. Quoted in David Crane, *Scott of the Antarctic*, p.180.

8 Charles Royds Diary, 14 June 1902. Quoted in David Crane, *Scott of the Antarctic*, p.180.

9 See David Crane, *Scott of the Antarctic*, p.179.

10 R.E. Priestley, 'The Psychology of Exploration', in *Psyche*, Vol. 2 (1921), p.20.

11 K.V. Blaiklock to the author, 14 June 2010.

12 Hal Lister Diary, 9 May 1957.

13 Hal Lister Diary, 17 August 1957.

14 Jon Stephenson, *Crevasse Roulette: The First Trans-Antarctic Crossing, 1957–58*, p.71.

15   P.G. Law, 'Personality Problems in Antarctica', in *The Medical Journal of Australia*, Vol. 1, No. 8 (20 February 1960), p.274.

16   Author's interview with Derek Williams, 5 July 2009.

17   See Palinkas, Cravalho & Browner, 'Seasonal variation of depressive symptoms in Antarctica', in *Acta psychiatrica Scandinavia*, Vol. 91, Issue 6 (1995), p.428.

18   H.W. Simpson, 'Field Studies of Human Stress in Polar Regions', in *The British Medical Journal*, Vol. 1, (1967), p.532.

19   Hal Lister Diary, 22–25 September 1957.

20   Author's interview with Richard Brooke, 8 August 2009.

21   Alexander Turnbull Library, MS90-304-2, J.H. Miller Diary, 13 March 1957.

22   Auckland Museum, MS 2010-1, Edmund Hillary Diary, 6 March 1957.

23   See Palinkas, Gunderson, Holland, Miller and Johnson, 'Predictors of Behavior and Performance in Extreme Environments: The Antarctic Space Analogue Program', in *Aviation, Space, and Environmental Medicine*, Vol. 71, No. 6 (June 2000), p.624.

24   See Mihaly Csikszentmihalyi, *Beyond Boredom and Anxiety: Experiencing Flow in Work and Play* (San Francisco: Jossey-Bass, 1975).

25   Palinkas, Gunderson, Holland, Miller and Johnson, 'Predictors of Behavior and Performance in Extreme Environments: The Antarctic Space Analogue Program', in *Aviation, Space, and Environmental Medicine*, Vol. 71, No. 6 (June 2000), p.624.

26   Author's interview with Richard Brooke, 8 August 2009.

27   Palinkas, Glogower, Dembert, Hansen and Smullen, 'Incidence of Psychiatric Disorders after Extended Residence in Antarctica', in *International Journal of Circumpolar Health*, Vol. 63, Issue 2 (2004), p.157.

28   P.G. Law, 'Personality Problems in Antarctica', in *The Medical Journal of Australia*, Vol. 1, No. 8 (20 February 1960), p.274.

29   Richard Byrd, *Alone* (1938 & 1984), p.107. Quoted by Barabasz, 'A Review of Antarctic Behavioral Research', in Harrison, Clearwater and McKay (eds), *From Antarctica to Outer Space: Life in Isolation and Confinement*, p.22.

30   Anonymous. Quoted by P.G. Law, 'Personality Problems in Antarctica', in *The Medical Journal of Australia*, Vol. 1, No. 8 (20 February 1960), p.274.

31 Cecil Madigan, AAE Diaries, 8 July 1913.

32 Mitchell Library, MSS382/2, A.L. McLean, AAE Diaries,
    11 July 1913.

33 F.H. Bickerton quoted in Cambridge University Library, MSS6762-
    6803, Stella Benson Diary, 23 April 1928.

34 See Beau Riffenburgh, *Aurora: Douglas Mawson and the Australasian
    Antarctic Expedition, 1911–14*, p.416.

35 Mawson Antarctic Collection, 68DM, Notebook 4, Mawson Diary,
    7 July 1913. Quoted in Riffenburgh, *Racing with Death: Douglas
    Mawson – Antarctic Explorer*, p.164.

36 Philip Ayres, *Mawson: A Life*, p.95.

37 For the most comprehensive analysis of Jeffryes' history, including
    his recruitment to the AAE, see Beau Riffenburgh, *Aurora: Douglas
    Mawson and the Australasian Antarctic Expedition, 1911–14*.

38 *The Times*, obituary for Stanley Kemp, 18 May 1945.

39 J.R. Stenhouse Diary, 24 October 1916. Courtesy of Patricia and
    Sarah Mantell.

40 From an unidentified newspaper cutting in the Stenhouse
    scrapbooks, 1923. Courtesy of Patricia and Sarah Mantell.

41 SPRI, MS100/57/1, Stanley Kemp to H.R. Mill, 18 October 1924.

42 SPRI, MS911/1, H.F.P. Herdman to D.D. Henderson, 1 November
    1925.

43 Stanley Kemp, 'Fourth Report on the Scientific Work of the RRS
    Discovery', p.1.

44 J.R. Stenhouse to Gladys Stenhouse, June 1926. Courtesy of Patricia
    and Sarah Mantell.

45 SPRI, MS 1284/4/6, J.R. Stenhouse to the *Discovery* Committee,
    19 August 1926.

46 SPRI, MS 1284/4/8, E.H. Marshall interviewed at a special meeting
    of the *Discovery* Committee, 2 December 1927.

47 *Ibid*.

48 SPRI, MS 1284/4/7, Stanley Kemp to E.R. Darnley, 10 October 1927.

49 SPRI, MS 1284/4/8, E.H. Marshall interviewed at a special meeting
    of the *Discovery* Committee, 2 December 1927.

50 E.R.G.R. Evans, 'How the Sailor Looks at the Surgeon and the
    Medical Aspect of Polar Exploration from a Sailor-Explorer's
    Viewpoint', in *The Journal of the Royal Medical Service*, Vol. 23
    (1937), p.24.

51 P.G. Law, 'Personality Problems in Antarctica', in *The Medical Journal of Australia*, Vol. 1, No. 8 (20 February 1960), p.275.

52 *Ibid.*, p.274.

53 University of Manitoba, MSS 108, Box 8, Folder 22, Andrew Taylor, 'Private Report on Personnel', 21 May 1945.

54 *Ibid.*

55 *Ibid.*

56 David James, *That Frozen Land*, p.110.

57 *Ibid.*

58 BAS, AD6/16/1986/4.1, transcript of an interview with Eric Back, 8 October 1986.

59 BAS, AD6/16/1987/2.1, transcript of an interview with Andrew Taylor, 14 October 1987.

60 See University of Manitoba, Archived Fonds, Box 10, Folder 20, Andrew Taylor, memorandum dated 1 September 1989.

61 H.R. Guly, 'Psychiatric illness and suicide in the heroic age of Antarctic exploration', in *History of Psychiatry*, 23(2), p.213.

62 Douglas Mawson, *The Home of the Blizzard*, p.xvii.

63 Andrew Taylor, *Two Years Below the Horn*, p.233.

64 BAS, AD6/1D/1945/K1/Appendix S, David James Diary, 23 August 1945.

65 Ron Roberts, 'Psychology at the End of the World', in *The Psychologist*, Vol. 24, Edition 1 (January 2011), pp.22–25.

66 J.R. Stenhouse Diary, 9 January 1915.

67 E.H. Shackleton, *South: A Memoir of the Endurance Voyage*, p.207.

68 P.G. Law, 'Personality Problems in Antarctica', in *The Medical Journal of Australia*, Vol. 1, No. 8 (20 February 1960), p.274.

69 *Ibid.*

70 BAS, G12/1/3/4, E.H. Back, 'Recommended Treatment for Lt-Cdr JWS Marr, RNVR', 8 February 1945.

71 BAS, AD6/10/1945/A, Andrew Taylor, Report to the Governor, December 1944–March 1945.

72 BAS Personnel File for Arthur Farrant (formerly FIDS/P/87).

73 BAS Personnel File for Arthur Farrant (formerly FIDS/P/87), Captain Stroud, Base B, to SECFIDS, 13 August 1952.

74 Telephone conversation between Ray Berry and the author, 15 July 2016.

75 BAS Personnel File for Arthur Farrant (formerly FIDS/P/87),

A.H. Farrant to SECFIDS, 26 March 1953.

76   *Ibid.*, SECFIDS to A.H. Farrant, 27 March 1953.

77   Davy Simmons to the author, 18 November 2004.

78   Tony Quinn to the author, 18 November 2004.

79   BAS Personnel File for Arthur Farrant (formerly FIDS/P/87), 'Inquest into the Death of Arthur H. Farrant', statement of Ian William Noel Clarke, 18 November 1953.

80   *Ibid.*, statement of Frank Aitchieson Hall, 19 November 1953.

81   *Ibid.*, statement of Ian William Noel Clarke, 18 November 1953.

82   *Ibid.*, statement of Arthur Frederick Lewis, 18 November 1953.

83   *Ibid.*, statement of Bernard Taylor, 18 November 1953.

84   *Ibid.*, statement of Douglas Colin Geoffrey Mumford, 18 November 1953.

85   BAS Personnel File for Arthur Farrant (formerly FIDS/P/87), Captain William Johnston to Sir Miles Clifford, 18 November 1953.

86   *Ibid.*, 19 November 1953.

87   BAS Personnel File for Arthur Farrant (formerly FIDS/P/87), Sir Miles Clifford to the Secretary of State for the Colonies, 30 December 1953.

88   Curiously, in a review of FIDS and BAS deaths on service, reference is made to Farrant having 'committed suicide due to receipt of letter from girlfriend indicating a breakdown in relations' (see AD3/2/121/143/30, 'Accidents – Bases Faraday, August 1982. Deaths in Antarctica since 1947', dated 1982). However, the contemporary report on Farrant's suicide makes no reference to receipt of such a letter. Such an omission may have been the result of an attempt to spare the feelings of those involved; or the story may have been a corruption of the facts. In either case, there can be no doubt that Farrant's state of mind was already extremely fragile, though such a letter might have provided the final spark. Farrant's grave and grave marker were swept away or buried by a mudslide during a volcanic eruption in 1969.

89   H.R. Guly, 'Psychiatric illness and suicide in the heroic age of Antarctic exploration', in *History of Psychiatry*, 23(2), p.213.

90   R.E. Priestley to Philip Brocklehurst. Quoted in Riffenburgh, *Nimrod: Ernest Shackleton and the Extraordinary Story of the 1907–09 British Antarctic Expedition*, p.304.

91   Apsley Cherry Garrard Journal, 4 October 1912. Quoted in Sara Wheeler, *Cherry: A Life of Apsley Cherry-Garrard*, p.140.
92   V.E. Fuchs, lecture at the National Education Conference, Durban, *c*. 1958, as reported in an unidentified South African newspaper.
93   Author's interview with Rainer Goldsmith, 3 May 2009.
94   V.E. Fuchs, lecture at the National Education Conference, Durban, *c*. 1958, as reported in an unidentified South African newspaper.
95   Author's interview with Derek Williams, 5 July 2009.
96   Mawson, *The Home of the Blizzard*, Vol. 1, p.16. Quoted by H.R. Guly, 'Psychology during the expeditions of the Heroic Age of Antarctic exploration', in *History of Psychology*, 23 (2), p.203.
97   E.H. Shackleton, 'The Making of an Explorer', in *Pearson's Magazine*, Vol. 38, pp.138–42. Summarised by H.R. Guly, 'Psychology during the expeditions of the Heroic Age of Antarctic exploration', in *History of Psychology*, 23(2), p.203.
98   P.G. Law, 'Personality Problems in Antarctica', in *The Medical Journal of Australia*, Vol. 1, No. 8 (20 February 1960), p.81.
99   Palinkas, Gunderson, Holland, Miller and Johnson, 'Predictors of Behavior and Performance in Extreme Environments: The Antarctic Space Analogue Program', in *Aviation, Space, and Environmental Medicine*, Vol. 71, No. 6 (June 2000), p.623.
100 Grant, Eriksen, Marquis, Orre, Palinkas, Suedfeld, Svensen and Ursin, 'Psychological Selection of Antarctic Personnel: The SOAP Instrument', in *Aviation, Space, and Environmental Medicine*, Vol. 78, No. 8 (August 2007), pp.793–800.
101 Ibid.
102 Peter Marquis to the author, 14 June 2016.
103 Lawrence A. Palinkas & Peter Suedfeld, 'Psychological effects of polar expeditions', in *The Lancet*, Vol. 371 (12 January 2008), p.160.
104 P.G. Law, 'Personality Problems in Antarctica', in *The Medical Journal of Australia*, Vol. 1, No. 8 (20 February 1960), p.282.
105 Ibid., p.281.

Chapter 5

1   'Minutes of the Inaugural Meeting of the General Committee of the Commonwealth Trans-Antarctic Expedition', 24 June 1954. Courtesy of Peter Fuchs.

2   *Flight*, 5 August 1911.

3   For full details of Bickerton's extraordinary career, see Haddelsey, *Born Adventurer: The Life of Frank Bickerton, Antarctic Pioneer.*

4   SPRI MS944/8, Frank Wild to Fred Pinfold, 30 October 1911.

5   'Dr Mawson's Return', *Advertiser*, 9 October 1911. Quoted by Lucas, Henderson, Leane and Kriwoken, 'A flight of the Imagination: Mawson's Antarctic Aeroplane', *The Polar Journal*, 1:1 (2011), pp.63–75.

6   *Ibid.*

7   Watkins continued to fly and was again injured in a crash in a Spencer biplane at Brooklands. He attended a Central Flying School (CFS) course on 17 January 1913 but served with the infantry throughout the First World War and not with the Royal Flying Corps. If he failed the CFS course this might lend some credibility to Mawson's rather belated doubts about his abilities as a pilot.

8   Quoted in Ralph Barker, *The Royal Flying Corps in World War I* (London: Robinson, 2002), p.9.

9   Frank Debenham, 'The Future of Polar Exploration', *The Geographical Journal*, Vol. 57, No. 3 (March 1921), pp.182–200.

10   *Ibid.*

11   *Ibid.*

12   *Ibid.*

13   *Ibid.*

14   See Haddelsey, *Shackleton's Dream: Fuchs, Hillary & the Crossing of Antarctica* (Stroud: The History Press, 2012), pp.110–11, and Edmund Hillary, *No Latitude for Error* (London: Hodder & Stoughton, 1961), p.83.

15   John Claydon, 'Report by Officer Commanding RNZAF Antarctic Flight, Trans-Antarctic Expedition, 1955–58', Appendix F.

16   John Grierson, *High Failure: Solo Along the Arctic Air Route* (London: Hodge & Co., 1936), p.99.

17   Richard E. Byrd, *Little America: Aerial Exploration in the Antarctic; The Flight to the South Pole* (New York: Putnams, 1930), p.123.

18   Lincoln Ellsworth, 'The First Crossing of Antarctica',
      The Geographical Journal, Vol. 89, No. 3 (March 1937), pp.193–209.

19   R.N. Rudmose-Brown, 'Some Problems of Polar Geography',
      The Scottish Geographical Magazine, Vol. 43, No. 5 (1927),
      pp.266–67.

20   Hubert Wilkins, 'The Wilkins-Hearst Antarctic Expedition, 1928–
      1929', *The Geographical Review*, Vol. XIX, No. 3 (July 1929), pp.353–76.

21   For the full story of the British Imperial Antarctic Expedition see
      Thomas W. Bagshawe, *Two Men in the Antarctic: An Expedition to
      Graham Land, 1920–22* and M.C. Lester, 'An Expedition to Graham
      Land, 1920–1922', *The Geographical Journal*, Vol. 62, No. 3 (September
      1923), pp.174–93. Bagshawe and Lester were the only two men, out of
      Cope's planned fifty-man party, to overwinter in the Antarctic.

22   Thomas W. Bagshawe, *Two Men in the Antarctic: An Expedition to
      Graham Land, 1920–22*, p.57.

23   Hubert Wilkins, 'The Wilkins-Hearst Antarctic Expedition,
      1928–1929', *The Geographical Review*, Vol. XIX, No. 3 (July 1929),
      pp.353–76.

24   *Ibid.*

25   *Ibid.*

26   John Grierson, *Challenge to the Poles: Highlights of Arctic and Antarctic
      Aviation*, p.180.

27   Hubert Wilkins, 'The Wilkins-Hearst Antarctic Expedition,
      1928–1929', *The Geographical Review*, Vol. XIX, No. 3
      (July 1929), pp.353–76.

28   *Ibid.*

29   *Ibid.*

30   *Ibid.*

31   *Ibid.*

32   *Ibid.*

33   H.R. Mill, 'The Significance of Sir Hubert Wilkins's Antarctic
      Flights', *Geographical Review*, Vol. 19, No. 3 (July 1929),
      pp.377–86.

34   R.N. Rudmose-Brown, 'Some Problems of Polar Geography',
      The Scottish Geographical Magazine, Vol. 43, No. 5 (1927), pp.266–67.

35   H.R. Mill, 'The Significance of Sir Hubert Wilkins's Antarctic
      Flights', *Geographical Review*, Vol. 19, No. 3 (July 1929),
      pp.377–86.

36 Leonard Brooks, G.C.L. Bertram, W.L.S. Fleming, J.M. Wordie, A.R. Hinks, and A. Stephenson, 'Graham Land and the Problem of Stefansson Strait: Discussion', *The Geographical Journal*, Vol. 96, No. 3 (September 1940), pp.174–80.

37 H.R. Mill, 'The Significance of Sir Hubert Wilkins's Antarctic Flights', *Geographical Review*, Vol. 19, No. 3 (July 1929), pp.377–86.

38 Lincoln Ellsworth, 'The First Crossing of Antarctica', *The Geographical Journal*, Vol. 89, No. 3 (March 1937), pp.193–209.

39 For full details of the development of the whaling factory ship, the reader is directed to Bjorn L. Basberg, 'The Floating Factory: Dominant Designs and Technological Development of Twentieth-Century Whaling Factory Ships', *The Northern Mariner/Le Marin du nord*, Vol. VIII, No. 1 (January 1998), pp.21–37.

40 *Flight*, 29 August 1929.

41 Alan Innes-Taylor, 'Empty Boots – A Whaling Story', *Arctic*, Vol. 37, No. 1 (March 1984), pp.87–90.

42 *Ibid.*

43 *Ibid.*

44 Riiser-Larsen and Finn Lützow-Holm represented the Norwegian Navy, and Lier and Tancred Ibsen the army, in the Danish Aeronautical Society's race to establish who could cover the greatest distance in six hours.

45 Hjalmar Riiser-Larsen, 'The *Norvegia* Antarctic Expedition of 1929–30', *The Geographical Review*, Vol. 20, No. 4 (October 1930), pp.555–73.

46 Alan Innes-Taylor, 'Empty Boots – A Whaling Story', *Arctic*, Vol. 37, No. 1 (March 1984), pp.87–90.

47 *Ibid.*

48 Byrd Diary, 26–28 December 1929. Quoted in Byrd, *Little America* (New York: Putnams, 1935) pp.361–62.

49 Hjalmar Riiser-Larsen, quoted in Bjarne Aagaard, *Fangst og Forskning I Sydishavet (Fishing and Research In the Southern Ocean)*, Vol. 2, p.804.

50 Alan Innes-Taylor, 'Empty Boots – A Whaling Story', *Arctic*, Vol. 37, No. 1 (March 1984), pp.87–90. In later years, Innes-Taylor would specialise in training the crews of civilian and military aircraft in cold weather survival techniques, and it is interesting to speculate

on whether this career choice was influenced by the loss of his friends in December 1929.

51   Russell Owen, 'Antarctic Tragedy', *The Barrier Miner*, 3 January 1930.

52   John Grierson, *Challenge to the Poles: Highlights of Arctic and Antarctic Aviation*, p.204.

53   Source: John Stewart, *Antarctica: An Encyclopedia*, pp.407–11.

54   Lisle A. Rose, *Assault on Eternity: Richard E. Byrd and the Exploration of Antarctica, 1946–47*, p.36. It could, of course, be argued that, since Operation Tabarin (1943–45) was an expedition launched under the overall control of the Royal Navy, Britain had already taken the first step towards the partial militarisation of South Polar research; however, on its post-war transformation into the Falkland Islands Dependencies Survey, continuing survey and science passed back to civilian hands.

55   James Haskin 'Robbie' Robbins, 'Antarctic Mayday' (1981). Courtesy of Gary Pierson, South-pole.com.

56   William H. Kearns and Beverley Britton, *The Silent Continent*, p.186.

57   James Haskin 'Robbie' Robbins, 'Antarctic Mayday' (1981). Courtesy of Gary Pierson, South-pole.com

58   *Ibid.*

59   *Ibid.*

60   William H. Kearns and Beverley Britton, *The Silent Continent*, p.187.

61   Quoted by Owen McCarty, 'Dead Men's Diary', *Saturday Evening Post*, Vol. 219, Pt 46 (17 May 1947).

62   William H. Kearns and Beverley Britton, *The Silent Continent*, p.187.

63   *Ibid.*

64   *Ibid.*, pp.187–88.

65   Owen McCarty, 'Dead Men's Diary', *Saturday Evening Post*, Vol. 219, Pt 46 (17 May 1947).

66   *Ibid.*

67   *Ibid.*

68   William H. Kearns and Beverley Britton, *The Silent Continent*, pp.187–88.

69   *Ibid.*, pp.188–89.

70   James Haskin 'Robbie' Robbins, 'Antarctic Mayday' (1981). Courtesy of Gary Pierson, South-pole.com

71   *Ibid.*

72   William H. Kearns and Beverley Britton, *The Silent Continent*, p.189.

73   Owen McCarty, 'Dead Men's Diary', *Saturday Evening Post*,
      Vol. 219, Pt 46 (17 May 1947).
74   William H. Kearns and Beverley Britton, *The Silent Continent*, p.191.
75   Owen McCarty, 'Dead Men's Diary', *Saturday Evening Post*,
      Vol. 219, Pt 46 (17 May 1947).
76   James Haskin 'Robbie' Robbins, 'Antarctic Mayday' (1981).
      Courtesy of Gary Pierson, South-pole.com
77   William H. Kearns and Beverley Britton, *The Silent Continent*, p.189.
78   *Ibid.*, p.192.
79   Owen McCarty, 'Dead Men's Diary', *Saturday Evening Post*,
      Vol. 219, Pt 46 (17 May 1947).
80   William H. Kearns and Beverley Britton, *The Silent Continent*, p.191.
81   Owen McCarty, 'Dead Men's Diary', *Saturday Evening Post*,
      Vol. 219, Pt 46 (17 May 1947).
82   William H. Kearns and Beverley Britton, *The Silent Continent*, p.195.
83   *Ibid.*, pp.195–96.
84   *Ibid.*, p.196.
85   Owen McCarty, 'Dead Men's Diary', *Saturday Evening Post*,
      Vol. 219, Pt 46 (17 May 1947).
86   James Haskin 'Robbie' Robbins, 'Antarctic Mayday' (1981).
      Courtesy of Gary Pierson, South-pole.com
87   William H. Kearns and Beverley Britton, *The Silent Continent*, p.198.
88   Owen McCarty, 'Dead Men's Diary', *Saturday Evening Post*,
      Vol. 219, Pt 46 (17 May 1947).
89   *Ibid.*
90   Andrew Taylor, *Two Years Below the Horn*, p.115.
91   Owen McCarty, 'Dead Men's Diary', *Saturday Evening Post*,
      Vol. 219, Pt 46 (17 May 1947).
92   James Haskin 'Robbie' Robbins, 'Antarctic Mayday' (1981).
      Courtesy of Gary Pierson, South-pole.com
93   Dick Conger, quoted in Owen McCarty, 'Dead Men's Diary',
      Saturday Evening Post, Vol. 219, Pt 46 (17 May 1947).
94   Richard E. Byrd, *Little America: Aerial Exploration in the Antarctic;
      The Flight to the South Pole* (New York: Putnams, 1930), p.123.
95   Byrd, 'Our Navy Explores Antarctica', *National Geographic Magazine*,
      Vol. XCII, No. 4 (October 1947), pp.429–522.
96   *Ibid.*
97   James Haskin 'Robbie' Robbins, 'Antarctic Mayday' (1981).

Courtesy of Gary Pierson, South-pole.com.

98   *Ibid.*

99   John Grierson, *Air Whaler* (London: Sampson Low, Marston & Co., 1949), p.225.

100 *Ibid.*

101 Quoted by Lisle A. Rose, *Assault on Eternity: Richard E. Byrd and the Exploration of Antarctica, 1946–47*, p.71.

Chapter 6

1   British Library, MS51035, Scott Diary, 29 March 1912.

2   *Ibid.*, 19 March 1912.

3   *Ibid.*, 29 March 1912.

4   Solomon, *The Coldest March: Scott's Fatal Antarctic Expedition*, p.288.

5   Susan Solomon and Charles R. Stearns, 'On the role of the weather in the deaths of R.F. Scott and his companions', *Proceedings of the National Academy of Sciences* (USA), Vol. 96, No. 23 (9 November 1999), pp.13012–16.

6   British Library, MS51035, Scott Diary, 11 February 1912.

7   *Ibid.*, 12 February 1912.

8   *Ibid.*, 17 February 1912.

9   *Ibid.*, 17 February 1912.

10 *Ibid.*, 26 February 1912.

11 *Ibid.*, 28 February 1912.

12 Solomon, *The Coldest March: Scott's Fatal Antarctic Expedition*, pp.293–94.

13 British Library, MS51035, Scott Diary, 3 March 1912.

14 S.C. Colbeck, 'A review of the friction of snow skis', *Journal of Sports Sciences*, Vol. 12, Issue 3 (1994), pp.285–95.

15 British Library, MS51035, Scott Diary, 4 March 1912.

16 Biem, Koehncke, Classen and Dosman, 'Out of the cold: management of hypothermia and frostbite', *Canadian Medical Association Journal*, 168 (3), (4 February 2003), pp.305–11.

17 See Crane, *Scott of the Antarctic: A Life of Courage and Tragedy in the Extreme South*, p.546.

18 British Library, MS51035, Scott Diary, 2 March 1912.

19 *Ibid.*, 5 March 1912.

20   *Ibid.*, 10 March 1912.

21   *Ibid.*, 16 or 17 March 1912.

22   *Ibid.*

23   Simpson, *Scott's Polar Journey and the Weather: Being the Halley Lecture, Delivered on 17 May 1923* (Oxford: Clarendon Press, 1926), p.24.

24   Scott, 'Message to the Public', 29 March 1912.

25   H.R. Guly, 'History of accidental hypothermia', *Resuscitation*, 82 (2011), pp.122–25.

26   Cherry-Garrard Diary, 12 November 1912, quoted in Cherry-Garrard, *The Worst Journey in the World: Antarctica, 1910–13*, pp.495–96.

27   Cherry-Garrard, *The Worst Journey in the World: Antarctica, 1910–13*, pp.497–98.

28   Henry Guly to the author, 3 March 2017.

29   Scott, 'Message to the Public', 29 March 1912.

30   Fuchs, telegram to TAE offices, 16 May 1957. Courtesy of Peter Fuchs.

31   Quoted in Lister Diary, 9 October 1957. Courtesy of Mrs Margaret Lister.

32   Victor, *Man and the Conquest of the Poles*, p.259.

33   These rituals were first observed by a FIDS party under Bernard Stonehouse on the Dion Islands in 1949.

34   André Prud'homme & Bernard Valtat, *Les Observations Meteorologiques en Terre Adélie, 1950–1952, Analyse Critique* (Paris: Secretariat d'état aux Travaux Publics et a L'Aviation Civile, 1957).

35   Marret, *Antarctic Venture: Seven Men Amongst the Penguins*, p.32.

36   Victor, *Man and the Conquest of the Poles*, p.278.

37   *Antarctic: A News Bulletin* (New Zealand Antarctic Society), Vol. 2, No. 2 (June 1959).

38   Yoshio Yoshida to the author, 3 August 2017.

39   *Antarctic: A News Bulletin* (New Zealand Antarctic Society), Vol. 5, No. 2 (June 1968).

40   Lister, *Ice – High and Low*, pp.98–99.

41   Ken Blaiklock in conversation with the author, 6 March 2017.

42   Ranulph Fiennes, foreword to Haddelsey, *Born Adventurer: The Life of Frank Bickerton*, p.vii.

43   Fuchs, *Of Ice and Men: The Story of the British Antarctic Survey, 1943–73*, p.271.

44   See BAS AD6/24/1/140/3, transcript of an interview with Terry Tallis, conducted by Chris Eldon Lee, 28 October 2011.

45   BAS AD6/2e/1966/H, T.H. Tallis, 'Accident Report', December 1966.

46   *Ibid.*

47   BAS AD6/2e/1966/H, T.H. Tallis Diary extract, 25 May 1966, in Tallis, 'Accident Report', December 1966.

48   BAS AD6/2e/1966/H, T.H. Tallis, 'Accident Report', December 1966.

49   BAS AD6/24/1/144, transcript of an interview with Neil Marsden, conducted by Chris Eldon Lee, 29 October 2011.

50   http://www.antarctic-monument.org/; Terry Tallis to the British Antarctic Monument Trust (undated). See entry for John Noel.

51   BAS AD6/2e/1966/K2, Holmes & Tallis, 'Journey Report of a Search Party, Northeast Glacier, June 1966'.

52   BAS AD6/24/1/144, transcript of an interview with Neil Marsden, conducted by Chris Eldon Lee, 29 October 2011.

53   BAS AD6/24/1/59, group interview with the 'Stonington Five' (Ken Doyle, Edward Madders, Ian Smith, Ian Sykes and Phil Wainwright), conducted by Chris Eldon Lee, 6 November 2009.

54   BAS AD3/1/AS/160/17B, Fuchs to next of kin, 9 June 1966.

55   BAS AD3/1/AS/160/17B, BAS press release, 10 June 1966.

56   BAS AD6/2e/1966/H, T.H. Tallis, 'Accident Report', December 1966.

57   BAS AD6/24/1/144, transcript of an interview with Neil Marsden, conducted by Chris Eldon Lee, 29 October 2011.

58   BAS AD3/1/AS/160/17B, BAS press release, 21 July 1966.

59   Fuchs, *Of Ice and Men: The Story of the British Antarctic Survey, 1943–73*, p.272.

60   See Elisabeth E. Tuck, 'Hypothermia', *Forensic Science, Medicine and Pathology* (2010), 6, pp.106–15.

61   P.G. Law & T. Burstall, *ANARE Interim Reports 7: Heard Island* (Melbourne: Antarctic Division, Department of External Affairs, 1953), p.6.

62   Lt Cmdr G.M. Dixon, 'Operation Orders', December 1947. Quoted by Arthur Scholes, *Fourteen Men: The Story of the Australian Antarctic Expedition to Heard Island*, p.31.

63   Arthur Scholes, *Fourteen Men: The Story of the Australian Antarctic Expedition to Heard Island*, pp.31–32.

64 Peter Lancaster Brown, *Twelve Came Back*, p.48.

65 *Ibid.*

66 P.G. Law & T. Burstall, *ANARE Interim Reports 7: Heard Island* (Melbourne: Antarctic Division, Department of External Affairs, 1953), p.8.

67 J.T. Carr, 'Working with Sledge Dogs in Antarctica', *The West Australian*, 9 May 1953.

68 Peter Lancaster Brown, *Twelve Came Back*, p.114.

69 *Ibid.*, pp.114–15.

70 *Ibid.*, p.115.

71 *Ibid.*

72 *Ibid.*, p.116.

73 John Lawrence Atkinson, quoted in Peter Lancaster Brown, *Twelve Came Back*, p.120.

74 John Lawrence Atkinson, quoted in *The Brisbane Telegraph*, 18 May 1953.

75 *Ibid.*

76 On 24 August 1952, Brown stumbled across the partial remains of Richard Hoseason, which had been washed up on the beach of Corinthian Bay. They consisted of parts of an arm and ribcage, the rest having been eaten by leopard seals and giant petrels. The remains were interred with Alistair Forbes' body beneath a concrete cross, close to the base. See Peter Lancaster Brown, *Twelve Came Back*, p.163.

77 John Lawrence Atkinson, quoted in Peter Lancaster Brown, *Twelve Came Back*, p.121.

78 *Ibid.*

79 *Ibid.*

80 *Ibid.*

81 J.T. Carr, 'Where Seven Minutes' Immersion Means Death', *The West Australian*, 23 May 1953.

82 Peter Lancaster Brown, *Twelve Came Back*, p.119.

83 J.T. Carr, 'Where Seven Minutes' Immersion Means Death', *The West Australian*, 23 May 1953.

84 *Ibid.*

85 Peter Lancaster Brown, *Twelve Came Back*, p.119.

86 *Ibid.*

87   Cherry-Garrard, *The Worst Journey in the World: Antarctica, 1910–13*, p.498.

88   See P.G. Law & T. Burstall, *ANARE Interim Reports 7: Heard Island* (Melbourne: Antarctic Division, Department of External Affairs, 1953).

89   See Elisabeth E. Tuck, 'Hypothermia', *Forensic Science, Medicine and Pathology*, 6, (2010), pp.106–15.

90   J.T. Carr, 'Where Seven Minutes' Immersion Means Death', *The West Australian*, 23 May 1953.

91   Peter Lancaster Brown, *Twelve Came Back*, p.118.

92   *The Argus* (Melbourne), 30 May 1952.

93   Peter Lancaster Brown, *Twelve Came Back*, p.122.

94   Marret, *Antarctic Venture: Seven Men Amongst the Penguins*, p.120.

95   J.T. Carr, 'Where Seven Minutes' Immersion Means Death', *The West Australian*, 23 May 1953.

Afterword

1   BAS Archives, Sir Donald Logan, 'A review of safety provisions for staff and property in the British Antarctic Survey with particular reference to operations in Antarctica', October 1982 (issued January 1983).

2   See, for instance, Matthew Barlow, *The Motives for Participation in High Risk Sport* (unpublished PhD thesis, Bangor University, 2012) and James Hardie-Bick and Penny Bonner, 'Experiencing Flow, Enjoyment and Risk in Skydiving and Climbing', *Ethnography*, 17 (3), (2016).

3   BAS Archives, Inquest No. BAT 1/66, 'Inquiry into the Deaths of David Wild, Jeremy Bailey and John Wilson, 16 February 1966'.

4   Robin Burns & Peter Sullivan, 'Perceptions of Danger, Risk Taking, and Outcomes in a Remote Community', *Environment & Behavior*, Vol. 32, Issue 1 (January 2000).

5   *Ibid.*, pp.60–61.

6   *Ibid.*, p.61.

7   Pete Salino to the author, 29 April 2017.

8   Ken Blaiklock interviewed by the author, 1 June 2009.

9   R.F. Scott, 'Message to the Public', 29 March 1912.

10   See, for instance, Sandeep Mishra & Martin L. Lalumière, 'Individual differences in risk-propensity: Associations between personality and behavioural measures of risk', *Personality and Individual Differences*, 50 (2011), pp.869–73.

11   P.G. Law, 'Personality Problems in Antarctica', in *The Medical Journal of Australia*, Vol. 1, No. 8 (20 February 1960), p.281.

12   NZ Defence Force Archives, Tom Couzens, NZ Army School, record of sick leave, 25 August 1949.

13   James Hardie-Bick and Penny Bonner, 'Experiencing Flow, Enjoyment and Risk in Skydiving and Climbing', *Ethnography*, 17 (3), (2016).

14   *Ibid.*

15   Pete Salino in conversation with the author, 31 March 2017.

16   BAS AD6/2F/1982/H, 'Faraday Winter Personnel with Relevant Travel Experience, 1982'.

17   Des Lugg to the author, 26 March 2017.

18   I am most grateful to John Hall MBE, BAS Head of Operations, for providing a valuable insight into BAS's current recruitment and retention procedures.

19   Pete Salino in conversation with the author, 31 March 2017.

20   H.R. Mill, *The Siege of the South Pole: The Story of Antarctic Exploration* (London: Alston Rivers, 1905), p.245.

21   Pete Salino in conversation with the author, 31 March 2017.

22   BAS Archives, Sir Donald Logan, 'A review of safety provisions for staff and property in the British Antarctic Survey with particular reference to operations in Antarctica', October 1982 (issued January 1983).

23   *Ibid.*

24   *Ibid.*

25   *Ibid.*

26   John Hall to the author, 6 January 2017.

27   *Ibid.*

28   BAS Archives, Sir Donald Logan, 'A review of safety provisions for staff and property in the British Antarctic Survey with particular reference to operations in Antarctica', October 1982 (issued January 1983).

SELECT BIBLIOGRAPHY

For full bibliographic detail of journal papers and primary sources (including diaries, correspondence, articles, reports and interviews conducted) please see the detailed notes section.

Aagaard, Bjarne, *Fangst og Forskning I Sydishavet (Fishing and Research in the Southern Ocean)* (Oslo: Gyldendal Norsk Forlag, 1930).

Airey, Len, *On Antarctica* (Highmount Books, 2001).

Anderson, W. Ellery, *Expedition South* (London: Evans, 1957).

Ashcroft, Frances, *Life at the Extremes: The Science of Survival* (London: Flamingo, 2001).

Ayres, Philip, *Mawson: A Life* (Melbourne: The Miegunyah Press, 1999).

Bagshawe, Thomas W., *Two Men in the Antarctic* (Cambridge: CUP, 1939).

Béchervaise, John, *Blizzard & Fire: A Year at Mawson, Antarctica* (London: Angus & Robertson, 1964).

Beltramino, Juan Carlos M., *The Structure & Dynamics of Antarctic Population* (New York: Vantage Press, 1993).

Bernacchi, L.C., *To the South Polar Regions: Expedition of 1898–1900* (London: Hurst & Blackett, 1901).

Boothe, Joan, *The Storied Ice* (Berkeley: Regent Press, 2011).

Borchgrevink, Carsten, *First on the Antarctic Continent: Being an Account of the British Antarctic Expedition, 1898–1900* (London: George Newnes, 1901).

Brotherhood, J.R., & C.J.H. Johnson, *Kurafid: The British Antarctic Survey Medical Guide* (Cambridge: BAS, 1982).

Brown, Peter Lancaster, *Twelve Came Back* (London: Robert Hale, 1957).

Burke, David, *Moments of Terror: The Story of Antarctic Aviation* (London: Robert Hall, 1994).

Byrd, Richard E., *Discovery: The Story of the Second Byrd Antarctic Expedition* (New York: Putnam, 1935).

Byrd, Richard E., *Alone* (New York: Putnam, 1938).

Charcot, Jean Baptist, *The Voyage of the Pourquoi-Pas: Journal of the Second French South Polar Expedition, 1908–10* (London: Hodder & Stoughton, *c.* 1911).

Cherry-Garrard, Apsley, *The Worst Journey in the World* (London: Pimlico, 2003).

Christie, E.W. Hunter, *The Antarctic Problem* (London: George Allen & Unwin, 1951).

Clarke, Basil, *Polar Flight* (London: Ian Allen, 1964).

Cook, Frederick A., *Through the First Antarctic Night, 1898–1899, A Narrative of the Voyage of the* Belgica *Among Newly Discovered Lands and Over and Unknown Sea About the South Pole* (New York: Doubleday & McClure, 1900).

Crane, David, *Scott of the Antarctic: A Life of Courage and Tragedy in the Extreme South* (London: HarperCollins, 2005).

De Gerlache, Adrien, *Voyage of the* Belgica: *Fifteen Months in the Antarctic* (Norwich: Erskine Press/Bluntisham Books, 1998).

Dewart, Gilbert, *Antarctic Comrades: An American with the Russians in Antarctica* (Columbus: Ohio State University Press, 1989).

Dodds, Klaus, *Pink Ice: Britain and the South Atlantic Empire* (London: I.B. Taurus, 2002).

Dufek, George J., *Operation Deepfreeze* (New York: Harcourt, Brace & Company, 1957).

Evans, E.G.R., *South with Scott* (London: Collins, n.d.).

Fisher, Margery & James, *Shackleton* (London: Barrie Books, 1957).

Fuchs, Sir Vivian, & Sir Edmund Hillary, *The Crossing of Antarctica: The Commonwealth Trans-Antarctic Expedition, 1955–58* (London: Cassell, 1959).

Fuchs, Sir Vivian, *Of Ice and Men* (Oswestry: Anthony Nelson, 1982).

Giaever, John, *The White Desert: The Official Account of the Norwegian–British–Swedish Antarctic Expedition* (London: Chatto & Windus, 1954).

Grierson, John, *High Failure: Solo Along the Arctic Air Route* (London: Hodge, 1936).

Grierson, John, *Air Whaler* (London: Sampson Low, Marston & Co., 1949).

Grierson, John, *Challenge to the Poles: Highlights of Arctic and Antarctic Aviation* (London: Foulis, 1964).

Haddelsey, Stephen, *Born Adventurer: The Life of Frank Bickerton* (Stroud: Sutton, 2005).

Haddelsey, Stephen, *Ice Captain: The Life of J.R. Stenhouse* (Stroud: The History Press, 2008).

Haddelsey, Stephen, *Shackleton's Dream: Fuchs, Hillary & the Crossing of Antarctica* (Stroud: The History Press, 2012).

Haddelsey, Stephen, with Alan Carroll, *Operation Tabarin: Britain's Secret Wartime Expedition to Antarctica, 1944–46* (Stroud: The History Press, 2014).

Hastings, Max, & Simon Jenkins, *The Battle for the Falklands* (London: Pan, 2010).

Hayes, J. Gordon, *The Conquest of the South Pole* (London: Thornton Butterworth, 1932).

Hemming, Henry, *Churchill's Iceman: The True Story of Geoffrey Pyke: Genius, Fugitive, Spy* (London: Arrow Books, 2015).

Huntford, Roland, *Shackleton* (London: Abacus, 2011).

Ignatov, V., *Where It's Coldest* (Moscow: Progress Publishers, 1965).

James, David, *That Frozen Land* (London: The Falcon Press, 1949).

Kearns, William H., & Beverley Britton, *The Silent Continent* (London: Gollancz, 1955).

Law, Phillip, & John Béchervaise, *ANARE: Australia's Antarctic Outposts* (Melbourne: OUP, 1957).

Mawson, Sir Douglas, *The Home of the Blizzard* (London: Heinemann, 1915).

Nasht, Simon, *No More Beyond: The Life of Hubert Wilkins* (Edinburgh: Berlinn, 2006).

Nordenskjöld, Otto, *Antarctica, or Two Years Amongst the Ice of the South Pole* (London: Hurst & Blackett, 1905).

Norman, Nelson, *In Search of Remote Health Care* (Self-published, 2010).

Richards, R.W., *The Ross Sea Shore Party, 1914–17* (Norwich/Huntingdon: Bluntisham Books/Erskine Press, 2003).

Riffenburgh, Beau, *Nimrod: Ernest Shackleton and the Extraordinary Story of the 1907–09 British Antarctic Expedition* (London: Bloomsbury, 2004).

Riffenburgh, Beau, *Aurora: Douglas Mawson and the Australasian Antarctic Expedition, 1911–14* (Norwich: The Erskine Press, 2011).

Rose, Lisle A., *Assault on Eternity: Richard E. Byrd and the Exploration of Antarctica, 1946–47* (Annapolis: Naval Institute Press, 1980).

Rymill, John, *Southern Lights* (London: Chatto & Windus, 1938).

Scott, Robert Falcon, *Scott's Last Expedition* (London: Smith, Elder & Co., 1913).

Shackleton, Ernest, *The Heart of the Antarctic: Being the Story of the British Antarctic Expedition, 1907–09* (London: Heinemann, 1909).

Shackleton, Ernest, *South: A Memoir of the Endurance Voyage* (London: Robinson, 1999).

Solomon, Susan, *The Coldest March: Scott's Fatal Antarctic Expedition* (Newhaven & London: Yale University Press, 2001).

Stephenson, Jon, *Crevasse Roulette: The First Trans-Antarctic Crossing, 1957–58* (New South Wales: Rosenberg Publishing, 2009).

Stewart, John, *Antarctica: An Encyclopedia* (Jefferson: McFarland & Co., 1990).

Swithinbank, Charles, *Foothold on Antarctica: The First International Expedition (1949–52) Through the Eyes of its Youngest Member* (Lewes: Book Guild Publishing, 1999).

Tait, Stephen, *Shambles* (Strategic Book Publishing, 2009).

Taylor, Andrew (Stephen Haddelsey, ed.), *Two Years Below the Horn: A Personal Memoir of Operation Tabarin* (Norwich: Erskine Press, 2017).

Taylor, Griffith, *With Scott: The Silver Lining* (Norwich: Bluntisham Books/Erskine Press, 1997).

Thomas, Lowell, *Sir Hubert Wilkins: His World of Adventure* (London: Arthur Barker, 1961/62).

Thomson, Robert, *The Coldest Place on Earth* (Wellington: Reed, 1969).

Thorson, Odd, *Kosmos Gjennom 25 Ar: En Epoke I Antarktis (Kosmos Through 25 Years: An Era in Antarctica)* (Oslo: Dreyers Forlag, n.d.).

Walton, E.W. Kevin, *Two Years in the Antarctic* (London: Lutterworth Press, 1955).

INDEX

If you enjoyed this book ...

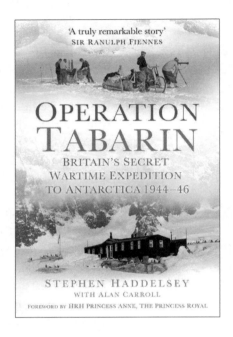

978 0 7509 6746 4

In 1943 Winston Churchill's War Cabinet met to discuss the opening of a new front, fought not on the beaches of Normandy or in the jungles of Burma but amid the blizzards and glaciers of the Antarctic. *Operation Tabarin* tells the story of the only Antarctic expedition to be launched by any of the combatant nations during the Second World War.

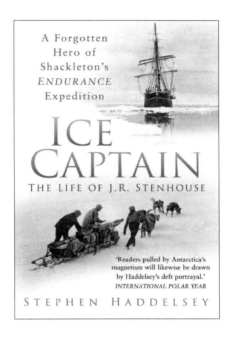

A Forgotten
Hero of
Shackleton's
ENDURANCE
Expedition

ICE
CAPTAIN
THE LIFE OF J.R. STENHOUSE

'Readers pulled by Antarctica's
magnetism will likewise be drawn
by Haddelsey's deft portrayal.'
INTERNATIONAL POLAR YEAR

STEPHEN HADDELSEY

978 0 7524 9779 2

Not long after Shackleton watched his ship *Endurance* become trapped in the ice floes of the Weddell Sea, the expedition's second ship, *Aurora*, suffered an equally terrifying fate. One hundred years on from the Endurance expedition of 1914–17, *Ice Captain* reveals the story of J.R. Stenhouse's achievements aboard the *Aurora*, and his many adventures in later life.

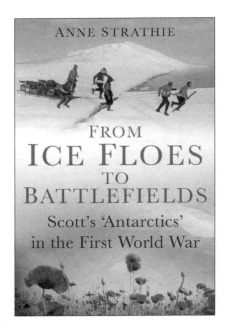

978 0 7509 6178 3

Scott's 'Antarctics' trade one adventure for another. By 1919 Scott's 'Antarctics' have fought at Antwerp, the Western Front, Gallipoli, in the Channel, at Jutland and in Arctic Russia. As in Antarctica, life is challenging and dangerous. As on the ice, not all survive.

The History Press

The destination for history
www.thehistorypress.co.uk